ROMANTIC PERIODICALS AND PRINT CULTURE

BOOKS OF RELATED INTEREST

MEDIEVALISM AND THE QUEST FOR THE "REAL" MIDDLE AGES
Edited by Clare A Simmons

WINSTANLEY AND THE DIGGERS, 1649–1999
Edited by Andrew Bradstock

NEWS, NEWSPAPERS AND SOCIETY IN EARLY MODERN BRITAIN
Edited by Joad Raymond

**THE INTERSECTIONS OF THE PUBLIC AND PRIVATE SPHERES
IN EARLY MODERN ENGLAND**
Edited by Paula R. Backscheider and Timothy Dykstal

ROMANTIC PERIODICALS AND PRINT CULTURE

Editor

Kim Wheatley

With a foreword by Stephen C. Behrendt

FRANK CASS

LONDON • PORTLAND, OR

First published in 2003 in Great Britain by
FRANK CASS AND COMPANY LIMITED
Crown House, 47 Chase Side, London N14 5BP, England

and in the United States of America by
FRANK CASS
c/o International Specialized Book Services, Inc.
920 NE 58th Avenue, Suite 300, Portland, OR 97213-3786

Copyright © 2003 Frank Cass & Co. Ltd.

Website: www.frankcass.com

British Library Cataloguing in Publication Data

Romantic periodicals and print culture
   1. English literature – 19th century – History and criticism
   2. English literature – 18th century – History and criticism
   3. Romanticism – Great Britain 4. Gender identity in
   literature 5. Periodicals – Great Britain – History – 19th
   century 6. Periodicals – Great Britain – History – 18th
   century 7. Great Britain – Intellectual life – 19th century
   8. Great Britain – Intellectual life – 18th century
   I. Wheatley, Kim, 1960–
   820.9′145

ISBN 0 7146 5437 X (cloth)
ISBN 0 7146 8437 6 (paper)

Library of Congress Cataloging-in-Publication Data

Romantic periodicals and print culture / editor Kim Wheatley.
   p. cm
Includes bibliographical references and index.
   ISBN 0-7146-5437-X (hardback) – ISBN 0-7146-8437-6 (pbk.)
   1. English prose literature–19th century–History and criticism. 2.
   English literature–19th century–History and criticism–Theory, etc.
   3. Periodicals–Publishing–Great Britain–History–19th century. 4.
   Criticism–Great Britain–History–19th century. 6. English
   periodicals–History–19th century. 8. Romanticism–Great Britain. I.
   Wheatley, Kim, 1960- II. Title.
   PR773.R66 2003
   820.9′007–dc21   2003011291

This group of studies first appeared in a Special Issue of *Prose Studies*
(ISSN 0144-0357), 25/1 (April 2002)
[Romantic Periodicals and Print Culture].

Printed in Great Britain by Antony Rowe Ltd., Chippenham, Wiltshire.

Contents

Foreword

STEPHEN C. BEHRENDT

Ours is not the first age to fuss about the role and function of "the media" in public – and therefore political – life. In the twenty-first century "the media" is increasingly both "mass" and electronic, but its powers – and the fears about them that arise from seemingly all quarters – bear some remarkable similarities to the situation that existed in Great Britain two centuries ago. The Romantic era witnessed a wholesale redefinition of the relationships of individual citizens to the various and sometimes (but not always) overlapping communities to which they belonged – including the nation. Typically defined by the religious, economic, ideological, intellectual, or aesthetic convictions of their members, these communities were invariably partisan, reflecting the volatility of any culture during times of social and political revolution and extended war-making. Vital to all such partisanship is a mechanism for rallying support and enthusiasm behind any group's principles and spokespersons and for demonizing its opponents and their spokespersons.

Periodical literature provided much of that mechanism during these years. While earlier periodicals had begun to transform the public sphere along the lines suggested some years ago by Jürgen Habermas, enfranchising increasing numbers of variously configured and largely male "publics" in a burgeoning discourse about ideas, the state, and civil institutions, the mid-eighteenth century periodical was nevertheless largely an eclectic, urbane, and masculinist organ that both presumed and therefore shaped a middle- to upper-class readership of well-rounded, largely cosmopolitan Britons. By the century's end, however, the situation was much altered. Rocked by political and ideological revolution, Western Europe presented new and eager audiences whose tastes ran far from the staid standard set by those earlier periodicals. Already were emerging in England what modern media studies call "niche publications," periodicals whose contents were defined by the particular readerships to which they were directed. This meant greater specialization and a partitioning of the general public readership into what are now called interest groups, a phenomenon against which William Godwin had warned already in *Political Justice* (1793). Partisanship became both more widespread and more aggressive under these conditions, as the total number of periodicals – and therefore of real or imagined sub-readerships – multiplied. Indeed, periodical literature at the dawn of the nineteenth century was remarkably adversarial in every sense, from the often witty conservatism of the *Anti-Jacobin* to the paid party politics of journals like the Whig *Edinburgh Review* and the Tory *Quarterly Review*. From there it was a natural step to the success during the Regency of the shrewd marketing (and carefully crafted idiom) of Cobbett's *Two-Penny Trash* or the wildly performative rhetoric of T.J. Wooler's radical weekly *Black Dwarf*, both of which aimed at demolishing the ideas and icons of the Establishment while raising up a more perceptive, self-aware citizenry capable of penetrating cant of whatever sort and finding its way to some apparently measurable "truth."

That truth lay, of course, largely in the convictions of the beholder. Periodicals existed, therefore, as instruments for shaping the competing versions of truth that they wished their readers to seem to discover for themselves – with the periodical's help, naturally. The success of the "new" Romantic periodical lay both in its enfranchisement of significantly larger numbers of readers – including the working classes – and in its consequent contribution to the spread of literacy among portions of the populace whose pretensions to literacy had routinely been repudiated by the political establishment. Now that establishment recognized – and not just from the example of revolutionary France – what it had to fear from an informed and therefore empowered citizenry. This helps to account for the energy expended in the more "traditional" (read "ideologically conservative") periodicals on decrying impropriety of one sort or another. For impropriety is inherently an attack on the privileged *status quo* and its institutions. It is "excess," apparent alike from its unconventional thinking and its rhetorical vigor. This is one reason why Cobbett and Wooler were so successful, and why William Hone and George Cruikshank's *Political House that Jack Built* (1819), like James Gillray's caricatures of two decades earlier, possessed such devastating impact.

Still, in the long view, perhaps the most important contribution of Romantic periodicals, and the one that has escaped serious notice for so long, was their unmistakable contribution to the "conversation in print" that is the distinguishing hallmark of British Romantic writing. Literary history long nourished an image of the Romantic writer (usually a poet) as a solitary, flower-sniffing devotee of unspoiled Nature. This myth entirely misses the reality that Romantic writers were characteristically directly involved in the leading social, political, economic, and ideological contests of their era. They immersed themselves in these issues and spoke their minds about them, both in the overtly "literary" works by which we remember a William Wordsworth or a Mary Robinson, a Percy Shelley or a Felicia Hemans, and in the surprising number of their contributions to the periodicals which they – along with their contemporaries – avidly read. Moreover, they knew one another's works well enough to respond to them – to engage them, intellectually and rhetorically – both in the periodical press and in their more conventionally published works. Further still, careful examination reveals that both the few canonical Romantic writers and many less familiar but equally active and committed writers knew the *periodicals* – and the authors who wrote for them – well enough to engage in a no less interactive conversation in print with them. This was true no less for women authors than for men: Mary Wollstonecraft contributed to Joseph Johnson's *Analytical Review*; Mary Hays to the *Monthly Magazine*; and Mary Robinson to the *Morning Post* and the *Monthly Magazine* in the 1790s, while Felicia Hemans and Letitia Landon were popular contributors to Regency and post-Regency periodicals.

The essays in this volume reveal some of how the vast and varied periodical literature of the Romantic era both shaped and energized literary, social, economic, spiritual, intellectual, and aesthetic discourse among large numbers of readers *and writers* whose contributions – whether they took the form of submissions (from genuine or spurious letters, squibs, poems, and essays) – or purchases fueled a conversation in print – and therefore a dynamic and diversified community of public discourse – that proved to be as irresistible (in every sense of the word) as it was unstoppable. Not the collection of isolated misanthropes and disaffected dreamers they have sometimes been styled, the Romantics were a fractious, well-read, and socially committed *community* of writers and thinkers who sought to empower their readers by validating their individual *and* collective independence of vision and of mind. This is their legacy, to which the body of Romantic periodical literature provides incontrovertible evidence.

Introduction

KIM WHEATLEY

"We must please to live, and therefore should live to please," asserted William Hazlitt in his 1823 article "The Periodical Press," an attempt to assuage – or possibly to intensify – contemporary anxieties about the expansion of periodical writing. "Therefore, let Reviews flourish –" Hazlitt added with a rhetorical flourish of his own, "let Magazines increase and multiply – let the Daily and Weekly Newspapers live for ever!"[1] Each of the categories of publication identified by Hazlitt had already taken on a new lease of life during the first two decades of the nineteenth century, in what amounts to a series of paradigm shifts within British print culture. Substantial "Reviews" or reviewing periodicals, lighter and more miscellaneous magazines, and of course newspapers had already increased and multiplied during the eighteenth century, especially the 1790s, but three developments in particular helped to shape the distinctive periodical culture of the Romantic era.

The first was the creation in 1802 of the Whig *Edinburgh Review*, which dispensed with the universal coverage and ostensibly objective criticism of the earlier *Critical Review* and *Monthly Review* and the more recent *Analytical Review*. The success of the selective and opinionated *Edinburgh* provoked the establishment of a Tory counterblast (some would say counterpart), the *Quarterly Review*, in 1809; these two elite quarterlies in turn would spark competition in the form of the radical *Westminster Review* in 1824.

The second major development lay in the heightening of the literary pretensions of the miscellaneous magazine, through the arrival on the scene of *Blackwood's Edinburgh Magazine* in 1817. The creativity of this playful and instantly notorious monthly publication generated imitators such as the *London Magazine* (founded in 1820) and the *New Monthly Magazine* (which began its second series in 1821).[2] (In contrast, the *Monthly Magazine*, founded in 1796, and associated with a radical dissenting milieu, had a much less literary bent.)

A third new departure can be seen in the directions taken by the weekly, if not the daily, newspaper.[3] At an ideological distance from the politically conservative *Blackwood's*, two weekly newspapers of the 1810s, Leigh Hunt's *Examiner* and William Cobbett's more populist *Political Register*, made reformist journalism more belletristic in one case, and more accessible in the other.[4] Relatively low in status yet fast gaining respectability, periodicals in early nineteenth-century Britain claimed a new degree of cultural influence at once admired and feared. Yet, as befits a genre that by definition never "live[s] forever," many of these publications have disappeared over the last two centuries into a sort of literary-historical oblivion. Nevertheless, their contents remain highly readable, entertaining, and illuminating, as many specialists in Romantic literature are now discovering. The present collection of essays builds on recent research on the Romantic-era periodical press and extends that research into some new directions.

Romanticists long neglected the periodicals that proliferated during the early nineteenth century, for specific reasons. What Jerome McGann has labeled the "Romantic ideology" stands for everything that periodical writing does not.[5] It elevates, among other things, inspired (and solitary) authorship over routine (and collaborative) composition; self-exploration or an ahistorical aestheticism over immersion in commodity culture; and immortal fame over transient publicity. The tendency to treat canonical Romantic writers as transcending their historical moment is itself a Romantic legacy.[6] The present revival of scholarly interest in the periodicals coincides with the prevalence of new historicist criticism, one of the initial impulses of which was to show how Romantic poetry, however idealistic, registers and helps to form its cultural – and especially political – context. One way of recovering that context is through the periodicals that reviewed the work of Romantic writers when it first appeared and in which many of the writers themselves published essays, poems and reviews. What might be called "old historicist" scholarship – in which history is unfurled as a sort of backdrop to literary history – paid sporadic attention to early nineteenth-century periodical writing, but always with the assumption that knowledge of such writing constituted "background."

Moving that background to the foreground, the first wave of Romantic new historicists undertook the important work of resituating well-known poems and essays within or against the periodicals in which they were originally published or reviewed. These critics tended to be attracted to the various feuds between the canonical Romantic poets and their reviewers, especially the campaign of *Blackwood's Magazine* against the "Cockney School," including John Keats and Leigh Hunt. Such feuds continue to fascinate present-day critics: the campaign of the *Edinburgh Review* against the "Lake School" of poets – Robert Southey, William Wordsworth, and Samuel Taylor Coleridge – is attracting renewed attention, as is the intriguingly ambivalent attitude of contemporary reviewers to the "Satanic School," namely Percy Bysshe Shelley and Lord Byron.

However, research on Romantic-era periodicals now also reflects new historicist scholarship's expanded scope – its aspiration to study the full spectrum of print culture, rather than literature narrowly defined. Much of this research depends on ongoing archival recuperation. The rediscovery of Romantic women writers, the main growth area in Romantic studies, goes hand-in-hand with the study of periodicals, since much work by women writers first appeared in periodicals and ephemeral annuals. Likewise, the recovery of Romantic-era working-class writers (male and female) inevitably proceeds alongside research into the populist political journalism of the period. The decentering of canonical literary texts can also be seen in criticism taking the periodicals as objects of study in their own right – criticism as likely to interpret a *jeu d'esprit* in *Blackwood's* as a review of Keats, or, if a review, as likely to address one of a long-forgotten work of non-fiction prose as one of a canonical poem. Lest a new hierarchy arise, privileging the *Edinburgh Review* over (say) the *Literary Gazette*, continuing new excavation work becomes necessary. In this introduction I will discuss how the contributions in this collection fit in with these various related approaches. First, though, I shall survey earlier criticism of Romantic-era periodicals, which tends to focus on the upmarket Reviews and magazines rather than the lower-status weekly or daily publications. I shall begin by mentioning some of the periodicals' own self-evaluations and appraisals of each other, which are frequently used as starting points for discussion.[7] Nothing if not reflexive, Romantic-era periodical writing offers an array of self-analyses to guide scholarly investigation.[8]

Recurring themes appear in early nineteenth-century comments on the periodical press: the idea that periodicals are detrimental to higher literary pursuits (partly because of the quality of their writing and partly because of their potentially all-encroaching extensiveness), their relentless politicization of discourse, their reliance on (and abuse of) anonymity, their indulgence in so-called "personality" or personal attacks and, last but not least, their sway over public opinion. The assemblage of such charges best-known to Romanticists appears in Coleridge's *Biographia Literaria* (1817) – not, of course, itself a periodical, but containing a chapter entitled "Remarks on the Present Mode of Conducting Critical Journals." The chapter purports to be a general analysis of reviewing practices, but is actually an attack on the *Edinburgh*, and in particular its editor, Francis Jeffrey, for his hostile reviews of Wordsworth's poetry. In a less serious vein, an 1818 article in *Blackwood's*, "Remarks on the Periodical Criticism of England," denounced the fierce partisanship of the two major quarterlies, claiming that "The author is a mere puppet in the hands of the critic."[9] The ostensible author, a fictitious German nobleman, characterized the *Edinburgh* as balefully influential, a danger to public morals. In the same year, Hazlitt published in the *Examiner* a far more scathing attack on the *Quarterly* editor William Gifford, an attack elaborated upon in Hazlitt's magnificent *Letter to William Gifford, Esq* (1819) and reprised in *The Spirit of the Age* (1825). The piece in the *Examiner* opens: "This little person is a considerable catspaw: and so far worthy of some slight notice. He is the Government Critic, a character nicely differing from that of a Government spy – an invisible link, that connects literature with the police."[10] Here as elsewhere Hazlitt succeeds in matching the *Quarterly*'s own vitriolic prose.

Hazlitt's 1823 "Periodical Press" article, which I quoted from earlier, is rather unusual in defending instead of attacking the genre, but it deals with the same topics as some earlier and later critiques of particular periodicals. Published anonymously in the *Edinburgh*, the article cannot really possess the critical distance to which it lays claim. Hazlitt begins with the question, "*Whether Periodical Criticism is, upon the whole, beneficial to the cause of literature?*" (349) and sidesteps the issue by "announcing a truism:" "*viz. That periodical criticism is favourable – to periodical criticism*" (349–50, his italics). Given the prevalence of such concerns, Hazlitt's "truism" can be read as a threat. In the course of his defense of periodicals, Hazlitt admits that reviewing is "too often made the engine of party-spirit and personal invective" (358) but, according to him, this "only shows the extent and importance of this branch of literature" in that "it has become the organ of every thing else" (359).[11] He does, however, assail the "base system of mean and malignant defamation" (378) associated for him with the Tory press, *Blackwood's* in particular. His article thus inevitably partakes of the partisanship to which he takes a *laissez-faire* attitude. A year after the publication of Hazlitt's article, a more detailed attack on the *Edinburgh* and the *Quarterly* appeared in the first numbers of the *Westminster Review*: in three long articles, James Mill and John Stuart Mill accused both major periodicals of supporting the status quo and deplored their hold over public opinion.[12] James Mill accused the *Quarterly* in particular of "dirt-flinging" – a standard allegation against periodicals from across the political spectrum.[13] More defensively, a lengthy Preface to the 1826 volume of *Blackwood's* attempted to refute the charges, so often raised against its writers, of "personality, insolence, impertinence, assassination, with many other crimes of similar atrocity" – the sources, many might think, of this magazine's reputation for brilliance.[14] The same Preface insisted that the political effect of *Blackwood's* was superior to that of the great quarterlies: "we Tories beat the Whigs in argument all to sticks, and … all the world acknowledged it" (x). As we shall see, early nineteenth-century writers' preoccupation – whether anxious or enthusiastic – with the power of periodicals has become a central concern of present-day studies of periodical writing.

The first full-length studies of Romantic-era periodicals, by contrast, were more concerned with the periodicals' content and self-presentation than with their effect on their readers – if *logos* and *ethos* can really be distinguished from *pathos*. These studies can be seen as an outgrowth of the periodicals' self-reflexive tendencies, being in-house productions. Samuel Smiles' *A Publisher and His Friends* (1891), a less-than-disinterested history of John Murray's publishing house, recounts the fascinating behind-the-scenes tale of the creation of the *Quarterly Review* and its subsequent success.[15] Taking a similar approach in *Annals of a Publishing House: William Blackwood and His Sons* (1897), Margaret Oliphant, herself a copious contributor to *Blackwood's*, enthusiastically described the advent of *Maga* and some of the early controversies that it incited.[16] Despite or because of their biases, these histories remain essential reading for students of the *Quarterly* and *Blackwood's*: both books bring to life the colorful personalities associated with the two major Tory periodicals. Later more scholarly studies continued Smiles' and Oliphant's diachronic approach, recounting the development of specific periodicals across time. Walter Graham's survey, *English Literary Periodicals* (1930), has a chapter on the early nineteenth-century Reviews and another on the magazines, placing them in the larger context of the history of British periodicals.[17] John Clive's *Scotch Reviewers* (1957) relates the founding of the *Edinburgh* and the fluctuation of its stances on political and economic issues.[18] Clive also gives a lively summary of the various schools of thought concerning Francis Jeffrey's feud with Wordsworth. No comparable study exists of the *Quarterly Review*.[19] In a different line of scholarly endeavor, over the course of the twentieth century work proceeded on the attribution of the authorship of the mostly anonymous articles in the periodicals – work culminating in the *Wellesley Index to Victorian Periodicals* (1966).[20] Meanwhile, scholars of reception history assembled collections of reviews of the major Romantic writers, at first with only limited contextualization.[21] The biggest undertaking of this kind, Donald Reiman's multi-volume *The Romantics Reviewed* (1972), includes reviews of minor writers such as Southey, Charles Lamb, Hazlitt, and Hunt, and prints the reviews in facsimile, a mode of presentation that gives a taste of the periodicals in which the articles first appeared.

Reiman's collection helped to spark new historicist studies on the relationship between canonical Romantic poetry and the periodicals. Jerome McGann was extremely influential in insisting on the importance of taking into account the circumstances of a text's initial publication – circumstances that in turn affect the manner of reception. His essay "Keats and the Historical Method in Literary Criticism" (1979) discusses the differences between the versions of Keats' ballad "La Belle Dame sans Merci" first published by Keats in Leigh Hunt's weekly literary periodical the *Indicator*, and the better-known version published posthumously in 1848. McGann suggests that "Keats means to share a mildly insolent attitude towards the literary establishment with his readers in *The Indicator*," an attitude responding to the attacks on Keats by Tory reviewers.[22] Following in the footsteps of McGann, Theresa Kelley, in "Poetics and the Politics of Reception: Keats's 'La Belle Dame sans Merci,'" argues that the sources behind and revisions to the poem show that Keats' attitude to his contemporary reviewers was both defiant and conciliatory.[23] Marjorie Levinson's *Keats's Life of Allegory* was especially decisive in resituating Keats in the context of the hostile reception of the Cockney School.[24] Levinson sees the extravagant language of the reviewers – notably John Gibson Lockhart writing for *Blackwood's* – as reflecting anxieties concerning class status. Levinson's brilliant study inspired a stream of interpretations of the Cockney School attacks.[25] In inviting critics to historicize and thus politicize the Romantic poet whose work most explicitly aspires to a timeless beauty, the Cockney School attacks would seem to exert an almost irresistible appeal. But Keats is of course not the only Romantic poet whose contemporary reviews reward close reading. Karen Swann's 1985 essay "Literary Gentlemen and Lovely Ladies: The Debate on the Character of *Christabel*" argues that early attacks on Coleridge's poem betray – and seek to allay – anxieties about the boundaries between high culture and mass culture (in this case, the Gothic). Like Kelley and Levinson, Swann brings in questions of gender definition and sexual identity, putting a feminist twist on the line of argument initiated by McGann.[26] Such questions have not always been pursued as vigorously as one might expect in subsequent work on the periodicals.

Studies approaching Romantic writers by way of periodical culture continue into the present decade. At the same time, as mentioned earlier, a related line of research takes the periodicals themselves as its primary focus. Jon Klancher's highly respected and widely cited *The Making of English Reading Audiences 1790–1832* (1987) was a groundbreaking achievement both in the breadth of its coverage and in its premise that periodicals are worthy of interpretation in their own right, although even Klancher does not entirely lose sight of the canonical Romantic writers.[27] Klancher examines periodicals from the 1790s, popular magazines of the 1820s like the *Penny Magazine*, and post-Waterloo radical newspapers, as well as the elite quarterlies and monthlies that had been the subject of earlier studies. This material at once de-emphasizes and reanimates the subject of his final chapter: Wordsworth's, Coleridge's and Shelley's idealistic theories of reading. Two of Klancher's arguments have proved particularly influential. The first is that the periodicals create various separate readerships with different assumptions about how to interpret words and the world. In his chapter on the major Reviews and magazines, for example, Klancher argues that these periodicals at once function to create middle-class intellectual desire and teach the social codes that help to define that class. The notion of disparate (even if overlapping) audiences has proved especially appealing to scholars working on reformist journalism, attempting to modify Jürgen Habermas' theory of the public sphere by elaborating the notion of a counter-public sphere.[28] Klancher follows earlier scholars such as Graham and Clive, however, in attempting to characterize readerships by way of the periodicals and not vice versa, though his emphasis is on "the collective audience" (11) rather than on the individual reader, actual or implied. Second, Klancher has also changed the way scholars think about Romantic-era periodicals through his contention that the Reviews and magazines offer a "transauthorial discourse" (52), a term that can also apply to the more popular journalism that he discusses. Instead of thinking in terms of separate writers for the periodical, Klancher treats the periodical itself as an agent, diffusing its influence through such characteristic practices as anonymity and collaborative authorship. Earlier critics had seen each periodical as stamped with a single voice: that of the editor.[29] Klancher takes this assumption and flips it over, seeing the monolithic voice as a corporate one, the magisterial "we" that subsumes the work of any individual contributor. One might object that each periodical has a distinctive voice because of the editorial practice of altering contributions to fit in with the ethos of the periodical. Yet the fact remains that, independent of editorial interference, individual writers' voices change in a periodical context: Southey, for instance, sounds more reactionary in the *Quarterly* than in his own *Letters from England* (1807), despite writing anonymously in both cases. David Latané commends Klancher for submerging the individual author but points out, "The question begged, of course, is to what extent … the anonymous author … really speaks as or for [a particular periodical]."[30] Latane calls for more, not less, information about specific contributors.

Several subsequent studies build on Klancher's claims about periodicals' carving out of Romantic-era audiences and about periodical writing having a "transauthorial" agency of its own. Marilyn Butler's 1993 account of the spectrum of Romantic-era periodicals stresses the role of the quarterlies – the *Edinburgh* in particular – in dividing up fields of knowledge in ways that affected writers as well as excluding certain classes of reader in the course of defining a new middle-class audience. Discussing James Mill's radical attack on the *Edinburgh* in the *Westminster Review*, Butler observes that "his point was partly subverted by the design and tone of the new journal – twelve long analytical articles, written in a voice of effortless superiority, in perfect mimicry of the prestigious quarterlies."[31]

The format of the *Westminster* thus implicitly conceded the quarterlies' dominance. Mark Schoenfield, in an article on the *Edinburgh* published in the same year as Butler's overview, also stresses the disciplinary function of the quarterlies, while conceding that "The *Westminster*'s analysis exaggerates the *Edinburgh*'s hegemony" (148).[32] Like Klancher, Schoenfield sees the voice of the periodical as subsuming the voices of individual contributors. In an earlier essay on the *London Magazine*, he had stressed the value of considering the dialogue between contributions in a single issue of a periodical: "voices together" sound different from voices apart.[33] Jerome Christensen's 1996 essay, "The Detection of the Romantic Conspiracy in Britain," complicates this assumption in examining the glaring contradiction between two review-articles in the opening number of the *Edinburgh*: Christensen asks, "is it a *self*-contradiction? What does it mean to think of a periodical in terms of a 'self'? … Does anonymity excuse contradictory articles, or should it operate as a stronger constraint upon contradiction?"[34] Such questions become even trickier when one considers the periodicals' seemingly self-conscious manipulation of the tensions between anonymous collective discourse and individual authorship. The best discussion of this issue as it applies to the monthly magazines is in Margaret Russett's book on Thomas De Quincey.[35]

Entire books are now being devoted to topics dealt with by Klancher in individual chapters or only in passing. Kevin Gilmartin's excellent study of popular journalism, *Print Politics* (1996), focuses unapologetically on non-literary print culture, including radical weekly periodicals such as the *Black Dwarf* (1817–24) and the *Republican* (1819–26). Downplaying the effect of radical discourse on its original readers in favor of sustained analysis of its rhetorical strategies and self-awareness concerning form, Gilmartin argues that Romantic-era radical journalism was at once constrained and energized by its oppositional stance.[36] Stephen Behrendt's 1997 collection, *Romanticism, Radicalism, and the Press*, aims to demonstrate "the extent to which the Radical press figured directly in the 'writing culture' we associate with both the canonized and the marginalized writers of British Romanticism."[37] One of Behrendt's contributors, Steven Jones, calls his essay on the *Black Dwarf* an "extended meditation on Klancher's astute observations" concerning the language of satire in Thomas Wooler's radical weekly.[38]

Addressing a different area of Romantic-era periodical culture, Mark Parker's *Literary Magazines and British Romanticism* (2000) takes the primary monthlies, *Blackwood's*, the *London*, and the *New Monthly*, to exemplify the contention that periodical discourse repays detailed attention of the kind formerly reserved for literary texts.[39] Parker accepts the argument of Klancher and Butler that the class-inflected discourse of the periodicals creates a particular kind of audience: he claims, for example, that the *New Monthly* helps to invent a bourgeois aestheticism, while at the same time its writers implicitly acknowledge the socioeconomic conditions that make possible such escapism. Parker modifies Klancher's concept of transauthorial discourse by reintroducing individual agency, that of the editor rather than the writer: showing how different contributions within a single issue of a magazine resonate against each other, he sees such resonances as the result of editorial manipulation. Parker admits that readers do not necessarily approach the contents of any given issue of a periodical in sequence but claims that "the historical record" offers no "evidence of such readerly freedom" (15). In the absence of such evidence, seemingly escapist essays by Charles Lamb ("Elia") can be seen as politicized by the circumstances of their original publication in the *London*. There is almost a Romantic pathos in Parker's retelling of the story of how John Scott of the *London* – for him, the exemplary strong editor – met his untimely end in a duel resulting from his attacks on *Blackwood's*.[40] Parker's book thus combines the kind of new historicist criticism inspired by McGann – resituating well-known Romantic authors within the context of production and reception – with the more recent impulse to demonstrate that periodical writing possesses an intrinsic interest.[41]

Klancher's argument that the periodicals helped shape their audiences carries over into recent work on Romantic-era women's magazines such as the *Lady's Magazine* (1770–1819), *La Belle Assemblée* (1806–32), and the *British Lady's Magazine* (1815–19). Edward Copeland writes that the *Lady's Magazine* helped to create "a narrative of shifting ideologies devoted to explaining just what it meant to be female and middle-class in a market economy."[42] Sonia Hofkosh, in her 1998 essay, "Commodities Among Themselves," sees such magazines as offering their female readers a "transformative potential," a space of exchange for women within and yet beyond patriarchal commercial culture.[43] Hofkosh discusses women's magazines again in her book *Sexual Politics and the Romantic Author* (1998), bringing out their intertwining of domestic and economic issues. In doing so, she sheds fresh light on the much-discussed Cockney School articles in *Blackwood's*, exploring connections between "Z"'s attacks on Leigh Hunt as a "tea-sipping milliner girl" and contributions to women's magazines of the period on the fraught subject of the working woman. Hofkosh argues that the Romantic so-called "deep self" itself depends on fantasies of female desire, articulated both in periodical writing and elsewhere. Analyzing essays by Hunt on female fashions and work in the *Examiner* and in his more literary periodical the *Indicator*, Hofkosh suggests that Hunt can be seen as invested in an autonomous Romantic individual self which excludes women. Other critics working on periodical literature written by male authors have been slower to address those authors' role in constructing and contesting gender identities. Following Hofkosh's lead, three of the contributors to the present collection, Andrea Bradley, Mark Schoenfield, and Lisa Niles, analyze figurations of gender in the mainstream periodicals, namely, the *Edinburgh*, the *Quarterly*, and *Blackwood's*.

Hofkosh states that her study "participates in the ongoing effort to elaborate a new romanticism being undertaken from a number of different perspectives: feminist, historical, materialist."[44] Whether continuing to recontextualize Romantic writers by way of the periodicals or treating periodicals as their primary texts, the essays in this collection all collaborate upon that effort. But what would it mean to see periodical writing as itself Romantic? For Hofkosh, periodical writing, whether by or for men or women, is not part of a countertradition but implicated in Romanticism as we know it. While some of the criticism that I have discussed assumes that Romanticism and the periodicals are at odds, a few earlier commentators had addressed what Parker terms "continuities" between the periodicals and "what we have come to call Romanticism" (182), mainly involving appreciation of Romantic innovation by the reviewers.[45] More recently, critics combining new historicist and formalist approaches have begun to attend to the literariness of periodical discourse. Christensen, for example, detects a Romantic element that he calls "dark Romanticism" in the "wild sarcasm" of the *Edinburgh Review*, a sarcasm that "marks the *felt* incapacity of the *Review* to comprehend its own social being and force."[46] It may now be time to pursue a broader quest for the Romantic in the Romantic-era periodical.

The first essay in the present collection gives us an example of how a new, expanded Romanticism can be seen to engage in dialogue with what has traditionally been thought of as Romanticism. Adriana Craciun's examination of Mary Robinson's four-part article on the "Present State of the Manners, Society, &c&c of the Metropolis of England" contributes to the vital ongoing project of establishing the extent of women writers' participation in turn-of-the-century literary culture. Robinson's hitherto almost entirely neglected defense of London print culture appeared in consecutive installments in the *Monthly Magazine* at the time when Wordsworth was composing his famous Preface to the second edition of the *Lyrical Ballads* (1800). Craciun argues that Robinson's "Metropolis" article challenges various tenets of Romanticism as defined by Wordsworth. Its vision of a burgeoning free press energized by the voices of continental and female writers runs counter to Wordsworth's anxiety about the corrupting effects of popular culture. Like the radical writers discussed by Gilmartin, Robinson sees the freedom of the press as liberating, not dangerous. Robinson's celebration of metropolitan culture in her *Monthly Magazine* piece also contrasts markedly with Wordsworth's negative depiction of urban life in the Preface and elsewhere in his poetry. Robinson's conception of art as public rather than private is similarly unWordsworthian (although like other Romantic-era poets, she values thoughts that arise in solitude). Craciun's description of the eventful afterlife of Robinson's "Metropolis" article in several cultural guidebooks to London attests to its appeal to the kinds of readers that Wordsworth's Preface refuses to take into account.

Andrea Bradley's and Mark Schoenfield's essays examine male reviewers' appraisals of women writers popular in their own time but only relatively recently being reconsidered as part of the Romantic canon. Both essays reconsider the disciplinary and supervisory role of the great quarterlies, revealing their stratification of writers – and, by implication, readers – along gender as well as class lines. Bradley sees the *Edinburgh*'s review of Amelia Opie's 1802 *Poems*, the only review of a woman poet in its inaugural issue, as exemplifying this periodical's gendered hierarchizing of literary genres. On the one hand, Opie is chosen for review because her popularity unsettles the *Edinburgh*'s sense of what should constitute "celebrity;" on the other hand, the reviewer exploits her vulnerability to chastisement. Bradley offers a detailed analysis of the rhetorical strategies through which an anonymous male *Edinburgh* reviewer keeps a woman writer in her place. Taking both a synchronic and a diachronic approach, she compares the first Opie review with a better-known article in the same number, Jeffrey's first attack on the Lake School of poetry in his review of Southey's *Thalaba*, as well as with a later *Edinburgh* review of Opie. Bradley identifies an unexpected connection between the *Edinburgh*'s aesthetic priorities and Wordsworth's version of Romanticism in that the first review of Opie values psychological depth; yet, as she notes, the *Edinburgh* may uphold the deep self in order to monitor it all the more thoroughly. Bradley follows Klancher in stressing the seamless corporate voice of the *Edinburgh* over the individual voices of its contributors, but suggests at the end of her essay that the hyper-confident tone of the *Edinburgh* masks its editor's own sense of insecurity about the periodical's financial and ideological success.

While Bradley catches the *Edinburgh* in the act of defining its role as the professional arbiter of print culture, Mark Schoenfield confirms the later solidification of that role although, as he notes, the quarterlies' hegemony would in due course be challenged by the monthly magazines, as well as by radical writers such as Cobbett. In examining responses in the *Edinburgh* and the *Quarterly* to two novels by women, Frances Burney's *The Wanderer* and Maria Edgeworth's *Patronage* (both published in 1814), Schoenfield analyzes particular maneuvers by which both major reviewing periodicals exert a quasi-legalistic power through their (gendered) aesthetic judgments. Situating the reviews of these two novels historically with reference to changing legal and economic definitions of marriage during the late eighteenth century and early nineteenth century, Schoenfield argues that Burney's and Edgeworth's resistance to patriarchal economic arrangements can be seen in scenes of female labor which the reviewers attempt to divest of their political critique. His essay suggests that, despite the *Edinburgh*'s reputation as more enlightened and skeptical and the *Quarterly*'s reputation as more reactionary and regressive, the two quarterlies, as Hazlitt put it in the Preface to his *Political Essays* (1819), "both travel the same road and arrive at the same destination."[47]

Bonnie Gunzenhauser shares her fellow-contributors' assumption that periodical writing repays careful rhetorical analysis, but in dealing with a very different kind of periodical, she makes a contrasting argument about its purpose and effects. She examines Cobbett's *Political Register* in the period from late 1816 to early 1817 when Cobbett transformed this middle-class radical weekly newspaper into the mass-circulation *Two-Penny Trash*. Rather than seeing this periodical as engaged in cultural definition, Gunzenhauser emphasizes Cobbett's effort to send out readers to change the (political) world. According to her, Cobbett is not just one more (loud) voice in a counter-public sphere; his commitment to the political objective of overthrowing "Corruption" places his publication outside commercial culture. In making this argument, she distinguishes Cobbett's reformulation of the novelistic discourse of sympathetic identification from that of Wordsworth, claiming that the readers of Wordsworth's Preface to the *Lyrical Ballads* are posited as mere consumers while Cobbett's readers are constituted as political actors. Nevertheless, Gunzenhauser contends that Cobbett exploits the notion of sympathy rather than rejecting it entirely; even his writing, then, aligns itself to some extent with contemporary literary discourse. She goes on to suggest that despite his well-known egotism and the fact that he was taken to personify radical politics, Cobbett, anticipating later critics, takes his periodical itself rather than the author to be an agent, one which blurs the boundaries between writer and reader. Gunzenhauser concludes that the *Two-Penny Trash* succeeded in creating a new political community. It would be easy to object that the efficacy of reading remains elusive, and that the implied opposition between consumption and action is idealistic. Yet even in inviting such objections, Gunzenhauser raises questions that all critics working on the political aspects of the periodicals must continue to confront.

The remaining essays in this collection concentrate on the genre that came to dominate the periodical market in the late 1810s and 1820s: the monthly magazine. Like Bradley and Schoenfield, Lisa Niles investigates the treatment of gender in periodical discourse. Rather than reviews of women writers, the texts she addresses are playful articles on feminized topics such as fashion and marriage, purportedly addressed to a female audience. Niles uses the gender dynamics within and around these articles, published between 1817 and 1819, to argue that *Blackwood's Magazine* serves primarily as the site of homosocial male relationships mediated by women both figurative and real. This site will take its most powerful imaginary shape in the series *Noctes Ambrosianae* (1822–35), set in Ambrose's tavern. The space of male bonding that is *Blackwood's* is presided over by the figure of the bachelor, who becomes, according to Niles – looking back to the eighteenth-century coffeehouse periodical, the *Spectator* – "a trope for periodical culture itself." In this analysis, periodical culture in the innovative form of *Blackwood's* remains as male-dominated as the world of the *Edinburgh* and the *Quarterly*, even when, or especially when, appealing to female readers and reminding those readers that it includes the work of actual female writers.

The next two essays continue the task, begun by a number of earlier new historicist critics, of re-entangling Romantic writers with the periodicals that helped to establish their reputations. David Higgins explores an episode in the development of William Wordsworth's fame, while Peter Manning returns Charles Lamb to the context of magazine publishing. Higgins discusses the multiple reasons for *Blackwood's Magazine*'s support of Wordsworth around 1820, one of which, he claims, was an attempt to distinguish the literary criticism of *Blackwood's* from that of the *Edinburgh*, as epitomized by Jeffrey's notorious hostility to Wordsworth. Higgins' essay puts an 1819 tribute to Wordsworth by John Wilson in the context of earlier and later attacks on Wordsworth in *Blackwood's*, which were also written by Wilson. This ambivalence reflects the *Blackwood's* ethos of inconsistency, but it is also shown to have a personal dimension, expressing Wilson's own mixed feelings towards Wordsworth. Higgins is thus concerned with the interplay between the input of an individual contributor and the collaborative discourse of the magazine. Higgins gives us a Romantic *Blackwood's* in that he stresses its promotion of the Romantic conception of genius. Yet, writing from a materialist perspective, he sees this cult of genius as in service of the self-conscious commercialism of the magazine. His essay points to a dark side of Romantic biography: the adulation of genius, like the culture of personality, involves the publicizing of private life. Even a panegyrical account of a poet can therefore be read as an insult.

Following in the footsteps of Schoenfield ("Voices Together") and Parker, Peter Manning restores essays by Lamb to their original context in the *London Magazine*, but unlike those previous critics, he suggests how Lamb's personality as a writer ultimately can be seen to transcend that context. Manning sets Lamb's "Detached Thoughts on Books and Reading," which appeared in the *London* in 1822, against an anonymous article "On Magazine Writers" published in the same issue. One of his quotations from the latter piece reads like a comment on Klancher's notion of transauthorial discourse:

> The general run of contributors [appear] in the least danger of suffering from any modifications in the character of magazines; inasmuch, as having no fixed and certain colours of their own, they imbibe, like the cameleon, the hues of their domiciles.[48]

The individual magazinist, that is to say, disappears into the periodical that is his (or her) home, while writing for the magazines becomes just another form of manufacturing. Manning contends that putting this article alongside Lamb's enables us "to see what appears most personal and spontaneous in Lamb as most typical and predetermined, an exercise in the form most favored by the conditions of publication." Yet according to Manning, Lamb preserves a unique self partly by invoking a world of *books* rather than magazines, and partly by inviting readers to speculate as to the identity of his persona, Elia. Lamb inhabits a space beyond "the accounts of materialist explanation" even if he needs Elia in order to do so.

Our final essay, by Nanora Sweet, turns to the major competitor of *Blackwood's* and the *London*: the second series of the *New Monthly Magazine*. The *New Monthly* has attracted less critical attention in the past than these other magazines, perhaps because they have been identified more with well-known Romantic writers. Given the prominence of Felicia Hemans in our ever-expanding picture of Romantic-era literary production, Sweet's essay could be seen as offering valuable background information concerning the periodical with which Hemans was most associated. But in addressing the huge text that is the *New Monthly* of the 1820s, Sweet, like other contributors to this collection, moves beyond any foreground–background distinction. The world that she conjures up bears a striking resemblance to Mary Robinson's vision of metropolitan culture in the article discussed by Craciun – open to female and continental contributors and with plenty of room for divergent political opinions. Sweet places the *New Monthly* in the context of reform-era politics, stressing its accommodationism rather than its ostensibly apolitical stance. Her essay brings out the tension between what Klancher calls "an essentially authorless text" (51) and the way in which the *New Monthly* took its identity from its editor, the Whig poet Thomas Campbell. The self-described "calm spot" in the periodical market was further ruffled, Sweet shows, by the differing agendas, political and otherwise, of the *New Monthly*'s other two "coadjutors:" its publisher Henry Colburn and its sub-editor Cyrus Redding. Beneath the surface of the commercially successful anonymous text, individual motivations swirl and jostle. Sweet's essay offers a reminder of the fact that, in studying the Romantic-era periodical, there are large numbers of people with whom we still need to become better acquainted.

Perhaps the most central Romantic assumption shared by the critics in this collection, as well as by the texts they have written on, is that the printed word has an effect on its audiences. These critics tend to discuss the impact of periodicals on implied readers rather than actual ones, however, which is understandable, since reactions by actual Romantic-era readers are not easy to come by. The occasional mention of a periodical in a diary entry or letter seems a slender basis on which to develop arguments about the extent to which periodicals enact or evade cultural tensions.[49] Nevertheless, even passing references to periodical reading in works of fiction or poetry may be worth taking into account. In Jane Austen's *Mansfield Park* (1814), for instance, some of the main characters at one point "lounge away the time as they could with sofas, and chit-chat, and Quarterly Reviews," a statement that implies an indiscriminate as well as idle perusal of the *Edinburgh* and the *Quarterly*.[50] Further research into non-canonical literary texts will presumably increase our understanding of Romantic-era periodicals – though I do not mean to imply that, in a mere reversal of priorities, we should unearth more literature simply in order to study the reception of the periodicals. Given the vast body of material, attention to the historical and fictional readers of periodicals represents only one potential avenue of future scholarly endeavor. Work on the daily newspapers of the Romantic period should yield more insights into the kinds of periodicals dealt with here, and vice versa. On a general level, improved access to periodical texts both in facsimile and online will inevitably stimulate more scholarship in this field.[51] Whether taking periodicals as primary or secondary objects of investigation, Romanticists will no doubt continue to attempt to present the fullest possible historical record even when returning to the Romantic possibility of transcendence.

NOTES

Editorial work on this special issue was supported by a summer grant from the College of William and Mary.

1. William Hazlitt, "The Periodical Press," *Edinburgh Review* 38 (1823), 349–78 (358). Further references in parentheses. For an analysis of this article, see Charles Mahoney, "Periodical Indigestion: Hazlitt's Unpalatable Politics," *Romantic Praxis* 1 (1997), 19 paras. Available online at: http://www.rc.umd.edu (9 July 2002). Mahoney suggests that the line about pleasing serves to "model the contemporary critic on the coquette" (para.6).

2. Of the monthly magazines, Hazlitt wrote, "if all their names were to be written down, one Article or one Number would hardly contain them." "Periodical Press," 369. Hazlitt dismissively mentioned another category of publication: "As to the Weekly Literary Journals, Gazettes, &c. they are a truly insignificant race … – insects in letters … We cannot condescend to enumerate them" (369).

3. Regrettably, the subject of daily newspapers in the Romantic era lies beyond the scope of this collection. For a discussion of the daily newspaper as a commercial phenomenon in the early nineteenth century, see Jonathan Mulrooney, "Reading the Romantic-period Daily News," *Nineteenth-Century Contexts* 24/4 (2002), 351–77.

4. In his 1823 essay, Hazlitt called the *Examiner* the "ablest" weekly periodical while unfortunately, in his view, "Cobbett stands first in power and popularity" ("Periodical Press," 368).

5. Jerome McGann, *The Romantic Ideology: A Critical Investigation* (Chicago, IL: University of Chicago Press, 1983).

6. The exemplary Romantic text in this regard is Percy Bysshe Shelley's elegy on John Keats, *Adonais* (1821), in which the wretched reviewer who had – according to Shelley – killed Keats is condemned to a mere earthly existence while the dead poet becomes a "portion of the Eternal" (l.340).

7. Several of the essays that follow address the periodicals' various statements of purpose and manifestos, so I will not linger over them here. These include the *Edinburgh Review*'s "Advertisement" to the first number which promised to take note only of deserving works (*ER* 1 [1802]); the *London Magazine*'s vow in its Prospectus to "convey the very 'image, form, and pressure'" of the "*mighty heart*" of the metropolis (*LM* 1 [Jan. 1820], iv) – a jab at the alleged provincialism of the *Edinburgh* and *Blackwood's*; and Thomas Campbell's Preface to the 1821 *New Monthly Magazine* announcing the "purely literary character" of the new series (*NMM* 1/1 [Jan. 1821], v).

8. See Margaret Beetham, "Open and Closed: The Periodical as a Publishing Genre," *Victorian Periodicals Review* 22 (Fall 1989), 96–100, on the "characteristically self-referring" nature of the genre (97). Beetham also discusses some of the methodological problems involved in studying periodicals.

9. Baron von Lauerwinkel [John Gibson Lockhart], "Remarks on the Periodical Criticism of England – in a Letter to a Friend," *Blackwood's Magazine* 2 (March 1818), 670–79 (671).

10. "The Editor of The Quarterly Review," *Examiner* 546 (14 June 1818), 378–9 (378).

11. For the same reason, Hazlitt claims, "the only authors who, as a class, are not starving, are periodical essayists." "Periodical Press," 359. Hazlitt takes up so much space paradoxically celebrating what he calls the "mediocrity of the age" (356) that after characterizing first the major newspapers, then magazines, he leaves himself no room to embark on "the ticklish chapter of *Reviews*" (378).

12. See James Mill, "Periodical Literature: 1. The Edinburgh Review, Vol.1, 2, &c," *Westminster Review* 1 (Jan. 1824), 206–49; John Stuart Mill, "Periodical Literature: The Edinburgh Review," *Westminster Review* 1 (April 1824), 505–41; and James Mill, "Periodical Literature: The Quarterly Review," *Westminster Review* 2 (Oct. 1824), 463–503.

13. Mill, "Periodical Literature: The Quarterly Review," 467.

14. John Wilson *et al.*, "Preface," *Blackwood's Edinburgh Magazine* 19 (1826), i–xxx (xi); further reference in parentheses. I have mentioned here some of the most often cited general discussions of the major periodicals; the periodicals' more specific attacks on each other are innumerable.

15. Samuel Smiles, *A Publisher and His Friends*, 2 Vols. (London: John Murray, 1891). Smiles also briefly discusses John Murray's connections with *Blackwood's*.

16. Margaret Oliphant, *Annals of a Publishing House: William Blackwood and His Sons*, 2 Vols. (New York: Charles Scribner's Sons, 1897).

17. Walter Graham, *English Literary Periodicals* ([1930] New York: Octagon Books, 1966). As the title of his book suggests, Graham is interested in particular periodicals' impact on literary history – and with none of a latter-day critic's skepticism about what the literary might be. Other studies of specific periodicals include Edmund Blunden's *Leigh Hunt's "Examiner" Examined, 1808–1825* (New York and London: Harper, 1928), which focuses on the more literary aspects of Hunt's weekly, and Josephine Bauer, *The London Magazine* (Copenhagen: Rosenkilde and Bagger, 1953).

18. John Clive, *Scotch Reviewers: The Edinburgh Review, 1802–1815* (Cambridge, MA: Harvard University Press, 1957).

19. Donald Reiman notes that the "history" of the *Quarterly Review* "has yet to be written, not

because there is too little information but because there is too much." See Reiman (ed.), *The Romantics Reviewed: Contemporary Reviews of British Romantic Writers*, 9 Vols. (New York and London: Garland Publishing, 1972), Part C, 2:751. Walter Graham's *Tory Criticism in the Quarterly Review 1809–1853* ([1921] New York: AMS Press, 1970) discusses the political, social, and literary leanings of the *Quarterly*, but this study is brief. For an account of the day-to-day workings of both major quarterlies during the mid-Victorian era, however, see Joanne Shattock, *Politics and Reviewers: The Edinburgh and the Quarterly* (Leicester: Leicester University Press, 1989).

20. See W.A. Copinger, *On the Authorship of the First Hundred Numbers of the Edinburgh Review* (Manchester: privately published at the Priory Press, 1895); Hill Shine and Helen Chadwick Shine, *The Quarterly Review Under Gifford: Identification of Contributors 1809–1824* (Chapel Hill, NC: University of North Carolina Press, 1949); and *The Wellesley Index to Victorian Periodicals, 1824–1900; tables of contents and identification of contributors, with bibliographies of their articles and stories*, ed. Walter Edwards Houghton, 5 Vols. (Toronto: University of Toronto Press, 1966–89). The work of the Shines has also been supplemented by a website, *The Quarterly Review 1809–1824: Notes, Contents, and Identification of Contributors*, available online at: http://www.dreamwater.com/edu/earlyqr/ (16 July 2002). Since the *Wellesley* begins its coverage of *Blackwood's* in 1824, Alan Lang Strout's *Bibliography of Articles in Blackwood's Magazine, 1817–1825* (Lubbock, TX: Texas Tech University Press, 1959) remains useful. Despite the date in its title, the *Wellesley* offers full coverage of the early years of the *Edinburgh*.

21. See, for example, Newman Ivey White, *The Unextinguished Hearth: Shelley and his Contemporary Critics* (Durham, NC: Duke University Press, 1938). As Marilyn Butler points out, "To assemble together the reviews of one poet (as in, say, the *Critical Heritage* volume on Coleridge or Keats) is to disjoin each review from an expressive and very pertinent original location." Butler, "Culture's Medium: The Role of the Review," in *The Cambridge Companion to British Romanticism*, ed. Stuart Curran (Cambridge: Cambridge University Press, 1993), 120–47 (147).

22. Jerome McGann, "Keats and the Historical Method in Literary Criticism," *Modern Language Notes* 94 (1979), 988–1032 (1002). For more recent work along these lines see, for example, John Kandl, "Private Lyrics in the Public Sphere: Leigh Hunt's *Examiner* and the Construction of a Public 'John Keats,'" *Keats-Shelley Journal* 44 (1995), 84–101; Paul Magnuson, *Reading Public Romanticism* (Princeton, NJ: Princeton University Press, 1998), 167–210.

23. Theresa M. Kelley, "Poetics and the Politics of Reception: Keats's 'La Belle Dame sans Merci,'" *ELH* 54 (1987), 333–62.

24. Marjorie Levinson, *Keats's Life of Allegory: The Origins of a Style* (Oxford: Basil Blackwell, 1988). Levinson builds on the insights of William Keach, "Cockney Couplets: Keats and the Politics of Style," *Studies in Romanticism* 25 (1986), 182–96.

25. See, for example, Kim Wheatley, "The *Blackwood's* Attacks on Leigh Hunt," *Nineteenth-Century Literature* 47 (June 1992), 1–31; Nicholas Roe, *John Keats and the Culture of Dissent* (Oxford: Clarendon Press, 1997); Emily Lorraine de Montluzin, "Killing the Cockneys: *Blackwood's* Weapons of Choice Against Hunt, Hazlitt, and Keats," *Keats-Shelley Journal* 47 (1998), 87–107; Jeffrey Cox, *Poetry and Politics in the Cockney School* (Cambridge: Cambridge University Press, 1998).

26. Karen Swann, "Literary Gentlemen and Lovely Ladies: The Debate on the Character of *Christabel*," *ELH* 52 (1985), 394–418.

27. Jon P. Klancher, *The Making of English Reading Audiences 1790–1832* (Madison, WI: University of Wisconsin Press, 1987). Further references in parentheses.

28. See, for example, Kevin Gilmartin, "Popular Radicalism and the Public Sphere," *Studies in Romanticism* 33 (1994), 549–57. For the notion of the early nineteenth-century English public sphere as divided into "multiple and contestatory publics," see also Jon Klancher's "Introduction" to the forum, "Romanticism and its Publics," in *Studies in Romanticism* 33 (1994), 523–5 (523).

29. Russell Noyes, for example, in *Wordsworth and Jeffrey in Controversy* (Bloomington, IN: Indiana University Publications, 1941) assumes that the *Edinburgh* spoke for Jeffrey.

30. David Latané, "The Birth of the Author in the Victorian Archive," *Victorian Periodicals Review* 22/3 (Fall 1989), 114.

31. Butler, "Culture's Medium," 137. The quarterlies' construction of their audience, then, would seem to be more social than political: Shattock, in *Politics and Reviewers*, suggests that people did not tend to read one of the two major quarterlies to the exclusion of the other (13); see also Butler, "Culture's Medium," 140.

32. Mark Schoenfield, "Regulating Standards: The *Edinburgh Review* and the Circulations of Judgment," *The Wordsworth Circle* 24/3 (1993), 148–51.

33. Mark Schoenfield, "Voices Together: Lamb, Hazlitt, and the *London*," *Studies in Romanticism* 29 (1990), 257–72.

34. Jerome Christensen, "The Detection of the Romantic Conspiracy in Britain," *South Atlantic Quarterly* 95 (1996), 603–27 (609–10). See also Jerome Christensen, *Lord Byron's Strength: Romantic Writing and Commercial Society* (Baltimore, MD: Johns Hopkins University Press, 1993), 28–31.

35. Margaret Russett, *De Quincey's Romanticism: Canonical Minority and the Forms of Transmission* (Cambridge: Cambridge University Press, 1997), 92–134. See also Peter Murphy's article on *Blackwood's*, "Impersonation and Authorship in Romantic Britain," *ELH* 59 (1992), 625–49, discussed by David Higgins in the present collection.

36. Kevin Gilmartin, *Print Politics: The Press and Radical Opposition in Early Nineteenth-Century England* (Cambridge: Cambridge University Press, 1996). See also Michael Scrivener, *Poetry and Reform: Periodical Verse from the English Democratic Press, 1792–1824* (Detroit, MI: Wayne State University Press, 1992).

37. Stephen C. Behrendt (ed.), *Romanticism, Radicalism, and the Press* (Detroit, MI: Wayne State University Press, 1997), 19.

38. Steven Jones, "The Black Dwarf as Satiric Performance," in Behrendt, *Romanticism, Radicalism, and the Press*, 203–14 (213).

39. Mark Parker, *Literary Magazines and British Romanticism* (Cambridge: Cambridge University Press, 2000). Further references in parentheses.

40. See, for example, [John Scott], "The Mohock Magazine," *London Magazine* 2 (Nov. 1820), 666–85.

41. See also Massimiliano Demata and Duncan Wu (ed.), *British Romanticism and the Edinburgh Review* (New York: Palgrave Macmillan, 2002), which did not appear in time for me to be able to discuss it here.

42. Edward Copeland, *Women Writing about Money: Women's Fiction in England, 1790–1820* (Cambridge: Cambridge University Press, 1995). See also Margaret Beetham, *A Magazine of Her Own?* (London: Routledge, 1996).

43. Sonia Hofkosh, "Commodities Among Themselves: Reading/Desire in Early Women's Magazines," *Essays and Studies* 51 (1998), 78–92 (86).

44. Sonia Hofkosh, *Sexual Politics and the Romantic Author* (Cambridge: Cambridge University Press, 1998), 9–10.

45. See, for example, J.H. Alexander, "*Blackwood's*: Magazine as Romantic Form," *The Wordsworth Circle* 15/2 (1984), 57–68. This essay focuses on the literary criticism of *Blackwood's*.

46. Christensen, "Detection of the Romantic Conspiracy," 625–6.

47. William Hazlitt, *Works*, ed. P.P. Howe, 21 Vols. (London: J.M. Dent and Sons, 1930–34), 11:127.

48. Peter G. Patmore, "On Magazine Writers," *London Magazine* 6 (July 1822), 23.

49. The Romantic-era diarist Henry Crabb Robinson, for example, sometimes mentions his reactions to periodicals. See Edith J. Morley (ed.), *Henry Crabb Robinson on Books and their Writers*, 3 Vols. (London, J.M. Dent, 1938), 1:279. Clive, in *Scotch Reviewers*, quotes an example of a diarist disagreeing with the *Edinburgh* (12). Lyn Pykett, in "Reading the Periodical Press: Text and Context," *Victorian Periodicals Review* 22 (1989), 100–8, calls for more information about actual readers of periodicals.

50. Jane Austen, *Mansfield Park*, ed. Claudia L. Johnson (New York: Norton, 1998), 74.

51. See, for example, *The Examiner 1808–1822*, 15 Vols. (London: Pickering & Chatto, 1996–98), a facsimile edition of a text long available to many scholars only on microfilm.

Mary Robinson, the Monthly Magazine, and the Free Press

ADRIANA CRACIUN

> Does not the liberty of the press present a thousand avenues for just and natural retaliation?
>
> Mary Robinson, *Walsingham; or, The Pupil of Nature* (1797)

Mary Robinson's essay on the "Present State of the Manners, Society, &c&c of the Metropolis of England,"[1] published in the *Monthly Magazine* shortly before the author's death in 1800, makes a significant statement on the volatile state of British print culture at the turn of the nineteenth century.[2] Robinson is now widely recognized as a major figure of the Romantic period, when her volumes of poetry, popular novels, and polemical pamphlets attracted both critical esteem and controversy. Robinson's large body of work is known to have influenced and been influenced by contemporaries such as Robert Southey, William Wordsworth, and especially Samuel Taylor Coleridge, who called Robinson "a woman of undoubted genius."[3] Robinson's little-known essay on the "Present State of the Manners and Society of the Metropolis" (hereafter "Metropolis"), as the first half of this essay will demonstrate, represents the increasingly radical author's contribution to the turn-of-the-century debate over the direction of print culture and fate of the free press. Perhaps the best-known contribution to this debate (at least to modern readers) is William Wordsworth's Preface to the *Lyrical Ballads* (1800). In the second half of this essay I examine the possibility that Wordsworth may have been influenced by Robinson's authoritative overview of British public culture, and perhaps composed his own countervision of art – nativist, introspective, and masculine – in some respects as an alternative to Robinson's celebration of London as a cosmopolitan and (proto)feminist sphere of public art. Regardless of any possible direct influence, the coeval origin of these two major manifestos attests to the urgency with which Romantic writers addressed the crisis in print and popular culture.

Published in four monthly installments, Robinson's "Metropolis" gives an overview of the rise of London print culture and its politically liberating effects through such institutions as libraries, publishing houses, newspapers, periodicals, and theaters, despite politically repressive measures and lack of aristocratic patronage. According to Robinson, whose early stage career remained central to her understanding of art, the theaters in particular ("open schools of public manners, which exhibit at all times the touchstone of the public mind" [36]) are central to metropolitan culture.[4] Moving through different kinds of public spectacles, in the second installment Robinson catalogs a series of fashionable vices and urban hazards: the late night suppers of "the effeminized race of modern nobility" (139); the "barbarity" of cattle driven through the city on their way to the slaughterhouses at Smithfield; the contrasts between modern British medicine and the sorry state of underfunded charity hospitals for the poor. Robinson's panoramic account is unflinching in its attention to the interconnectedness of civility and squalor, splendor and misery (a characteristic theme of her poems and novels). The nobility in particular are severely rebuked here and throughout the essay for their indifference to the suffering of the poor (and of artists), yet Robinson also resolutely defends the cultural fruits of leisure, refinement, and wealth.

Focusing on the phenomenon of what she terms the "Aristocratic Democrat," Robinson in the third installment launches her most vitriolic attack on the leisured classes' hypocritical relationship to public culture and its democratizing potential. Robinson critiques the hypocrisy of those who claim to embrace the democratic principles of cross-class contact available uniquely in the metropolis. An Aristocratic Democrat "talks loudly of the rights of mankind; extols the blessings of universal liberty," and "ridicules the distinctions" of inherited wealth and titles, yet only superficially (219). "If a man of the less exalted classes of society meets the ARISTOCRATIC DEMOCRAT in the public streets," writes Robinson, "he is coldly saluted, or perhaps, wilfully unseen" (219), much like the former prostitute Jemima was ignored by the enlightened philosopher in Wollstonecraft's *The Wrongs of Woman* (1798). The Aristocratic Democrat is thus a travesty of the (ostensibly disinterested) cosmopolitan citizen of the public sphere, enjoying the praise he might gain from championing a meritocracy, but reinforcing the hierarchies of rank for his own selfish ends. By not allowing "his wife or daughters, or any of the female branches of his family" to associate with women of inferior rank, he reveals himself as the most retrograde of patriarchs as well, strictly policing women's access to the benefits of the public sphere (219). As we will see, women were central to Robinson's metropolitan manifesto.

The aristocracy remains a formidable barrier to this metropolitan, cosmopolitan ideal that Robinson elaborates, a significant departure from earlier eighteenth-century notions of cosmopolitanism. In the final installment of Robinson's essay, she returns to the central argument regarding the democratizing, cross-class potential of metropolitan culture, despite the hypocrisy and debauchery of its elite. Robinson attempts to carve out of the overwhelming heterogeneity of metropolitan London a version of the public sphere that more closely resembles her ideal, borrowing from continental models as alternatives, and focusing on the free press as the chief means of reform:

> There never were so many monthly and diurnal publications as at the present period; and to the perpetual novelty which issues from the press may in great measure, be attributed the expansion of mind, which daily evinces itself among all classes of the people. The monthly miscellanies are read by the middling orders of society, by the *literati*, and sometimes by the loftiest of our nobility. The daily prints fall into the hands of all classes: they display the temper of the times; the intricacies of political manoeuvre; the opinions of the learned, the enlightened, and the patriotic. ... The press is the mirror where folly may see its own likeness, and vice contemplate the magnitude of its deformity [305].

This self-referential gesture makes visible the cultural matrix in which Robinson's manifesto takes shape, and the actual audience she hopes to reach in the *Monthly Magazine* – "the middling orders of society, ... the *literati*, and sometimes ... the loftiest of our nobility."

The contrast between Robinson's celebration of public and print culture as democratizing and Wordsworth's anxiety regarding popular culture is instructive. Wordsworth in his Preface famously engages in a literally reactionary project to establish (he might say restore) imaginative literature – Milton, Shakespeare, and by extension Wordsworth himself – as a bulwark against the dehumanization caused by "the increasing accumulation of men in cities."[5] As Jon Klancher argues:

> This Romantic writer yearns to return to the space of "reception" (symbolic exchange) from the historical ground of "consumption" (commodity exchange). Yet to restore the reading of Milton and thus to save literature itself, Wordsworth must ultimately produce the most paradoxical sense of "literature" – a discourse which can be "received" only in the absence of a real social audience.[6]

Robinson's "Metropolis" essay offers an alternative model for Romantic "literature," one that reveals what Wordsworth in his Preface is manifestly uncomfortable in addressing: the conditions of cultural production in which it is itself forged and received. The periodical press in particular emerges in Robinson's essay, as in her other prose works, as the most significant engine of political and intellectual liberty in the contentious 1790s. The "real social audience" that Wordsworth (paradoxically) fears is openly and successfully sought out by Robinson in "Metropolis." By publishing her manifesto in the reformist and popular *Monthly Magazine*, as well as other essays in other periodicals, Robinson helps build the Republic of Letters that she sets out to document.

ROBINSON AND THE *MONTHLY MAGAZINE*

Robinson's "Metropolis" essay crystallizes her increasing commitment to the free press as the most potent engine of political reform, and its publication in Richard Phillips' *Monthly* invites us to consider more comprehensively her political writings in the periodical press. The *Monthly Magazine*, with its "situational" "liberal or radical principles," was the natural venue for Robinson's increasing confidence as public intellectual and outspoken political thinker.[7] Founded in 1796 by Richard Phillips and Joseph Johnson,[8] the *Monthly* was edited until 1806 by the prominent Dissenter Dr John Aikin, a central figure in the Warrington Academy of radical Unitarians whose associates included Joseph Priestley, William Taylor, Gilbert Wakefield and Anna Laetitia Barbauld.[9] With a circulation of 5,000 in 1797, the *Monthly* was easily one of the most popular periodicals in the 1790s, outselling the *Gentleman's Magazine*, *British Critic* and *Critical Review*.[10] The *Monthly* was known for its "cosmopolitan, 'continental' frame of mind," covering foreign literature in detail as well as controversial debates on the rights of women, non-human animals, and the insane.[11] Mary Hays wrote a number of feminist essays in the *Monthly*'s "Enquirer" series of debates between readers, and Wordsworth and Coleridge famously intended to write "The Ancient Mariner" for the *Monthly* in hopes of earning £5.[12] The "*Monthly* collected readers and writers as interchangeable participants," writes Jon Klancher, into "a new kind of ideologically cohesive discursive community:" "not a 'society of the text' in the eighteenth-century sense, but a 'polity' of the text" characterized by a "philosophical radicalism."[13] Unrepentantly Francophilic and anti-war throughout the Romantic period, the *Monthly Magazine* was thus well-suited to Robinson's increasingly radicalized politics and her cosmopolitan feminism. In addition to "Metropolis," Robinson also published in the *Monthly* essays on French political figures (the Duc d'Orleans, Marie Antoinette)[14] and poems later incorporated in her unfinished political epic *The Progress of Liberty*.[15]

"Metropolis" is generically innovative, not surprisingly for a writer whose final volume of poems, *Lyrical Tales* (1800), has been credited by Stuart Curran as representing "the single most inventive use of metrics in English verse since the Restoration."[16] Robinson builds on earlier eighteenth-century models of urban writing, as well as more recent examples in the *Monthly*. In addition to influential earlier accounts such as

Defoe's *Tour Through the Whole Island of Great Britain* (1724–26), contemporary British travel books were clearly a source of Robinson's inspiration, such as her friend Samuel Pratt's *Gleanings of England*, which she admired and celebrated in verse.[17] An earlier essay in the *Monthly*, a "Sketch of the Present State of Society and Manners in Plymouth," fits well with the periodical's consistent interest in what we would today describe as cultural diversity, from foreign periodicals and literature to provincial manners.[18] After Robinson's "Metropolis," numerous other such urban accounts appeared in the *Monthly*, none as long or as ambitious as hers. Robinson expanded the scope of her metropolitan essay to that of a cultural manifesto, though others who followed her example in the *Monthly* did not take this further step into cultural critique. The "Account of the State of Society and Manners in Liverpool," for example, is written as a tourist guide to Liverpool, as were most of the other such accounts, and lacks the critical edge of Robinson's overview of metropolitan culture, which is quite frank about London's excesses and hazards.[19]

Robinson's essay thus grew out of the contemporary taste for such panoramic urban accounts, and grew into a new form of cultural critique, bringing together her accumulated interests in art, politics, and print culture. Robinson had published several earlier essay series that are in some respects proto-versions of the "Metropolis" essay, though smaller in scope, such as her series of *Morning Post* essays signed "Sylphid" and gathered posthumously in the *Memoirs*. The Sylphid essays are not overtly political but more social in nature, giving an overview of the aristocracy's (particularly women's) pretensions and hypocrisy. They also nicely illustrate the unfolding trajectory of her Metropolis project, at one point incorporating the titles of the two series that would follow: "Behold me at the Close of the Eighteenth Century, in the metropolis of England."[20] Between the Sylphid essays early in 1800 and the Metropolis series later in the year, Robinson also wrote an unsigned essay series titled the "Close of the Eighteenth Century," published from August to September 1800 in the *Morning Post* and to my knowledge not previously attributed to her. Robinson builds on her Sylphid critique of fashionable life, adding an appreciation of women writers and artists which she had recently expounded in her feminist *Letter to the Women of England* (1799).[21]

The final essay on the "Close of the Eighteenth Century" begins by condemning the vanity of portrait painting among the aristocracy, and ends with a celebration of authors and the Republic of Letters, a nice transition from the concerns of the earlier Sylphid to the "Metropolis." Robinson finds particularly irksome the hypocrisy of the wealthy, who do not patronize the arts and yet affect their attributes in their portraits:[22]

Men, who have never read five volumes, beyond the literature of the
Race-Course, or a Court-Calendar, pourtrayed in pensive attitudes,
with books surrounded, as proudly as Macaenas: while women, who
can scarcely write an epistle, are displayed with pens in their hands,
and with a solemnity of countenance that marks the very extent of
modern philosophy: Dull, empty, vain, and imposing! There have
been instances of silly females sitting for their pictures crowned with
laurels! Some have attempted to personify Hebe, Minerva, Cleopatra,
Sappho![23]

"As Authors (at least good ones), deserve the highest honours," she
continues, "so those who are mere pretenders cannot be too severely
censured." The essay concludes with a tribute to British authors: "the
Republic of Letters will fix a splendid data to the superior and augmenting
powers of the human mind, evinced at the close of THE EIGHTEENTH
CENTURY." This would become the central concern of the *Monthly*'s
"Metropolis" essay, which began publication just as the "Close of the
Eighteenth Century" ended.

What began as acute social critique of fashionable foibles and hypocrisy
in the *Morning Post*'s Sylphid and the "Close of the Eighteenth Century"
becomes a radical critique of press and political repression, and the political
(not merely social) corruption of the wealthy, in the *Monthly*'s
"Metropolis." Robinson skillfully designs each series to fit the publication's
distinct content and audience. For the two series in the *Morning Post*,
Robinson concentrates on fashionable society because that newspaper, like
most, regularly covered the comings and goings of high society, from royal
levees, to official functions, balls, and dances, including detailed
descriptions of the fashions worn. The Sylphid and "Close of the Eighteenth
Century" essays are juxtaposed deliberately and ironically with such
accounts of high society in the *Morning Post*. In the *Monthly Magazine*,
Robinson expands her argument to one suitable for that quintessentially
"serious" and philosophical periodical,[24] sharpening the political argument
beyond a more acceptable anti-luxury critique, to a reformist and anti-
aristocratic one. This range of materials and audiences shows Robinson at
her entrepreneurial best, juggling numerous publishing ventures under
different guises (and pseudonyms),[25] but it also illustrates how much more
we need to learn about the extent and underestimated political range of her
periodical publishing.

Unjust restrictions on the press and on writers were a growing concern
for Robinson and appear as a theme throughout her novels. *The Natural
Daughter* (1799) in particular is deeply involved in print culture debates,
featuring as its heroine a writer who encounters a full range of difficulties
while publishing. Here Robinson is able to put to use her considerable

experience of diverse print media, venues, and genres, particularly regarding the periodical press. Her narrative illustrates a cross-section of different kinds of periodicals read by her female characters, distinguishing their content, audience, and the corruptions they are prey to, including: a county paper, whose owner is menaced with prosecution; a society paper, where marriages of the wealthy are pompously announced; and the "diurnal prints" available in circulating libraries, where women keep up with events in Bath high society, as well as the developments in the war with France. In *The False Friend* (1799), Robinson dramatizes how the treason laws and climate of paranoia were abused for selfish and criminal ends while regulating the circulation of writings. The heroine Gertrude is detained before a Lord Justice, charged by a scheming landlady with possessing a packet of treasonous papers (in reality, papers legitimizing her lineage): "the packet is a most suspicious packet: it looks and it smells like treason," says the landlady, "and it is the duty of every loyal subject to be careful, and to examine all writings that pass through their hands; and to give information where they find such symptoms of guilt."[26] Robinson's *Natural Daughter*, *The False Friend* and especially *Walsingham* have begun to attract critical attention, though generally this focuses on the feminist sexual politics of the novels, not on their engagement with reform and print politics.[27]

Excerpts from Robinson's novel *Walsingham; or, The Pupil of Nature* (1797) published in the *Morning Post* illustrate the political acumen with which Robinson addressed freedom of the press in different publishing contexts. *Walsingham*'s complex plot centers on a disinherited orphan Walsingham Ainsworth, whose cousin Sidney inherits the family estates and title instead of him because s/he cross-dresses as a man. Robinson demystifies sexual and class privilege, and despite the "happy" marriage ending (of the excessively sensitive Walsingham and the newly feminized Sidney, who nevertheless possesses a masculine education and manly virtues), *Walsingham* is one of Robinson's most politically controversial novels. *Walsingham* was rightly identified by the *Anti-Jacobin* as a dangerously philosophical novel, and its inclusion (along with the *Monthly Magazine*) in Gillray's "The New Morality" cartoon placed this novel of cross-dressing and social critique squarely in the camp of fellow radicals like Godwin and Wollstonecraft. Robinson clearly invited such political readings of her novels, excerpting controversial passages from *Walsingham* in the pro-reform *Morning Post* in order to raise political issues as well as sell more copies. Robinson had long used the *Morning Post* as a platform for publicizing her works and popularizing her social critique (for example, in the London columns and her sharp-edged "Tabitha Bramble" poems). In *Walsingham*, however, she spoke out even more boldly, as for example in this excerpt from the novel published in the *Morning Post* as "On the Diurnal Prints:"

"What right have the *canaille* to know the transactions of the upper world?"

"That right which is the scourge of overbearing licentiousness, which raises the bulwark of freedom above the chaos of folly and deception, and illumines the low hovel of honest industry, equally with the loftiest abode of pride and dissipation. Heaven forbid that the time should ever approach when the source of public information, which has so long been the pride of Englishmen, shall be closed and annihilated!"[28]

Here Walsingham defends the freedom of the press in a debate with an aristocrat, describing newspapers as "the bulwark of freedom" because "they are not so bought over to the service of unjust condemnation," that is, to bribery and influence. "The daily papers are too cheap," and "their price should be raised above the pockets of the vulgar," replies the aristocrat (3:253). Of course that is precisely what happened with Pitt's Stamp Tax, as the *Morning Post* reminded its readers each day for years by listing both its original price (three pence) and its doubled price due to "Mr Pitt's Tax."[29]

A second excerpt from *Walsingham* in the *Morning Post* similarly highlights the free-press issue, with Robinson declaring that "the most powerful of the human race, in these momentous times, are *men of letters*, not men of *titles*: those who can guide the *pen*, and *influence the country by the genuine language of truth and philanthropy*."[30] Robinson's inflated rhetoric here and elsewhere should not be mistaken for abstraction, because her targets are specific to the post-treason trials 1790s, and she is not afraid to name names. Lest there should be any confusion about the nature of her new novel, Robinson frequently alludes to its critique of "men of titles" in notes inserted in the *Morning Post* in 1797 and 1798, and singles out Lord Kenyon in particular: *Walsingham* "should have been dedicated to Lord Kenyon," she writes in the *Post*.[31] Lord Kenyon was the Chief Justice and Master of the Rolls,[32] and had presided over several key English treason trials of publishers and writers, namely those of John Frost, Daniel Eaton, Thomas Williams (for printing Paine), and the *Morning Chronicle*. In the 1794 *Morning Chronicle* case, Kenyon summed up by saying that "I think this paper was published with a wicked, malicious intent to vilify the Government, and to make the people discontented," adding that "the minds of the people of this country were much agitated by these political topics, of which the mass of the people never can form a true judgment."[33] The main thrust of Walsingham's disputes with the aristocracy, and specifically in the excerpts Robinson includes in the *Morning Post*, systematically attacks the persecution of the free press that Kenyon enacted on publishers, writers, and "diurnal prints" like the *Morning Chronicle*.

Like *Walsingham*, Robinson's "Metropolis" also refers to the treason trials and other repressive measures that the government used to police the Republic of Letters:

> Works of extensive thought and philosophical research have been watched with more malevolence than justice. Political restrictions have been enforced, to warp the public taste; and the gigantic wings of Reason have, at times, been paralyzed by their augmenting severity [Aug. 1800, 36].

"Even our prisons have been illumined by the brilliancy of talents," continues Robinson (36). The consequences of such repression of the free press can be deadly, as the repentant aristocratic hero of her French Revolution novel, *Hubert de Sevrac* (1796), finally realizes: "Had the tongues of my countrymen been at liberty, their swords had been unstained with blood!"[34] Walsingham echoes this conviction: "Does not the liberty of the press present a thousand avenues for just and natural retaliation?" (3:252). What remains unsaid in Walsingham's rhetorical question – the possibility of violent retaliation – is precisely what Robinson had addressed in a 1794 letter defending the founders of the British Convention against charges of treason.

In January 1794, Robinson, writing under her well-known pseudonym "Tabitha Bramble," wrote a remarkable letter to the Lord Advocate of Scotland, Robert Dundas, defending the convicted founders of the British Convention in Edinburgh and attacking governmental repression: "On the one hand, we have the Reformers contending for certain principles, & certain renovations which every body allows to be founded in Justice. On the other, Government persecuting in a rigorous manner such honest endeavours."[35] Robinson then evokes the example of the Glorious Revolution, and concludes with a warning citing a more recent precedent of governmental terror and the retaliation that it inspires:

> The sanguinary harsh measures employed against the Reformers, are with some degree of Propriety, attributed to you. Mr Muirs, & now Mr Skirvings & Margarots cruel treatment have added to your Lordships unpopularity: a few more will render you perfectly odious. It will then be reckoned honourable to deprive Society of such a *Pest*. Some Male, or rather more likely some Female hand, will direct the Dagger that will do such an important Service; and Britain shall not want a Female Patriot emulous of the fame of *M. Cordet* [*sic*].[36]

William Skirving and Maurice Margarot, leaders of "The British Convention of the Delegates of the People, associated to obtain Universal Suffrage and Annual Parliaments," had been convicted of treason earlier that month and sentenced to transportation, virtually a death sentence.[37] Thomas Muir, founder of the Friends of the People in Edinburgh, had been convicted (along with the Revd Thomas Palmer) of sedition in the autumn of 1793 and also sentenced to transportation. Such sanguinary measures, warns Robinson, have inspired terrible acts of revenge in English and French history – among them the assassination of radical journalist Jean-Paul Marat by Charlotte Corday. Corday assassinated Marat in July 1793 in retaliation for the Jacobins' earlier coup against the Girondins, one of the precipitating events leading to the Terror. A chain of escalating violence is precisely what restricting freedom of the press, of speech, and of association sets in motion according to Robinson, who went as far as calling for a British Corday, a "Female Patriot," to defend such liberties.[38]

Robinson's engagement with the treason trials, particularly in matters of the free press, is significant, and due to restrictions of space I have only discussed it here in the context of her writings in the *Monthly Magazine* and very briefly in the *Morning Post* and the later novels. Freedom of the press increasingly occupied Robinson's mind throughout the 1790s, and we see in her subtle use of different media – both monthly and daily papers, and novels – that she was keen to exploit different formats to highlight the urgency of the situation. Having examined Robinson's "Metropolis" in this larger context of political reform and repression, and in relation to other forms of publication such as "diurnal prints" and novels, I turn now to a more detailed account of that essay's claims, and their significance for her audience, from (perhaps) William Wordsworth to a large number of posthumous readers.

ROBINSON'S "METROPOLIS" AND WORDSWORTH'S PREFACE

Robinson's poetic practice has been put forward by Stuart Curran, Jerome McGann, Judith Pascoe and others as a significant alternative to the Wordsworthian poetic model under which Romantic studies have so long labored. Thus McGann, referring to Robinson's Preface to *Sappho and Phaon* (1796), in which she elevates feminine sensibility to the highest poetic calling, persuasively argues: "Well might Wordsworth, in the face of such a consciously feminized prophecy, step slightly back and try to re-establish poetry as the discourse of a 'man speaking to men.'"[39] In her 1800 "Metropolis" essay, I suggest, Robinson goes farther than in her 1796 poetic manifesto, and offers a critical overview of British public culture as a whole. Resolutely urban, democratic, and cosmopolitan, Robinson's essay amounts to a manifesto of metropolitan culture, one in which women are central agents of change. Building on this scholarship that has returned Robinson to the center of critical accounts of Romanticism and, more specifically, that sees her as representing a powerful alternative to

Wordsworth's influential model of Romantic poetry, I want to compare her "Metropolis" essay to Wordsworth's Preface to the *Lyrical Ballads*. In exploring the connections between these texts, my intention is not to re-establish Wordsworth and his Preface as the philosophical center of "Romanticism" (as is often the case in traditional accounts) and Robinson as an "alternative." Rather, I am interested in seeing how Robinson's manifesto, like Wordsworth's that followed, resonated with competing Romantic models of art and its relations to the social.

As mentioned earlier, Robinson's essay was published in the *Monthly* in four parts – 1 August, 1 September, 1 October, and 1 November 1800. Wordsworth wrote his Preface in September and October and revised it as late as December; the 1800 *Lyrical Ballads* did not actually appear until January 1801.[40] During this same time, Robinson and Coleridge enjoyed an ongoing poetic correspondence in the *Morning Post* (where Robinson served as poetry editor). We know that Coleridge (and perhaps Wordsworth) also read Robinson's novels, and that after reading "Kubla Khan" in manuscript, Robinson published the first known reference to that poem in her tribute "To the Poet Coleridge."[41] Wordsworth's relationship to Robinson was more conflicted, as he had tried to change the title of the second edition of *Lyrical Ballads* once he heard that Robinson's *Lyrical Tales* would also be published by Longman's in London and printed by Cottle in Bristol.[42] Nevertheless, Wordsworth's "The Solitude of Binnorie" (known later as "The Seven Sisters"), which acknowledges the influence of Robinson's "The Haunted Beach," was published in the *Morning Post* of 14 October.[43] This was followed by another poem of Wordsworth's, "Alcaeus to Sappho," submitted by Coleridge and published in the *Morning Post* on 24 November 1800.[44] These are just a few of the literary interchanges that establish the great extent to which Wordsworth and Robinson (as well as Southey and Coleridge) were mutually influenced at this time when, as Curran has argued, Robinson was "by far the best known of these four poets."[45]

I suggest that, in addition to these acknowledged poetic affinities and influences, Robinson's "Present State of the Manners and Society of the Metropolis of England" may have been an inspiration for Wordsworth's Preface. Regardless of any possible influence, these manifestos merit reading alongside each other as instances of two Romantic writers developing their divergent models of art and its social functions and origins. Wordsworth considered providing his own "account of the present state of the public taste in this country,"[46] and one can trace in his essay a series of counterarguments to four central arguments in Robinson's "Metropolis." First, as we have seen, Robinson envisions turn-of-the-century London as the world's leading Republic of Letters, generating intellectual, aesthetic and political improvement across class and gender lines:

> The wide expansion of literature has been an augmenting fountain of knowledge ever since priestcraft and bigotry became palsied by those energies of mind which have, of late years, burst forth with an invincible … dominion. Every man, nay, almost every woman, now reads, thinks, projects, and accomplishes. The force of human reflection has taken off the chain which once shackled the mind. … London is the busy mart of literary traffick. Its public libraries, its multitudes of authors, its diurnal publications, and its scenes of dramatic ordeal, all contribute to the important task of enlarging and embellishing the world of letters [Aug. 1800, 35–6].

What for Robinson "embellish[es] the world of letters" and liberates people from "priestcraft and bigotry" – public theater and popular print culture – for Wordsworth are among the forces that "blunt the discriminating powers of the mind," reducing it "to a state of almost savage torpor."[47] For Robinson, the instrument of all this social reform is the free press:

> There never were so many monthly and diurnal publications as at the present period; and to the perpetual novelty which issues from the press may in great measure, be attributed the expansion of mind, which daily evinces itself among all classes of the people. … The daily prints fall into the hands of all classes [305].

Compare this to Wordsworth's well-known anxiety over the unpredictable effects of print media on the public and their degenerating taste, exacerbated by the "rapid communication of intelligence" in the mass media. In contrast, Robinson's commitment to the democratic effects of a free press is bracing, and in line with radical reformers of the time who according to Kevin Gilmartin "were convinced that the press necessarily promoted liberty and reform."[48] Robinson's firmly forward-looking "Metropolis" essay combines older eighteenth-century notions of commerce as contributing to refinement with contemporary radical rhetoric praising the free press as a "bulwark which REASON has raised … round the altar of immortal LIBERTY!" (305). Robinson perhaps echoes the language (and certainly the sentiment) of the Society for Constitutional Information, who in their publicized 1789 celebration of the English Bill of Rights affirmed that "The Liberty of the Press" is "the bulwark of liberty."[49]

In addition to this vision of metropolitan print culture as fundamentally democratizing, Robinson's cultural ideal is cosmopolitan. She repeatedly compares British cultural practices (often unfavorably) to European ones, and is generous with praise for French and German influence on British literature, theater, architecture, art, language, and fashion. For example, she notes that "The great number of emigrants who have become our inmates since the French revolution, have contributed to this wide circulation of knowledge," adding that "some of the best translations from the German have been the productions of female pens" (221). Robinson then praises Anne Plumptre, whose popular translations of Kotzebue were precisely what Wordsworth warned against a few months later when he complained about an influx of "sickly and stupid German tragedies."[50] Like Charlotte Smith, Helen Maria Williams, and other feminist contemporaries, Robinson had long looked to continental Europe (where she lived for some time) as a refuge from British provincialism and its suffocating sexual mores and legal hypocrisy. In "Metropolis," the bed-ridden and isolated Robinson, suffering in the last stages of the illness that would end her life in a few months, makes a powerful case for seeing London as a cosmopolitan and European metropolis, full of all the predictable excesses of wealth and squalor, but also a world capital, giving its citizens access to the widest possible cultural influences.[51]

Central to this cosmopolitan vision, which Wordsworth would explicitly reject in his nativist focus on English rural simplicity, is the role of women as cultural producers:

> The women of England have, by their literary labours, reached an altitude of mental excellence, far above those of any other nation. The works, which every year have been published by females, do credit to the very highest walks of literature. ... We have also sculptors, modellers, paintresses, and female artists of every description [39].

Throughout her works, Robinson characterized this "altitude of mental excellence" as an "Aristocracy of Genius,"[52] distinct from an aristocracy of wealth or privilege, as she clarified in *The Natural Daughter*: "the aristocracy of wealth had little to do with the aristocracy of genius" (1:249). Robinson also disassociates the Aristocracy of Genius from would-be "Aristocratic Democrats" who hypocritically reinforce hierarchies of (economic and sexual) power, upon whom she heaps scorn in "Metropolis." Women are central to this "Aristocracy of Genius," and as in her earlier feminist tract, *A Letter to the Women of England on the Injustice of Mental Subordination* (1799), Robinson is always careful to name Wollstonecraft, by then notorious, as a fellow traveler in this metropolis.[53] As Betsy Bolton and Judith Pascoe have argued, for the increasingly feminist Robinson, London – far from the frightening place of dislocation we find in *The Prelude* – offers women the professional opportunities that are their only hope for economic and sexual independence.[54]

These three emphases throughout Robinson's overview of London – urban print culture, cosmopolitanism, and women's central role therein – contribute to her overall vision of art as fundamentally public (not private, as in Wordsworth), both in its creative origins and its ideal sphere of influence. Robinson's vibrant metropolis, despite being riddled with predictable excesses (largely the aristocracy's), is simultaneously an unrivaled, if idealized, vision of the public sphere at the turn of the nineteenth century – that is, precisely when according to Habermas the public sphere was in decline. Habermas' theory of a monolithic (and masculine) bourgeois public sphere has met with numerous recent challenges; Robinson's "Metropolis," focusing as it does not only on the bourgeois literary public sphere, but also across gender and class lines, is further evidence of women's participation in this diverse sphere.[55] Trained in the theater and known as "Perdita" because of her role in *The Winter's Tale* which had attracted a young Prince of Wales in 1779, Robinson always retained a fascination with theatricality in her writings and self-presentation, which, as Pascoe has persuasively argued, allows us to imagine an alternative, unWordsworthian Romanticism "founded on theatrical modes of self-presentation and the corollary that women played active and influential roles in public life."[56] Robinson's essay overwhelms us with a tour through London as public spectacle, from its promenades "thronged with pedestrians of all classes" (138), through its cattle markets, gambling houses, charity hospitals, museums, and theaters. The emphasis is always on the public and (ostensibly) universally accessible nature of these spaces and art forms, from the public art in cathedrals and parks, to the cheap daily papers that "fall into the hands of all classes" and both genders. This will be Wordsworth's final and perhaps most significant departure in the Preface, in his consistent rejection of public, urban culture, and retreat into an idealized and introspective rural solitude. Robinson anticipated Wordsworth's withdrawal into "emotion recollected in tranquility" when she acknowledged that:

> The mind which is absorbed in the contemplation of public events, has no leisure to cherish the meliorating powers of sober, rational delight – It is in the solitude of peaceful thought alone that man becomes something far above the common hord [*sic*] of humanity [Aug. 1800, 37].

Nevertheless, Robinson consistently associates genius with the idealized public sphere: "A public exhibition is one of the most fostering spheres for the expansion of genius" (37). And "in arguing for the expansive power of the exhibit and the theatrical event," Pascoe reminds us, "Robinson provides a vindication of the exhibition of female talents."[57]

CONCLUSION: THE AFTERLIFE OF ROBINSON'S "METROPOLIS"

The "Metropolis" essay was one of the last writings published by Robinson in her lifetime, and its curious afterlife in Phillips' publishing house attests to its significance as a key Romantic representation of London print culture. Phillips, who had served three years in jail for printing seditious material and was known for publishing such radicals as Paine, Thomas Holcroft, Mary Hays, and Joel Barlow, also published the posthumous editions of Robinson's *Poetical Works* (1806) and *Memoirs* (1801), and her daughter's tribute volume, *The Wild Wreath* (1804).[58] In 1802 he began a new and profitable venture, a cultural guidebook to London called *The Picture of London*. Each year saw new editions, and the series was taken over by Longman's in 1815 and continued until the 1820s; later there would emerge competing editions such as *Leigh's New Picture of London* (1818) and *Mogg's New Picture of London* (1838), each following the model that Phillips had set out.[59]

Phillips' *Picture of London* contains the whole of Robinson's "Metropolis" essay, uncited and unacknowledged, and it seems possible that Robinson had contemplated writing such a comprehensive overview of London herself. Phillips' *Public Characters of 1800–1801* states that "Mrs Robinson ... has nearly completed her own memoirs, in the form of 'Anecdotes of distinguished Personages, and Observations on Society and Manners, during her Travels on the Continent and England.'"[60] Robinson died before completing this ambitious project (her memoirs were probably finished by her daughter). Perhaps had Robinson published them in her lifetime, she would have given the memoirs this title and larger scope, one echoed in her essay on the "Present State of the Manners, Society, &c&c of the Metropolis of England." Robinson's "Metropolis" is included, complete, in the *Picture of London for 1802* and for 1803, and by the 1806 edition, Phillips excerpts the essay chiefly as a section on periodicals and newspapers. By the 1815 edition only one paragraph remains of Robinson's essay (again on the periodical press), and in the 1818 competing *Leigh's New Picture of London* this paragraph is still discernible, though paraphrased, in a section on the "General State of Literature and the Arts in the Metropolis."

Phillips clearly saw the marketability of such a project, and in 1804 published a more lavish and expensive version of his guide, *Modern London; Being the History of the Present State of the British Metropolis.*[61] This guide is even more dependent on Robinson's (again uncited) "Metropolis," as its title suggests, with Robinson's essay no longer printed whole but excerpted in distinct sections, for example on publishing, promenades, art exhibits, and theater, making the volume an expanded form of Robinson's original vision. The numerous copper plates also illustrate for a more genteel audience the delights of London, many of which Robinson's essay had highlighted, such as the promenade in St James Park and the theaters. One of the illustrations of Drury Lane Theatre in particular seems to allude to Phillips' absent collaborator, for we see a woman selling a play bill for *Hamlet*, and readers of Robinson may have remembered that she played Ophelia at Drury Lane in 1777–78, a highlight of her theatrical career.

Phillips' reprinting of Robinson's essay introduced more revisions and excisions as the years went on: removing Robinson's critiques of the aristocracy and the government, and of the hazards of urban life, as well as her celebrations of women's (especially foreign women's) contributions to British culture. For example, while excerpting the (October 1800) "Metropolis" essay for his third chapter, Phillips omitted a large section containing Robinson's characteristic complaint of how men and women of letters are "neglected, unsought and alienated," particularly "enlightened women." Similar sections from "Metropolis" (on the contribution of women's salons to the French Revolution; on the positive influence of foreign theater and foreign women's fashions) are also omitted in *Modern London*, thus losing Robinson's overtly cosmopolitan and feminist critique of British culture.[62] And her critiques of the nobility and government are also excised or muted, so that, for example, Phillips does not risk offending national pride by reprinting unchanged Robinson's concluding remarks in "Metropolis" that we are "at a period when all kingdoms have exhibited the horrors of massacre and the outrages of anarchy" (306). "*Almost* all kingdoms," Phillips clarifies in *Modern London* (149). Robinson's warnings against the dangers of repression and censorship do not appear in *Modern London*, nor do her feminist celebrations of women of genius. What we have instead is a profitable and patriotic template, complete with illustrations, for what would become the thriving guidebook industry. Phillips owes his relative success as a publisher in part to his versatility, both political and generic, publishing reformist periodicals like the *Monthly Magazine* (and before that the radical *Leicester Herald*), and later such guidebooks as well as works for children, both aimed at larger, politically diffuse audiences.[63]

I have traced one possible genealogy of "Metropolis" and its continuing influence: from earlier cultural critiques in the *Morning Post* such as the "Sylphid" and "Close of the Eighteenth Century;" to its expanded form in the *Monthly Magazine* where it was firmly engaged with the cosmopolitan politics of that radical journal and with Robinson's consistent championing of the free press; to its resonance with Wordsworth's Preface to the *Lyrical Ballads*; and finally to Phillips' (and others') popular guides to the metropolis. It is perhaps fitting that Robinson's essay and its celebration of public culture and the free press proliferated in this manner, unattributed yet widely read by a large urban audience, while Wordsworth's Preface gathered about itself an aura of radical originality and revolutionary change, yet far fewer contemporary readers. The differences between their manifestos are thus ideological as well as (and because they are) generic. Robinson characteristically seeks the widest possible audience by publishing in a popular periodical her outward-looking vision of a heterogeneous metropolis and the public art uniquely available in it. Wordsworth's Preface, in contrast, signals his increasingly self-regarding desire to fashion the jointly-authored *Lyrical Ballads* into his own "Romantic vision of modernity."[64] Modern criticism is partly responsible for accepting Wordsworth's "revolutionary" self-representations at face value (an instance of the "Romantic Ideology"[65] at work), to the detriment of our understanding of his own work and that of his contemporaries. Robinson's "Metropolis" is an important theoretical statement on art and its relations to the public sphere, and a central document in the Romantic Republic of Letters. Its widespread dissemination through different genres, periodicals, and even authors testifies to the impressive vitality of that republic.

NOTES

For their helpful comments on earlier versions of this essay, I am grateful to John Logan, Kari Lokke, Kim Wheatley, and Duncan Wu.

1. "Present State of the Manners, Society, &c&c of the Metropolis of England," *Monthly Magazine* (Aug. 1800), 35–8; (Sept. 1800), 138–40; (Oct. 1800), 218–22; (Nov. 1800), 305–6; subsequent citations will be given in the text as page numbers. The entire text of Robinson's essay is reprinted in a forthcoming issue of *PMLA* as part of their Little-Known Documents series, with my introduction. The essay is signed "M.R." and Robinson refers to her authorship of it in a 5 Aug. 1800 letter to the novelist Jane Porter: "Tell your brother to read my first paper on *Society and Manners in the Metropolis of England* page 35 of the Monthly Magazine" (MS 2290, Carl H. Pforzheimer Collection of Shelley and His Circle, New York Public Library, Astor, Lenox and Tilden Foundations). Judith Pascoe cites Robinson's essay and letter in a note to her fine edition of Robinson's *Selected Poems* (Peterborough: Broadview, 2000), 30.
2. For an overview of this crisis, see Paul Keen, *The Crisis of Literature in the 1790s* (Cambridge: Cambridge University Press, 1999).
3. Samuel Taylor Coleridge to Robert Southey, 25 Jan. 1800, *Collected Letters of Samuel Taylor Coleridge*, ed. Earl Leslie Griggs, Vol.1 of 6 (Oxford: Clarendon, 1966–71), 1:562.
4. On Robinson and the theater, see Judith Pascoe's *Romantic Theatricality: Gender, Poetry and Spectatorship* (Ithaca, NY: Cornell University Press, 1997), which also discusses "Metropolis" (138–9). See also the account of Robinson in Philip Highfill, Kalman Burnim and Edward Langhans (ed.), *A Biographical Dictionary of Actors, Actresses, Musicians, Dancers, Managers and Other Stage Personnel in London, 1660–1800* (Carbondale, IL: Southern Illinois University Press, 1973–93), 13:30–47. On Robinson's theatrical self-presentation, see Anne Mellor, "Making an Exhibition of Herself: Mary 'Perdita' Robinson and Nineteenth-Century Scripts of Female Sexuality," *Nineteenth-Century Contexts* 22 (2000), 271–304.
5. William Wordsworth, Preface to the 1800 *Lyrical Ballads*, in *Literary Criticism of William Wordsworth*, ed. Paul Zall (Lincoln, NE: University of Nebraska Press, 1966), 21.
6. Jon Klancher, *The Making of English Reading Audiences, 1790–1832* (Madison, WI: University of Wisconsin Press, 1987), 143.

7. Ibid., 40.
8. Like Johnson, Phillips was a radical as well as a committed vegetarian, who published on animal rights as well as prison reform (I discuss him further in the conclusion). See Richard Phillips, *Memoirs of the Public and Private Life of Sir Richard Phillips. By A Citizen of London* (London: J. Dean, 1808), and A. Boyle, "Portraiture in *Lavengro* II: The Publisher – Sir Richard Phillips," *Notes and Queries* 196 (1951), 361–6.
9. Geoffrey Carnall, "The *Monthly Magazine*," *Review of English Studies* n.s. 5 (1954), 158–64. See also "The *Monthly Magazine*," in *British Literary Magazines: The Romantic Age 1789–1836*, ed. Alvin Sullivan (Westport, CT: Greenwood, 1983), 314–19.
10. Richard Altick, *The English Common Reader* (Chicago, IL: Chicago University Press, 1957), 392.
11. Carnall, "The *Monthly Magazine*," 161. On the *Monthly*'s comprehensive literary reviews, see David Chandler, "'A Sort of Bird's Eye View of the British Land of Letters:' The *Monthly Magazine* and its Reviewers, 1796–1811," *Studies in Bibliography* 52 (1999), 169–79.
12. Burton Pollin, "Mary Hays on Women's Rights in the *Monthly Magazine*," *Etudes Anglaises: Grande Bretagne, Etats-Unis* 24 (1971), 271–82. These "Enquirer" essays are signed "M.H." and published in 1797, shortly after Hays published her feminist novel *The Memoirs of Emma Courtney* (1796). Hays' obituary of Wollstonecraft was also published in the *Monthly*. On other essays in the "Enquirer" series, see Lewis Patton, "Coleridge and the 'Enquirer' Series," *Review of English Studies* 16 (1940), 188–9.
13. Klancher, *The Making of English Reading Audiences*, 39.
14. "Memoirs of the Late Duc de Biron" (Feb. 1800); "Additional Anecdotes of Phillipe Egalité, late duke of Orleans, by one who knew him intimately" (Aug. 1800); "Anecdote of the Late Queen of France, by the same" (Aug. 1800). After Robinson's death, the *Monthly* also printed a long memoir of Robinson in this series of "Eminent Persons," with detailed responses to individual works (Feb. 1801, 36–40).
15. We know Robinson was working on a long poem before her death, and it seems this was to be the blank verse "Progress of Liberty," which her daughter compiled posthumously from a series of poems published between 1798 and 1800 in the *Morning Post* and *Monthly Magazine*. In the 1800 *Monthly* she published "The Hermit of Mont Blanc" (Feb.) and "The Italian Peasantry" (April), which were republished in *The Progress of Liberty*, as well as two poems that were not: "Lines Supposed to be Written Near the Monument of the Rev. John Parkhurst" (July) and "The Old Shepherd and the Squire" (Sept.).
16. Stuart Curran, "Mary Robinson and the New Lyric," *Women's Writing* 9 (2002), 17. This volume of *Women's Writing* is a special issue devoted to Robinson and edited by Jacqueline Labbe.
17. Samuel Pratt (1749–1814) was also a poet and novelist, and the author of Robinson's epitaph. In a 24 July 1799 letter to Pratt, she praised his *Gleanings of England*: "I am up to the brain in your Gleanings – ! I *admire*!! I am *amused* beyond expression!!" (*Shelley and His Circle 1773–1822*, ed. Kenneth Neill Cameron [Cambridge, MA: Harvard University Press, 1961], 1:209). In her 31 Aug. 1800 letter to Pratt she assured him of her support of his work via her influence at the *Morning Post*: "I have already taken care, I believe *twice*, to announce the Gleanings &c&c and on their publication I will do everything that is right, and just, and handsome about them" (*Shelley and His Circle*, 1:232; this letter is reproduced in full in the Romantic Circles electronic edition of Robinson's *Letter to the Women of England*; see note 21 below). See also her "Lines on Reading Mr Pratt's Volume 'Gleaning through England,'" *Morning Post* (25 July 1799).
18. Signed "A.A." and published June 1800 (426–7). In addition to its monthly overviews of foreign (crossdisciplinary) literature, in 1800 the *Monthly* also published the following accounts: "View of the State of the Stage in Germany" (Feb.); "Account of the Political Journals in … Denmark," in the Ottoman Empire (May), in Sweden and Russia (June); "Description of the City of Macao" (Aug.); "Account of the Present State of Society and Manners in Dublin" and "Sketch of Amsterdam" (Oct.); "Sketch of Exeter" (Nov.); "Some Account of Newspapers Published in Spain" (Dec.). In 1801, accounts of Liverpool, Woodstock, Newcastle upon Tyne, Copenhagen, and Portsmouth followed.

19. Signed "OBSERVATOR," the "Account of ... Liverpool" was published in the Jan. 1801 *Monthly Magazine* (497–9). The account of Dublin (Oct. 1800) is an exception to the celebratory tourist tendency, and instead focuses on the health hazards of urban living and especially (animal) diet. For other examples see previous note. Some of these subsequent accounts, such as "Sketch of Kendal" (March 1801) and of Exeter, are written as letters to the editor of the *Monthly* by readers who had enjoyed previous accounts. Some letters to the editor took issue with specific accounts, for example with "A.A."'s description of the religious makeup of Plymouth (Aug. 1800).

20. *The Sylphid* II, in *Memoirs of the Late Mrs Mary Robinson*, 4 Vols. (London: R. Phillips, 1801), 3:16.

21. Signed "Anne Francis Randall" in its first edition, *A Letter to the Women of England on the Injustice of Mental Subordination* (London: Longman, 1799) is a feminist treatise openly allied with her friend Mary Wollstonecraft, and focused on women's physical and intellectual liberty. The *Letter* celebrates women's intellectual accomplishments throughout history, across Europe, and concludes with a special acknowledgement of British women's genius, followed by a list of eminent living women writers (reproduced in the 1998 Romantic Circles annotated edition of the *Letter* at www.rc.umd.edu/editions/robinson/cover.htm). On the relationship between the first (pseudonymous) and reprint (signed, with different title) editions of the *Letter*, see the Romantic Circles edition.

22. Robinson was, of course, herself the subject of portraits by the leading artists of the age, such as Reynolds, Gainsborough, Romney, and the sculptor Flaxman. See Joseph Grego, "'Perdita' and the Painters: Portraits of Mrs Mary Robinson," *The Connoisseur* 5 (1903), 99–107; also, Robinson's *Monody to the Memory of Sir Joshua Reynolds* (London: J. Bell, 1792) as an example of her writings on painting.

23. *Morning Post*, 5 Sept. 1800. Robinson was known as the English Sappho, and this reference to the fashionable practice of posturing as Sappho is characteristic of her "continual self-reference and elision" (Ashley Cross, "From *Lyrical Ballads* to *Lyrical Tales*: Reputation and the Problem of Literary Debt," *Studies in Romanticism* 40 [2001], 571–605 [578]). The first installment of the "Close of the Eighteenth Century" was published 12 Aug. 1800. The series is unsigned but incorporates elements of both the "Sylphid" and "Metropolis" essays, and is clearly Robinson's in style and content. An aristocrat in her novel *The Natural Daughter* echoes this particular passage: "If I had the arrangement of things, all the volumes in the kingdom should be burnt, excepting the Racing Calendar. Reading only makes men stupid and women insolent" (Dublin: Brett Smith, 1797, 1:58–9).

24. Klancher, *Making of English Reading Audiences*, 39.

25. There exists a good body of work on Robinson's use of poetic pseudonyms in newspapers like the *Morning Post* and the *Oracle* by Stuart Curran, Judith Pascoe, Jacqueline Labbe, and Lisa Vargo, among others.

26. Mary Robinson, *The False Friend*, 4 Vols. (London: Longman & Rees, 1799), 3:297. The Judge (an unreformed libertine) dismisses the charges against Gertrude, sexually assaults her, and warns that "Law is a dangerous weapon when it is in the hands of the vulgar" (4:41).

27. See, for example, Eleanor Ty, *Empowering the Feminine: The Narratives of Mary Robinson, Jane West, and Amelia Opie* (Toronto: Toronto University Press, 1998); Sharon Setzer, "The Dying Game: Crossdressing in Mary Robinson's *Walsingham*," *Nineteenth-Century Contexts* 22 (2000), 305–28, and "Romancing the Reign of Terror: Sexual Politics in Mary Robinson's *The Natural Daughter*," *Criticism* 34 (1997), 531–55; Chris Cullens, "Mrs Robinson and the Masquerade of Womanliness," in *Body and Text in the Eighteenth Century*, ed. Veronica Kelly and Dorothea von Mucke (Stanford, CA: Stanford University Press, 1994), 266–89.

28. *Morning Post* (21 Dec. 1797); the excerpt is from *Walsingham*, 3:253–4. A note in the *Morning Post* (probably written by Robinson herself) predicts the reaction of critics due to *Walsingham*'s demystification of publishing corruption: "The *Critics*, like a nest of *hornets*, are probably roused in a phalanx to assail Mrs Robinson's *Walsingham*. She must expect *every degree of* ABUSE for her developement [*sic*] of their mysteries: every REVIEWER will take the lesson to himself; and every AUTHOR will applaud that spirit which could expose the *tricks of modern criticism*," that is, its political and personal biases (1 Jan. 1798).

29. On press restrictions such as the Stamp Tax and the Royal Proclamation of 1792, see Lucyle

Werkmeister, *The London Daily Press 1772–1792* (Lincoln, NE: University of Nebraska Press, 1963); Robert Rea, "'The Liberty of the Press' as an Issue in English Politics, 1792–1793," *The Historian* 24 (1961), 26–43. For a dissenting opinion against the "reign of terror on the press" interpretation, see Jeremy Black, *The English Press in the Eighteenth Century* (London: Croom Helm, 1987).

30. *Morning Post* (18 Dec. 1797), original emphasis. The excerpt is from *Walsingham* 3:260.

31. *Morning Post* (2 Dec. 1797).

32. Kenyon tried (and found guilty) Thomas Williams for blasphemous libel for printing Paine's *Age of Reason* in 1797. In that trial Kenyon's Charge to the Jury proclaimed the incompatibility of free speech and Christianity (*Speeches of the Honourable T. Erskine and S. Kyd on June 24, 1797* [London, 1797]). After fleeing to France, Paine had written to Kenyon to defend his publication of the earlier *Rights of Man* (see William Cobbett, ed., *Complete collection of State Trials*, compiled by T.B. Howell, 34 Vols. (London: R. Bagshaw, 1809–28), XXII: 397–8).

33. George Kenyon, *Life of Lloyd, First Baron Kenyon* (London: Longman's, Green, 1873), 297. Despite Kenyon's instructions, the jury acquitted the editor and printer of the *Morning Chronicle*; they had been charged with seditious libel for printing an address of the Society for Political Information. The otherwise positive *Public Characters of 1799–1800* noted that Kenyon had "exhibited … a mind heated and exasperated by the politics of the day" ([London: Richard Phillips, 1807], 584).

34. Mary Robinson, *Hubert de Sevrac, a Romance of the Eighteenth Century*, 4 Vols. (London: Hookham & Carpenter, 1796), 2:208–9.

35. Robinson ("Tabitha Bramble"), letter to Robert Dundas, 23 Jan. 1794 (Public Record Office, HO/102/10).

36. Robinson's threat to Dundas is echoed years later in the *Morning Post* note announcing *Walsingham*'s critique of Chief Justice Lord Kenyon: "she never before rendered so essential a service to society" as in that satire (*Morning Post*, 2 Dec. 1797).

37. On the British Convention and treason trials, see Albert Goodwin, *The Friends of Liberty* (London: Hutchinson, 1979), and John Barrell, *Imagining the King's Death* (Oxford: Oxford University Press, 2002).

38. On Robinson's praise of Corday in the larger context of British responses to Corday, see my "The New Cordays: British Representations of Charlotte Corday, 1793–1800," in *Rebellious Hearts: British Women Writers and the French Revolution*, ed. Adriana Craciun and Kari Lokke (Albany, NY: State University of New York Press, 2001), 193–232. On Robinson and women's violence, see my "Violence Against Difference: Mary Wollstonecraft and Mary Robinson," in *Making History: Textuality and the Forms of British History*, ed. Greg Clingham (Lewisburg, PA: Bucknell University Press/Associated University Presses, 1998), 111–41. On Robinson's politics, see M. Ray Adams, "Mrs Mary Robinson, A Study of Her Later Career," in *Studies in the Literary Backgrounds of English Radicalism* (Lancaster, PA: Franklin and Marshall College, 1947), 102–29.

39. Jerome McGann, *The Poetics of Sensibility: A Revolution in Literary Style* (Oxford: Clarendon, 1996), 102. Roger Lonsdale makes a similar point in his Introduction, *Eighteenth-Century Women Poets* (Oxford: Oxford University Press, 1990), xl–xli. For extended discussions of Robinson and Wordsworth, see Stuart Curran, "Mary Robinson's *Lyrical Tales* in Context," in *Re-visioning Romanticism: British Women Writers 1776–1837*, ed. Carol Shiner-Wilson and Joel Haefner (Philadelphia, PA: University of Pennsylvania Press, 1994); Pascoe, *Romantic Theatricality*; Cross, "From *Lyrical Ballads* to *Lyrical Tales*."

40. Of course, Wordsworth insisted that he wrote the Preface "solely to gratify Coleridge;" Mary Moorman, *William Wordsworth: A Biography. The Early Years* (Oxford: Clarendon, 1957), 1:492. Duncan Wu confirms that Wordsworth and Coleridge would have agreed by 24 July 1800 that Wordsworth would write a Preface; Wu, *Wordsworth: An Inner Life* (Oxford: Blackwell, 2002), 171. As Wordsworth actually began writing in September, my suggestion is that Robinson's first installments could have played a part in his thinking.

41. Coleridge reviewed Robinson's *Hubert de Sevrac* in the *Critical Review* (March 1797) and had *Walsingham* from 28 Jan. 1798, meaning that Wordsworth may also have seen it

(Duncan Wu, *Wordsworth's Reading 1770–1799* [Cambridge: Cambridge University Press, 1993], 160). In "Metropolis," Robinson acknowledges the value of provincial cities like Bristol (her birthplace, and site of *Lyrical Tales'* printer Cottle) and of "Coleridge, the exquisite poet" (35). On Coleridge and Robinson, see Cross, "From *Lyrical Ballads* to *Lyrical Tales*;" Curran, "Mary Robinson's *Lyrical Tales*;" Earl Leslie Griggs, "Coleridge and Mrs Mary Robinson," *MLN* 45 (1930), 90–95; Susan Luther, "'A Stranger Minstrel:' Coleridge's Mrs Robinson," *Studies in Romanticism* 33 (1994), 391–409; Daniel Robinson, "From 'Mingled Measure' to 'Ecstatic Measures:' Mary Robinson's Poetic Reading of 'Kubla Khan,'" *Wordsworth Circle* 26 (1995), 4–7; Lisa Vargo, "The Claims of 'Real Life and Manners:' Coleridge and Mary Robinson," *Wordsworth Circle* 26 (1995), 134–7.

42. Dorothy Wordsworth wrote to John Marshall in Sept. 1800 that William "intends to give them [the *Lyrical Ballads*] the title of 'Poems by W. Wordsworth' as Mrs Robinson has claimed the title and is about publishing a volume of *Lyrical Tales*. This is a great objection to the former title, particularly as they are both printed at the same press and Longman is the publisher of both works." *Letters of William and Dorothy Wordsworth: The Early Years, 1787–1805*, ed. Ernest de Selincourt (Oxford: Clarendon, 1935), 297. Stuart Curran notes that "it is clear that neither Joseph Cottle nor Thomas Longman saw Robinson's title as a usurpation of Wordsworth's rights; indeed, from the refusal of Longman to accede to Wordsworth's request we may conjecture that this highly successful firm had its eye shrewdly on the marketplace" ("Mary Robinson's *Lyrical Tales*," 19). Robinson had already published a number of works with Longman's. On 17 June 1800 she wrote to an unnamed publisher offering for purchase a "small volume" that "will consist of Tales, serious and gay, on a variety of Subjects in the manner of Wordsworth's Lyrical ballads" (MS in "Original Letters of Dramatic Performers," f.156, Garrick Club).

43. On the complexity of Wordsworth and Coleridge's collaboration in this poem (along with its prose introductory note, probably written by Coleridge), see Carol Landon, "Wordsworth, Coleridge, and the *Morning Post*: An Early Version of *The Seven Sisters*," *Reviews in English Studies* 11 (1960), 392–402. On the interchange between the *Lyrical Ballads* and newspaper verse, see also Robert Mayo, "The Contemporaneity of the *Lyrical Ballads*," *PMLA* 69 (1954), 486–522; Robert Woof, "Wordsworth's Poetry and Stuart's Newspapers: 1797–1803," *Studies in Bibliography* 15 (1962), 149–89; Wu, *Wordsworth's Reading*.

44. See Robinson, *Selected Poems*, ed. Pascoe, 376. Pascoe's edition reprints the poetic exchange.

45. Curran, "Mary Robinson's *Lyrical Tales*," 19.

46. Wordsworth, Preface, 17.

47. Ibid., 21.

48. Kevin Gilmartin, *Print Politics: The Press and Radical Opposition in Early Nineteenth-Century England* (Cambridge: Cambridge University Press, 1996), 24.

49. This SCI address was reprinted in *Gentleman's Magazine* LIX (1789), 1121–5. In the earlier excerpt from *Walsingham* (3:253–4) reprinted in the *Morning Post*, Walsingham also refers to the free press as the "bulwark of freedom." All of these accounts probably allude to John Wilkes' famous declaration that "the liberty of the press is the birthright of a Briton, and is justly esteemed the firmest bulwark of the liberties of this country" (quoted in Rea, "The Liberty of the Press," 26).

50. Judith Pascoe makes a related and significant point that: "In what serves to anticipate and counter Wordsworth's disparagement of German tragedies in the Preface to the *Lyrical Ballads*, she acknowledges that public taste has 'at times turned from our own rich and national feast of rational sentiment, to sicken itself on the high-seasoned treat of a German salmagundi,' but she still champions the theater's exhibition of 'the most sublime efforts of the dramatic art'" (*Romantic Theatricality*, 139). I suggest that the overall tenor of "Metropolis" is deliberately cosmopolitan (as well as theatrical, as Pascoe argues), however, and that in this additional respect significantly different from Wordsworth's work.

51. Robinson was paralyzed and isolated in Egham when she wrote "Metropolis." Pascoe notes the significant irony of Robinson's earlier "Sylphid" essays, also written while Robinson was bed-ridden and isolated in her daughter's cottage, yet celebrating an idealized social and physical mobility in the city: "One can read Robinson's adoption of the 'airy form' of the

Sylphid with her unlimited range of movement, as an escape from the body, … so crippled at the time that she had to be carried by servants." Judith Pascoe, "The Spectacular *Flâneuse*: Mary Robinson and the City of London," *Wordsworth Circle* 23 (1992), 170.

52. Robinson used this phrase throughout her works, for example in *Sight*: "Yet with an unconquerable enthusiasm, / I shall pay homage to the FIRST of all distinctions, – the ARISTOCRACY OF GENIUS!" Mary Robinson, *Sight* (London: T. Spilsbury & Son, 1793), 8; and also in "Metropolis:" "The cabinets of our statesmen are closed against the aristocracy of genius" (220). I discuss Robinson's "Aristocracy of Genius" in *Fatal Women of Romanticism* (Cambridge: Cambridge University Press, 2003), Ch.3.

53. Robinson was friends with both Wollstonecraft and Godwin, whose works she admired and politics she shared. In "Metropolis," she writes: "The monumental tablet (placed by the hand, and bedewed by the tears, of friendship) points out the tomb of Mrs Wollstonecraft Godwin; yet illiberal malice and unmanly abuse has disgraced the pages of literature; while it failed to sully the treasures of mental splendour, which this illustrious woman has bequeathed to posterity!" (221).

54. Pascoe argues that "Book seven of *The Prelude* excludes a literary society increasingly dominated by females represented by … Mary Robinson" ("Spectacular *Flâneuse*," 166). See also Betsy Bolton for an excellent comparison of Robinson and Wordsworth's poetic representations of urban London; Bolton, "Romancing the Stone: 'Perdita' Robinson in Wordsworth's London," *ELH* 64 (1997), 727–59. On earlier representations of women in London, see Elizabeth Bennett Kubek, "Women's Participation in the Urban Culture of Early Modern London," *The Consumption of Culture 1600–1800* (London: Routledge, 1995).

55. See Elizabeth Eger *et al.* (ed.), *Women, Writing and the Public Sphere 1700–1830* (Cambridge: Cambridge University Press, 2001), and Craig Calhoun (ed.), *Habermas and the Public Sphere* (Cambridge, MA: Harvard University Press, 1992).

56. Pascoe, *Romantic Theatricality*, 7.

57. Ibid., 139. Robinson also consistently laments the fate of genius (especially female genius) toiling in obscurity and neglect (including in "Metropolis," in her critique of aristocracy), though her stated ideal remains genius celebrated in the public sphere.

58. On Phillips, see Phillips, *Memoirs of the Private and Public Life of Sir Richard Phillips*; Carnall, "The *Monthly Magazine*;" Pollin, "Mary Hays on Women's Rights."

59. Phillips' *Picture of London* spawned numerous similar volumes which by the early Victorian period had become tour guides to the metropolis. In addition to Leigh's and Mogg's competing editions of the *New Picture of London*, which themselves went through many editions, there were companion volumes such as *Rowlandson's Characteristic Sketches of the Lower Orders, Intended as a Companion to the New Picture of London* (London: Leigh, 1820).

60. *Public Characters of 1800–1801* (London: Richard Phillips, 1802), 340.

61. I am grateful to Markman Ellis for suggesting that I investigate the possibility of *Modern London*'s connection to Robinson (*Modern London: Being the History and Present State of the British Metropolis* [London: R. Phillips, 1804]).

62. Compare, for example, Robinson's sentence with Phillips' revision: "Dress has also been considerably improved by our intercourse with foreign nations" (Robinson, "Metropolis," 305); "The progress of good sense and good taste is no less visible in the improvement of dress" (Phillips, *Modern London*, 143).

63. Phillips began publishing the *Juvenile Library*, a children's periodical, in 1800; see Alan Rauch, "Preparing the 'Rising Generation:' Romanticism and Richard Phillips's *Juvenile Library* 1800–1803," *Nineteenth-Century Contexts* 15/1 (1991), 3–27. Rauch comments on the compatibility of radicalism and a desire for profit in Phillips' ventures, qualities which I think are equally applicable to Robinson: "No less an entrepreneur than an ideologue, Phillips saw no contradiction in trying to make a good living by way of ideologically motivated journalism" (5).

64. Thomas Pfau, *Wordsworth's Profession: Form, Class, and the Logic of Romantic Cultural Production* (Stanford, CA: Stanford University Press, 1997), 238.

65. See Jerome McGann, *The Romantic Ideology: A Critical Investigation* (Chicago, IL: Chicago University Press, 1983).

Correcting Mrs Opie's Powers: The Edinburgh Review of Amelia Opie's Poems (1802)

ANDREA BRADLEY

Thomas Brown's review of Amelia Opie's *Poems* (1802) in the inaugural issue of the *Edinburgh Review* is remarkable, certainly, for a number of aesthetic and formal reasons, but also for its singular occasion: the article is the only one in the first issue to review the work of a woman and the only one, at least for the first ten issues, to review the work of a woman poet.[1] In succeeding numbers, the *Edinburgh* reviews the works of Amelia Opie's female contemporaries – from Madame de Staël's novels to Joanna Baillie's plays of the passions to Maria Edgeworth's tales of moral instructions and even Opie's own collected tales[2] – yet the uniqueness of the 1802 review provokes questions about the *Edinburgh*'s interest in marking the boundaries of genre and gender. In a debut number of 29 reviews featuring articles about travel narratives, political economy, religious writing, scientific discovery, and historical reconstruction, the discussion of poetry assumes a small but significant place.[3] The sole review of poetry written by a woman assumes an even more striking place among these various discourses and compels a consideration of the relationship of this discourse on women's poetry to those which surround it. An analysis of the content, style, and ideology of Brown's criticism of Opie will place the individual article within the larger review and within the greater project of the *Edinburgh* itself. The discussion of Opie offers a model of the periodical's practices of reading women's poetry and enacts its strategies of creating not only the *Edinburgh* reader and reviewer, but also the *Edinburgh* author. The critique of genre in the Opie article genders not only the writer under review – demarcating the bounds of appropriate form, style, and sentiment – but also genders by implicit comparison both the reader of the periodical and the *Edinburgh* reviewer: masculine, Whig, and committed to the maintenance of corporate identity.[4]

Of all the volumes of poetry to appear in 1802, or in the years preceding the periodical's debut, the *Edinburgh* deliberately chose Opie's slim volume for review. With the works of such contemporaries as George Dyer, Thomas Holcroft, M.G. Lewis, Lady Morgan, Sir Walter Scott and Charlotte Smith as well as Wordsworth and Coleridge available for review, the editors chose instead a minor female figure celebrated far more for her sentimental novels

than for her occasional poetry. Why did the *Edinburgh* choose to bring
Amelia Opie and her poems within what Mark Schoenfield describes as its
"circulations of judgment?"[5] A hint is given in the first issue's
"Advertisement" – as a principle of their plan of selection, "the Conductors
of the EDINBURGH REVIEW propose to ... confine their notice, in a great
degree, to works that either have attained, or deserve, a certain portion of
celebrity." Opie's established popularity among the reading public might
have prompted their critical interest; this is a justification, however, equally
applicable to such writers as Scott, Smith, and Wordsworth. Something
more than Opie's "celebrity" must stimulate the periodical's critical interest,
something disturbing in her particular popularity that provokes not only the
periodical's attention but also its anxiety and calls for the submission of
Opie's much-bought work to the disciplinary criticism of the *Edinburgh* and
its editors in order to allay that anxiety. Although we cannot conflate a
periodical with its editors by projecting their quite real anxieties onto an
inanimate production, there are grounds, however, for speaking of the
Edinburgh Review as having a psychology similarly vexed by the risky
nature of its enterprise.[6] First the corporate anxiety of the *Edinburgh*'s
founders and later the corporate identity of Francis Jeffrey and his
contributors facilitated the periodical's assumption of, self-evidently, an
aesthetic position, but also of a particular psychology. The collective fear of
the founding, the risking of income, status, and reputation, communicated
itself in the unified stance of the review – anxious to establish itself in the
face of political opposition and, in the initial case of Amelia Opie, the
perceived challenge of a feminine aesthetic.

In the review of Samuel Jackson Pratt's *Bread*, an article that closely
precedes Brown's review of Opie, the reviewer indicates the success of the
poem among the reading public – a success akin to Opie's, perhaps – as
enough reason for its inclusion to trump the volume's otherwise insipid
poetry and ill-informed political philosophy:

> We thought it extremely probable that [Pratt's poetry and philosophy]
> would be entirely forgotten before the First Number of this
> publication could issue from the press ... In this idea, we have been
> so much mistaken, that we ought to be more cautious how we indulge
> such conjectures in future ... If a work was passed over, which, in the
> course of a few months, has received so strong a mark of public
> approbation, it might justly be attributed to the obscurity of the
> Reviewers, not of the poem [1/1, 109].

Appearing as a bow to public opinion, the review actually seizes the
opportunity for the periodical to practice its surveillance of taste. By setting
forth Pratt's *Bread* and, by extension, Opie's *Poems* for review, the editors

of the *Edinburgh* can begin to subsume the reading habits of its potential buyers within its editorial sweep, a move which will eventually enable their transformation of such counterfeit tastes into the genuine article of *Edinburgh* opinion.

In his study of nineteenth-century periodical culture, *The Making of English Reading Audiences, 1790–1832*, Jon P. Klancher argues for the consciously shaping force of the periodicals' relationships to their readers.[7] Whatever their format, periodicals were never simply collections of articles, essays, and reviews; they were always meant to have an effect on their readers' habits of reading, thinking, and behaving in their relative social spheres. The texts under review in such a publication as the formidable *Edinburgh* offer its reviewers opportunities not so much for textual criticism as for political discourse; whether they be works of political economy, travel, history, or poetry, the surface subjects of the issues' articles operate more substantially as pretexts for scrutinizing and even unraveling various social fabrics for the purpose of analyses predominantly political at heart. A singular review such as Brown's critique of Opie, then, functions on a level beyond that of literary criticism: the discussion of her *Poems* offers an occasion for the *Edinburgh* to establish its critical principles not just on the topic of poetry or even of women's poetry, but also on the cultural and political import of women writing poetry at all.

As Brown points out through his odd and circuitous introduction to the review of the *Poems*, before making her foray into published poetry, Opie published a novel, *The Father and Daughter: A Tale in Prose*, in 1801, a work which he praises briefly as "one which excites a very high interest" (1/1, 115).[8] "But the merit of that novel does not consist in its action, nor in any varied exhibition of character" (1/1, 115), formal and tonal weakness which have clearly carried over to the *Poems*, as the reviewer begins to assert. The first four pages of the article establish a number of formal binaries, into whose lesser terms he routinely assigns Opie's work, with unevenness of success as the overall result: the poems are "of very various species of composition, and are perhaps still more different, in merit, than in subject" (1/1, 114). When confining herself to a small space of appropriate form and content, the circumscription of which will prove the *Edinburgh*'s critical object, Opie's poems achieve "uncommon elegance" (1/1, 114), but when ranging beyond the boundaries of skill and sense, they assume a "dissimilarity of character [from] ... the sweetness of the simpler pictures" (1/1, 114) in her more appropriate compositions.

Among the first and most condemnatory of the reviewer's aesthetic binaries is that of impulsive feeling and sustained effort. When Opie captures the solitary instant of a character's "gentler grief" in a brief burst of tender emotion, the poem offers real pleasure; when she attempts to draw out that grief – over lyric time or throughout other characters – the result is inadequate, sketchy, and unanchored to narrative context. "Mrs Opie's mind," he finds, "is evidently more adapted to seize situation, than to combine incidents … we do not think that she is well fitted for bringing before us the connected griefs and characters of the drama" (1/1, 114–15). This argument applies to poetic form as well: when Opie composes "tender song[s] of sentiment and pathos," she writes in her successful element, but when she assays longer poems, "which require dignity, or even terseness of expression, and an easy development of thoughts, which rise complicated in the moment of fancy" (1/1, 114), she cannot sustain the effort or develop the poignant moment of the song into the coherent time of the higher verse.

The critique of dignity – or, more precisely, its absence – in Opie's poetry becomes for the reviewer a discussion of synthesis and depth, literary and epistemological notions much to the point of the *Edinburgh*'s self-presentation. This question of dignity appears as a common trope among its reviews of women's poetry, serving as an absent ideal set against the inadequate attempts of Opie's and Felicia Hemans' verse. In this first review of the former's work, the achievement of dignity in poetry is drawn out against tenderness, sentiment, pathos, elegance, and even feeling. In the *Edinburgh*'s second review of Opie in 1806, editor Francis Jeffrey finds that her *Simple Tales*, while representing "admirably every thing that is amiable, generous, and gentle," fail to ascend the heights of literary practice, a failure not altogether lamented but decidedly tied to the continued absence in her poetry of dignity: "She can do nothing well that requires to be done with formality; and, therefore, has not succeeded in copying either the concentrated force of weighty and deliberate reason, or the severe and solemn dignity of majestic virtue" (8/16, 467). The choice of the word "copying" in this critique, as opposed to other words signifying originality, suggests a fundamental deficiency in women's poetry. Associating formality with dignity and invention, Jeffrey links these poetic goals in clearly gendered terms: "the concentrated force of weighty and deliberate reason," "the severe and solemn dignity of majestic virtue" belong to the masculine poet and to the masculine reviewer, whose "weighty reason" leads him to critique a woman poet's failure to "copy," let alone originally depict, the "majestic virtue" which marks all mature and laudable poetry.

This deficiency finds expression in the recurrent discussion of the role of reason in writing poetry not only in the reviews of Amelia Opie, but also in that of another distinctly popular woman poet, Felicia Hemans. In Opie's first review, Brown finds her "wholly unfit for that poetry, which endeavours to reason while it pleases" (1/1, 115) and by her second notice, she seems to have made little progress, at least according to Jeffrey: "She does not reason well; but she has, like most accomplished women, the talent

of perceiving truth, without the process of reasoning" (8/16, 467). If we turn
to the discussion of another one of these "accomplished women," Felicia
Hemans, we find Jeffrey, again, kindly but relentlessly demarcating the
boundaries of women's access to reason in poetry.[9] This remarkable article,
appearing 27 years after the initial review of Opie's *Poems*, begins with a
patronizing assessment of women's capabilities, literary and otherwise:

> Women, we fear, cannot do every thing; nor even every thing they
> attempt. But what they can do, they do, for the most part, excellently
> – and much more frequently with an absolute and perfect success,
> than the aspirants of our rougher and more ambitious sex [50/99, 32].

Jeffrey then traces the genealogy of women's "disabling delicacy" and
arrives at some restrictions which resonate with the limitations cited for
Opie and Hemans' work; women are:

> incapable of long moral or political investigations, where many
> complex and indeterminate elements are to be taken into account, and
> a variety of opposite probabilities to be weighed before coming to a
> conclusion ... the questions with which they have to deal ... may
> generally be better described as delicate than intricate; – requiring for
> their solution rather a quick tact and fine perception than a patient or
> laborious examination [50/99, 32].

Because they are neither trained nor inclined to carry out sustained mental
effort, to exercise "the concentrated force of weighty and deliberate reason,"
their poetry must reflect this inexperience. Opie, then, is better suited to
"seize situation, than to combine incidents" (1/1, 114), to compose short
songs of quick pathetic perception rather than longer lines of sustained
heroic investigation.

Drawing on traditionally gendered spheres of poetic mood and import,
Brown likewise praises Opie's poems of sentiment but faults her pieces
aiming at higher modes of dignity. He willingly accords her "verses of
feeling" the faint praise of being "among the best in our opuscular poetry,"[10]
but inflicts the punishment of "illustrating, by specimens of an opposite
nature, our unfavourable opinion of her heroic verse" (1/1, 115–16). His
continuing judgment – "it is probably because Mrs Opie has not succeeded
in verses of dignity and reflection, that she has succeeded in the verses of
simple feeling" (1/1, 117) – while of dubious logic, further cements his
division of Opie's poetic accomplishments. As another example of the
Edinburgh's place-assigning approbation of women's poetry, we might
compare Opie's "opuscular" accomplishments to Hemans' later, but
similarly confined, achievements. To end his review of Hemans' work,
Jeffrey offers the following restrictive encouragement: "For we do not

hesitate to say, that she is, beyond all comparison, the most touching and accomplished writer of occasional verses that our literature has yet to boast of" (50/99, 47). Though couched in superlative language, Jeffrey's commendation nevertheless restricts this "fine exemplification of Female Poetry" to the smaller branches of poetical form, the verse forms more suited to a woman poet's "softness and delicacy of hand" (50/99, 34).

Implicitly aligning the feminine with the impulsive, the small, the shallow, and the underdeveloped, Brown introduces other excluding pairs of aesthetic judgment and poetic form in his 1802 review. In addition to impulsive and sustained, he invokes individual and group: Opie can "represent, with powerful expression, the solitary portrait," but she cannot synthesize a "connected assemblage of figures" (1/1, 114). As an instance of this review's suggestion of significance beyond its own borders, its contrast of the solitary with the connected here reveals the *Edinburgh*'s stake in promoting an image of itself as just such a "connected assemblage of figures." The construction of periodical voice is accomplished by a number of methods – anonymity of authorship, similarity of style, use of the first person (nearly monarchical) plural, and central authority of editorial direction, to name a few – aimed at cultivating what Schoenfield calls the "corporate identity of the *Edinburgh* reviewer."[11] The *Edinburgh* seeks to collapse the "connected assemblage" of such figures as Jeffrey, Brown,[12] Sydney Smith, Henry Brougham, and Francis Horner into the "solitary portrait" of the corporate author.

As Mark Parker argues for literary magazines in general, the division of labor for a quarterly review like the *Edinburgh* is a concern not only in its pages, but also in its very composition.[13] Naming one of the leading figures of Scottish intellectualism, Parker links the mode of periodical production to its "ideological commitment" to promoting "breadth of knowledge" in its pages and its readers:

> the format of the magazine offers a suggestive parallel to what Adam Smith famously considered the motive force of the Industrial Revolution: the concept of division of labor. A quick look at the table of contents of almost any magazine of the period shows how much specialization had begun to creep into the medium [13].

A quick look at the table of contents of Jeffrey's collected contributions to the *Edinburgh Review* also shows how Jeffrey, whose professional and educational "specializations" would seem to fit him for such topics as rhetoric, politics, and the law, took on the reviews of subjects which would more reasonably fall within the bounds of literature and the humanities: besides two moderate sections on "Philosophy of the Mind, Metaphysics, and Jurisprudence" and "General Politics," the remainder of Jeffrey's sizable volume is devoted to reviews of "General Literature and Literary Biography," "History and Historical Memoirs," "Poetry," and "Novels, Tales, and Prose Works of Fiction."[14] As Jeffrey notes in his Preface to the collection of his contributions, which he assembled himself, the work of literary criticism always gestures outward to the larger business of leading a responsible social, political, and cultural life:

> refusing to confine itself to the humble task of pronouncing on the mere literary merits of the works that came before it, [the *Edinburgh Review*] professed to go deeply in *the Principles* on which its judgments were to be rested [v].

The traces of such division of labor which makes possible its production, however, are precisely what the *Edinburgh Review* wants to erase in its quest to create the uniform and authoritative voice of the Edinburgh reviewer, and it is this erasure which raises contradictions in its treatment of poetical valuations of individual and group.[15] While the individual poet or poetical subject may run the risk of insipidity, social irresponsibility, or self-love, that individual's association with the wrong group runs even worse risks. The discussion of group and individual in Brown's critique of Opie finds additional expression in the *Edinburgh*'s reviews of poetry by her male contemporaries, specifically Jeffrey's treatment of Southey's *Thalaba*, also in the first issue, and his discussion of Wordsworth's *The Excursion*, 12 years later.[16] Jeffrey's denunciation of *Thalaba* begins as an attack on Southey's affiliation with a dangerous political and poetical group: "The author who is now before us, belongs to a *sect* of poets, that has established itself in this country within these ten or twelve years, and is looked upon, we believe, as one of its chief champions and apostles" (1/1, 63). Recalling the issue's first article's consideration of blame for the *philosophes* whose public thinking helped to precipitate the Revolution,[17] Jeffrey castigates Southey and the school to which he belongs for promoting "false taste" in poetry in language approaching the accusation of treason: "They constitute, at present, the most formidable conspiracy that has lately been formed against sound judgment in matters poetical" (1/1, 64). The dangers posed by Southey's group, characterized as conspiratorial, lie in their belligerent collectivity: their abuses of "vulgar" language, meant to suggest the speech of the "lower orders," reveal their rebellion against the proper recognition of social classes.[18] Refusing to accept Jeffrey's dictum that the "different classes of society have each of them a distinct character, as well as a separate idiom" (1/1, 66), Southey and his heretical friends propose to stand outside the class system, to abstract themselves from the social order, and to confuse the clearly delineated strata of society. Jeffrey finds such poetical posturing ridiculous: "It is absurd to suppose, that an author should make use of the language of the vulgar, to express the sentiments of the refined" (1/1, 66). For Jeffrey, the aesthetically reprehensible tendencies of Southey's school manifest their politically irresponsible stances.[19] Although Opie is not affiliated with any particular group within the body of Brown's review, she may pose the threat of biographical connection with such radicals as William Godwin and Mary Wollstonecraft, with whom she associated in her youth and early married life.[20] The denigration of individualism, whether in social action or poetical portraiture, applicable to Opie as well as to Southey, carries not so much the critique of gender, then, as generic tendencies to political confusion. Far better to be associated with the right group (such as the *Edinburgh* reviewers) than to fall in with a dangerous or irresponsible one.

Related to this dimensional critique of misguided association is one of depth: Opie can offer a brief, probably shallow glimpse into a character's occasional emotion, but she cannot so well "represent each in its most striking situation, so as to give, as it were, to the glance of a moment, the events and feelings of many years" (1/1, 114). The reviewer inserts a related critique of Opie's inability to turn incident into sustained narrative with respect to her novel, *The Father and Daughter*: "we are almost tempted to believe, that the scene in the wood occurred first to the casual conception of the author, and that, in the design of fully displaying it, all the other events of the novel were afterwards imagined" (1/1, 115). This critique of depth in Brown's review of Opie gestures outward to the larger Romantic project of constructing models of subjectivity. As Andrea Henderson argues in her study of Romantic selfhood, *Romantic Identities*, more than one model of subjectivity appeared in the period's cultural discourse to challenge the Wordsworthian paradigm which has dominated not only the period of its inception but also the history of Romantic criticism.[21] The quintessential legacy of Romanticism, "its characterization of the self in terms of psychological depth" (1), was initially promulgated not only by Wordsworth in such works as *The Prelude* and *The Excursion*, but also, as the Opie article indicates, by his strange bedfellows, the *Edinburgh* reviewers. Though Jeffrey will later rebuke the great poet for his cultivation of individual psychological depth to the exclusion of healthy social and critical intercourse, in the Opie review at least, his periodical upholds what Henderson identifies as the "depth model of subjectivity" (2), the ideological investment in each "glance of a moment" containing the "events and feelings of many years." What Jeffrey and the *Edinburgh* value in such a "depth model," Henderson explains, is "the disciplinary potential of a self understood to develop and deepen with time" (2), a self whose political and poetical development the critic can monitor and guide, just the kind of self which Opie and her poetry do not offer to the regulatory eye of the *Edinburgh* reviewer.

In contrast to the depth model, Henderson proposes the proliferation of "other, competing models of the self that were produced during the period:" among them, a "commercial model of identity" which elevates "exchange value" above a canonically grounded "use value;" a "context-based identity;" a material or body-based identity; and a "marketplace" identity (2, 6–10). It is the second of these competing alternatives, the "context-based" identity, that seems especially applicable to the work of Amelia Opie and the *Edinburgh*'s critique of it. En route to a reading of Byron and *The Prisoner of Chillon*, Henderson considers the political philosophy of William Godwin: the author of *Enquiry Concerning Political Justice* "is insistent upon the non-existence of innate character attributes ... argues that identity has less to do with the externalization of interior and innate tendencies than with passive responses and interactions," and believes that "not only is identity formed by external influences, but 'internal' and 'external' never become powerfully opposed categories" (60–61). Her discussion of Godwin, Opie's good friend, social affiliate, and reputedly ardent admirer, offers insight into the reviewer's objection to what he reads as Opie's depiction of subjectivity as flat and fleeting.

Several of Opie's poems do rise from the specific occasions of their speakers' or subjects' narrative moments: graveside laments, near-death repinings, supplications for mercy or assistance, lovers' betrayals, and dated occurrences like New Year's Day or the Peace of Amiens. Perhaps because they are "occasional" or because they flow from a voice of a speaker not meant to be read as "Amelia Opie," the pieces offer models of psychological behavior rising from the context of the moment and not sustained from poem to poem. The context-based model of subjectivity offered by Opie's work challenges the period's dominant paradigm of selfhood as psychologically profound and plumbable by lyrical introspection, a paradigm typified by Wordsworth's poetically rendered ramblings. On a deeper ideological level, however, the "Revolutionary ideology" which Henderson identifies, one which promoted a "non-hierarchical, 'horizontal' system wherein identity is based on context,"[22] might seem to Jeffrey to flout the very *raison d'être* of the *Edinburgh* itself: the idea of an unstable, shifting self, poetical or otherwise, contradicts the periodical's real investment in such notions as history, narrative, linearity, and development. While a topographical model of subjectivity might locate temporary authority in one's response to changing contexts, the kind of geological model which founds the *Edinburgh*'s sense of its own enterprises stakes authority in what Jerome Christensen terms the "prudent" stance of its "stress on the instrumental cultivation of belief."[23] Contextual subjectivity resists the regulation of standards of behavior and judgment – not only a cultivation but an inculcation of belief – which the *Edinburgh* wishes to impose as its singular critical and cultural prerogative. As with the critique of the "solitary portrait," Brown's discussion of Opie's poetical portraits of subjectivity turns on a distinction which is both manifestly political and latently gendered.

After such pairs as impulsive and sustained, individual and group, and shallowness and depth, a final aesthetic binary – natural versus unnatural – leads Brown into the critical focus of the 1802 article and it is one which, because gendered, highlights the strange gendering of the ensuing critique. As the final item in a list of Amelia Opie's failed poetic attempts, the reviewer cites her ill handling of the heroic couplet: "a line of ten syllables is too large for the grasp of her delicate fingers; and she spans her way along, with an awkward and feeble weariness, whenever she lays aside the smaller verse" (1/1, 115).[24] Despite its offending judgment, the metaphor of a weak woman musician is a forceful one, and it has the effect of making heroic verse not only aesthetically prohibited to Opie but even physically unattemptable and decidedly *unnatural*. The final adjective of the phrase, moreover, captures the essential element of this critical circumscription:

> It is in the smaller verse of eight syllables, which requires no pomp of sound, and in the simple tenderness, or simple grief, to which the artlessness of such numbers is best suited, that the power of Mrs Opie's poetry consists [1/1, 115].

Stick to the small, the simple, and the almost silent, Mrs Opie – the reviewer warns – and we shall be pleased to commend you. Similarly, in his much later review of Hemans' poetry, Jeffrey cautions the otherwise acceptable female poet to forswear the publication of poems and volumes too lengthy for critical approbation:

> She must beware of becoming too voluminous; and must not venture again on any thing so long as the Forest Sanctuary. But, if the next generation inherits our taste for short poems, we are persuaded it will not readily allow her to be forgotten [50/99, 47].

The gentle scolding of Jeffrey's tone effectively marks the literal and metaphoric boundaries of women's verse through the implicitly gendered direction of its condescension to the woman poet under inquisition.

Back in the initial review of Amelia Opie, Brown begins to narrow his focus toward the bottom of the fourth full page of the article. Having praised the sufficiently smaller verse of Mrs Opie's volume, he steps back to ascertain the darker errors of her work: her neglect of the "true artifice of that poetry, which consists in a happy artlessness" (1/1, 117). Definitions of what counts as "natural" occupy much space in the *Edinburgh*'s analyses of poetry.[25] In Jeffrey's review of Southey's *Thalaba*, for example, the greatest offenses against poetic naturalness take the form of an "affectation of great simplicity and familiarity of language" (1/1, 64). Proposing to "bring his compositions nearer to the true standard of nature" (1/1, 66), Southey succeeds only in concocting verses which are decidedly unnatural, uneven, and frequently ridiculous. Pratt, too, accomplishes only caricature in his attempt to preach a perverted political economy beneficent to the poor: his vision of the island's merry, deserving destitute is a "monstrous assemblage … as never, perhaps, was brought together before, by the most distempered imagination. No one feature of it resembles the poor of England, or any other country" (1/1, 110). As is the case with Southey, the distortion of political reality to suit the poet's radical or irresponsible ends produces unnatural images and language.

The two reviews of Opie's poetry, however, focus attention on the poet's violation of natural decorum in poetry, and because they are rendered without the explicit political implications of Southey and Pratt's reviews, their treatment of her poetry seem particularly gendered. Naturalness for the *Edinburgh* again means the "true artifice of that poetry, which consists in a happy artlessness" (1/1, 117). "Natural" as artlessness whose artifice has been concealed informs the standard which judges Opie's failure, for example, in "The Orphan Boy:"

> [the] sudden death of his mother … is, like all sudden grief-strokes, narrative or dramatic, founded on observations so rare in real nature, that, when adopted as poetic incidents, they strike us as made for the poem, rather than as deduced from truth [1/1, 120–21].

The mother's sudden death *is*, of course, *made for the poem*, as all poetic incidents are, but Opie's error lies in not concealing the incident's creative genealogy. The critic's recourse to "real nature," however, returns in Jeffrey's later review of Opie's *Simple Tales*, in which she seems to have made some progress in the artlessness of artifice: her "personages," though not original, have the "incomparably superior" merit of being "strictly true to general nature" (8/16, 465–6). This praise of Opie's characters gives Jeffrey a chance to lay out the *Edinburgh*'s policy on naturalness in literary compositions:

> We have always been of opinion, indeed, that no character can be natural, unless it be pretty common. … It will be found accordingly, we believe, that almost all the fine traits of natural expression that are quoted and remembered … derive their whole beauty from this perfect and beautiful conformity to general and universal nature … they express the concentrated and appropriate emotion, which it is natural for persons in such circumstances to feel [8/16, 466].[26]

The elevation of naturalness as being "true to general nature" – another version of "perfect and beautiful conformity" – suggests the notion of "copying" which Jeffrey will pick up again in relation to the masculine "force of weighty and deliberate reason," an evaluative turn which implicitly genders Opie's "copying" of "general nature" as appropriately feminine. This definition of naturalness as "true to general nature" – both circular and dependent on the reviewer's understanding of what constitutes "general nature" – then turns into a praise of Opie's own naturalness which is decidedly gendered by her poetry's ambiguous artfulness:

> There is something delightfully feminine in all Mrs Opie's writings; an apparent artlessness in the composition of her narrative, and something which looks like want of skill or of practice in writing for the public, that gives a powerful effect to the occasional beauties and successes of her genius [8/16, 467].

Jeffrey is either forgetting that the *Edinburgh* did not always find "all" her writing "delightfully feminine" (it may have found her early popularity disturbingly feminine) or he is deliberately recasting the trajectory of her literary output to conform to the arc of Brown's initial critique. The seductive "want of skill" which seemed to attract the reviewer's anxious attention and motivate his critical faculties in the 1802 review now makes Opie charming to Jeffrey and easily containable. While readers may debate the justness of his estimation of Opie's "want of skill," they are certainly on solid ground in doubting the truth of his description of her writing career. Not only had Opie produced a number of novels and volumes of poetry by the time of this 1806 review, but she had also been contributing verses to periodical publications since her teens.

Despite Jeffrey's praise of her artful naturalness in the 1806 *Simple Tales*, Opie's earlier blunders in artless artifice (or artificial artlessness) consist, according to Brown, in "three great faults; her abuse of *reflection*, of *inversion*, and of *personification*" (1/1, 117). Her authorial intrusions into her characters' reflections are disruptive and unnatural; her expressive inversion is forced and delinquent; and her frequent personifications are excessive, affected, and fatal. The examples of her poetic transgressions, however, are not so remarkable as are the reviewer's descriptions of them; the terms of his criticism – "injurious," "abuse," "delinquent," "forced," "violates," "fatal" – are violent, brutal, almost criminal. Having just faulted the poet for her strained and unladylike couplets, the critic now takes her to task for transgressing the legal bounds of civilized poetry, and in language usually reserved for the descriptions of masculine crimes.

A masculine crime is very much the issue, however, in Jeffrey's review of the decidedly masculine Thomas Moore's *Epistles, Odes, and other Poems*

(1806), an article which immediately precedes that treating Opie's *Simple Tales*.[27] After having named him "the most licentious of modern versifiers, and the most poetical of those who, in our times, have devoted their talents to the propagation of immorality" (8/16, 456), Jeffrey goes on to detail the unprecedented "crime" of Moore's publication in a remarkable harangue:

> There is nothing, it will be allowed, more indefensible than a cold-blooded attempt to corrupt the purity of an innocent heart; and we can scarcely conceive any being more truly despicable, than he who, without the apology of unruly passion or tumultuous desires, sits down to ransack the impure places of his memory for inflammatory images and expressions, and commits them laboriously to writing, for the purpose of insinuating pollution into the minds of unknown and unsuspecting readers [8/16, 456].[28]

The real danger of Moore's verse, Jeffrey warns, is its potential attractiveness to female readers, a class of persons wholly unfit to distinguish its perverted seductions from the reality of quotidian amorous interaction. Male readers will know better, he admits,[29] but the delicacy of women's training and nature "renders them peculiarly liable to be captivated by the appearance of violent emotions, and to be misled by the affectation of tenderness or generosity" (8/16, 458). Having disarmed potential female readers of their wit and resistance, Jeffrey ends by making the classic sexist argument about gender and the national welfare which places the burden of social health on the mental and sexual purity of women:

> There can be no time in which the purity of the female character can fail to be of the first importance to every community; but it appears to us, that it requires at this moment to be more carefully watched over than at any other [8/16, 459].

Not only are women "now beginning to receive a more extended education, to venture more freely and largely into the fields of literature, and to become more of intellectual and independent creatures" (8/16, 459), the dubious wisdom of which social changes Jeffrey gravely implies, but also the publication of such licentious work as Thomas Moore's makes women's literary education doubly dangerous. "In these circumstances," Jeffrey claims, "it seems to be of incalculable importance, that no attaint should be given to the delicacy and purity of [women's] expanding minds" (8/16, 459). The experience of the woman reader of Moore's poetry forms the negative version of the experience of the woman writer/reader of the *Edinburgh* reviewer: while the female readers of Thomas Moore receive a false education in social, sexual, and literary relations, the female readers of the *Edinburgh Review* (who also include female writers like Amelia Opie) will receive an improving and disciplining education in similar topics, with an emphasis on the relations between gender and genre. While the male writer (Moore) abuses the trust of his female readers, the male reviewer of the *Edinburgh* (Jeffrey) regulates the minds of *his* female readers to contain their expansion within appropriate bounds.[30]

These final assessments, then, of Opie's poetic errors – her "abuse of *reflection*, of *inversion*, and of *personification*" – as unfeminine, unnatural, take us some way towards conceiving an idea of the critical project in the *Edinburgh*'s first review of her work. Opie's errors, in this case as in all others, are not only literary but also, and more saliently, philosophical: she is intrusive when she ought be invisible; unnatural when she ought be unaffected; and immoderate when she ought to be restrained. Her formal errors of categorization, Brown intimates, arise from her epistemological ones and stand in need of *Edinburgh* regulation. Excessive and melodramatic personifications in Opie's poetry, moreover, draw attention to their status as formal artifice and so threaten or call attention to the also artificial personification of the *Edinburgh* reviewer which bolsters the corporate identity of the periodical itself. As all the *Edinburgh* reviewers are enjoined to do with each critique, Brown here concerns himself with policing the boundaries of genre and, uniquely, of gender. What is the proper scope of women's poetry? What are its proper skills and concerns? With Opie at least, the *Edinburgh* focuses more fully on treatment than on subject matter, praising the author for those poems of smaller verse and of feeling which "accord better with the character of her imagination," faulting those which attempt a tone or form or sustained mood beyond "the character of her powers" (1/1, 115). A poet capable of pathetic sentiment but not of heroic dignity, Opie is "therefore wholly unfit for that poetry, which endeavours to reason while it pleases" (1/1, 115) – the *Edinburgh*'s judgment in a nutshell, implicitly, prohibitorily, gendered.

But if Pratt, too, in *Bread* fails to reason while he pleases and Southey, at least in Jeffrey's reading, fails in *Thalaba* to do either, what serves to mark the critic's reading of Opie as particularly gendered? His paternal injunction that she "accept advice" while he "direct[s] her attention" (1/1, 118) to the poems' errors, for one, seems singular among the issue's other articles for its heavy-handedness and condescension. Male writers working in all genres receive their share of criticism, sarcasm, and forced advice in the *Edinburgh Review*, but they are treated as ones who should have known better.[31] Mrs Opie, on the other hand, is treated by Brown as one who clearly did not know better and so has chanced, through publication, upon the opportunity to be instructed in her art by the wise reviewer. He counsels Opie to defer her poetic gifts to the pictorial ones of her artist-husband, the Cornish painter John Opie, whom she married in 1798. The fact of her marriage having occurred four years prior to the *Edinburgh*'s review of her *Poems* and the equally demonstrable fact of her having established something of a literary reputation under her maiden name makes the *Edinburgh*'s effort to contain her feminine poetic outpouring and suppress her literary career both anxious and belated. Brown finally urges the womanly submission of her art to her own learned self-pruning: "submit to abandon all idle decoration, and … give her whole fancy to simplicity and tenderness" (1/1, 121). The injunction, almost matrimonial in its exhortation to chaste restraint, bases its success on Mrs Opie's having "rightly learned her own powers" (1/1, 116) through the instruction of the reviewer's sound judgment – a relational and discursive dynamic ultimately central to the *Edinburgh*'s larger enterprise.

This first issue of the *Edinburgh Review* constantly engages discussions of authority; because it requires sure footing for the establishment of its position as critical center, the periodical reveals a near obsession with authority of all kinds – aesthetic, financial, social, legal, but above all, cultural authority. The issue raises, implicitly and explicitly, questions of the management of power and the consequences of deploying particular modes of art, thought, and feeling. This is manifested in the repeated distinction of treatment and subject matter and the potentially conflicting (de)merits of both: a writer may bring good treatment to an unfit subject matter or treat ill highly fit subject matter. Distinction, moreover, signals the *modus operandi* of the periodical's reviewers; they are highly invested in the distinction of categories from one another and the successes from the lamentable attempts.[32] Brown's review of Opie's *Poems*, then, plays out this critical investment, relying on its editorial imposition of poetic categories for the unassailable soundness of its judgment.

In addition, the reviewer's adoption of a firmly critical but condescendingly benevolent tone performs the discursive aims of the *Edinburgh Review*. In order to gain its coveted power of cultural pronouncement, the periodical must obtain the willing submission of its readers' individual opinions to that judgment, and it does so through the illusion of intimate conversation, the fine and learned talk of culturally literate acquaintances. Brown assumes a kindly orality of tone and diction throughout his review of Opie's work, meant to co-opt his readers as wise sharers of his assertions. This "cultural conversation" which the *Edinburgh* seems to promote aspires to be a discussion between reviewer and reader marked by accord rather than debate; David Bromwich describes its stance as the "presumption of consensus, from questions of politics to questions of taste."[33] In fact, as Christensen argues in his situation of the *Edinburgh*'s cultural and political project in the context of a post-revolutionary Britain in which "both who the people were and what the people wanted were matters of opinion," "whatever opinion mattered would, if the future worked out as planned, be subject to the judgment of the *Edinburgh Review*" (620). The success of the periodical's future, then, depends critically on its success in establishing public reading habits consistent with those of the *Edinburgh* itself.

Ideal *Edinburgh* readers, in this view, will be those who read like *Edinburgh* reviewers. This body of readers, though, possibly includes Amelia Opie herself – a potential inclusion which impressively lengthens the reach of the *Edinburgh*'s aims. The periodical is clearly bent on creating and sustaining an *Edinburgh* reader, but as the reviews under discussion here indicate, the periodical wants to form the *Edinburgh* author as well. In *Literary Magazines and British Romanticism*, Parker urges us to consider periodical literature in "broadly cultural terms, as attempts to organize the spectrum of cultural production" (11). The *Edinburgh*, however, wants to do more than "organize the spectrum of cultural production;" as its addresses to such authors as Southey, Pratt, Opie, Hemans, Moore, and Wordsworth signal, the periodical wants to contain that spectrum within its own critical reach, bringing all species of cultural work within the circulation of its discursive system.[34] If the *Edinburgh* interests itself not only in monitoring but also in controlling the production of culture, then its reviews – particularly of Southey, Moore, and Wordsworth – carry more weight, at least for the reviewers, than a mere critique, even an angry one. When the reviewer castigates the poet for abusing his powers – spending them in affected simplicity, licentious rot, or self-regarding isolation – he speaks not so much to the waste of literary creativity as to the dangerous mismanagement of political influence.

Both registers of discourse, however, also resonate with the reviewers' economic and social worlds, and the tone they adopt of assured and authoritative pronouncement may disguise their real anxiety about the maintenance and well-being of those worlds. The reviewers, after all, perhaps Jeffrey especially, had real reputations and financial circumstances bound up in the success of the periodical's undertaking. Jeffrey's early biographer, Lord Cockburn, makes much of the gloom which shadowed his letters on the subject of starting the review: "Our Review has been postponed till September," Cockburn quotes from a letter to Robert Morehead, "and I am afraid will not go on with much spirit even then. Perhaps we have omitted the tide that was in our favour" (*Life*, 104). To his brother, Jeffrey expresses a similar foreboding about the periodical's chances of either financial or social success:

> Our Review is still at a stand. However, I have completely abandoned the idea of taking any permanent share in it, and shall probably desert after fulfilling my engagements, which only extend to a certain contribution for the first four numbers. I suspect that the work itself

will not have a much longer life. I believe we shall come out in October, and have no sort of doubt of making a respectable appearance, though we may not perhaps either obtain popularity, or deserve it [*Life*, 104–5].

Jeffrey's epistolary pessimism, his hesitance to continue with a failing venture, offers a contrast to the confident corporate voice which speaks in the pages of the debut *Edinburgh*. Thus the paternalistic tone of Brown's critique of Amelia Opie (nine years his senior) works not only to establish an unassailable posture for the *Edinburgh*'s future literary critics, but also to suppress the anxiety attendant upon any significant political and cultural project – a project which, in Jeffrey's own recollection, "aimed high from the beginning" (*Contributions*, v). Insecurities about the periodical's abilities to generate income and public confidence might have been further sharpened by consideration of a poet, a *woman* poet, who had already "obtained popularity," whether or not she had "deserved" it. By casting Opie as the audience of his just, liberal, and improving remarks, the reviewer can co-opt the rest of his reading audience as unresisting subscribers to the correctness of the *Edinburgh*'s social and political discourse.

The *Edinburgh*'s initial review of Opie, finally, is as much forward-thinking instruction as it is current critique, as much an exhortation to Opie to constrain her poetry to appropriate registers, lines, and themes as a faulting judgment on her present (largely unsuccessful) attempts. So why, again, does the *Edinburgh* choose the work of this particular woman poet for one of its three founding literary articles? How does the perusal of her literary output contribute to the periodical's political aims of cultural production? "We cannot place Mrs Opie," Jeffrey concludes in his 1806 review of her *Simple Tales*, "so high in the scale of intellect as Miss Edgeworth; nor are her Tales, though perfectly unobjectionable on the score of morality, calculated to do so much good" (8/16, 470). Precisely because she is *not* Miss Edgeworth (or Mr Wordsworth, for that matter) can the *Edinburgh* "do much good" through its review of her work that her own work cannot perform. In his article on the periodical's poetical "ordinances," Bromwich claims that "Jeffrey was friendly to anomalous books or writers, provided he could associate them with reliable virtues" (10). This willingness of Jeffrey's to review minor writers for the purposes of literary didaction is evident in the periodical's first and later reviews of Opie: though he must fault her for attempting what lies beyond her capacity, he is pleased to grant her the poetical accomplishment of such "reliable virtues" as tenderness, pathos, simplicity, and grace, virtues that he decidedly makes reliably *feminine*.

In the final lines of his 1802 review, the *Edinburgh* reviewer bids Amelia Opie to learn the scope of her own powers by the mechanism of his beneficent corrections, and he promises future praise conditional on formal improvement: "we own, that a little selfishness has been mixed with our censure; as, in correcting the misapplication of Mrs Opie's powers, we looked forward to the enjoyment which they must afford us, whenever they are exerted on their proper objects" (1/1, 121). A *little* selfishness: the reviewer proposes the creation of a woman poet praiseworthy by the *Edinburgh Review* for her expected submission to its restraining poetic principles. A little nervous self-interest, too, might be evident in the review(er)'s repeated denouncement of Amelia Opie's failed poetic attempts: for the first number of a periodical which has set for itself the occupation of such mammoth cultural importance, the fear of failed attempts might be paramount indeed.

NOTES

1. Thomas Brown, "*Poems*. By Mrs Opie," *Edinburgh Review* 1/1 (Oct. 1802), 113–21. All subsequent references will be cited within the text; all identifications of authorship come from Walter E. Houghton (ed.), *The Wellesley Index to Victorian Periodicals, 1824–1900* (Toronto: University of Toronto Press, 1966).

2. Sydney Smith, "*Delphine*. By Madame de Staël-Holstein," *Edinburgh Review* 2/3 (April 1803), 172–7; Francis Jeffrey, "*A Series of Plays, in which it is attempted to delineate the Stronger Passions of the Mind; each Passion being the subject of a Tragedy and a Comedy.* By Joanna Baillie," *Edinburgh Review* 2/4 (July 1803), 269–86; Jeffrey, "*Popular Tales.* By Maria Edgeworth, author of Practical Education, Castle Rackrent, &c &c," *Edinburgh Review* 4/8 (July 1804), 329–37; Jeffrey, "*Simple Tales*: By Mrs Opie," *Edinburgh Review* 8/16 (July 1806), 465–71.

3. Three articles in the first issue (*Edinburgh Review* 1/1 [Oct. 1802]) review works of poetry: Francis Jeffrey, "*Thalaba, the Destroyer*: A Metrical Romance. By Robert Southey" (63–83); J.A. Murray, "*Bread; or, The Poor*. A Poem. By Mr Pratt, Author of Sympathy, Gleanings, &c" (108–12); and Brown's "*Poems*. By Mrs Opie."

4. For a brief consideration of the literary associations and attendant politics of the term "Whig," see Clare A. Simmons, *Eyes Across the Channel: French Revolutions, Party History and British Writing, 1830–1882* (Amsterdam: Harwood Academic, 2000), 1–62.

5. Mark Schoenfield, "Regulating Standards: The *Edinburgh Review* and the Circulations of Judgment," *Wordsworth Circle* 24/3 (1993), 148.

6. Most accounts of the founding, however contradictory in their casting, record the uncertain and even dangerous political climate of the moment: Lord Cockburn, in his *Memorials*, recalled that "the suppression of independent talent or ambition was the tendency of the times. Every Tory principle being absorbed in the horror of innovation … no one could, without renouncing all his hopes, commit the treason of dreaming an independent thought." Henry, Lord Cockburn, *Memorials of His Time*, ed. Karl F.C. Miller (Chicago, IL: University of Chicago Press, 1974), 161. In the preface to his collected works, Sydney Smith also remembered the fearful political environment: "it is impossible to conceive a more violent and agitated state of society." Sydney Smith, *Works of the Rev. Sydney Smith*, Vol.1 (London: Longman, Brown, Green, and Longmans, 1848), iii; quoted in Sheldon Halpern, *Sydney Smith* (New York: Twayne Publishers, 1966), 29. For more accounts of the founding of the *Edinburgh Review*, see Alan Bell, *Sydney Smith* (Oxford: Clarendon Press, 1980), 34–40; Henry, Lord Brougham, *The Life and Times of Henry Lord Brougham Written by Himself*, Vol.1 (Edinburgh: William Blackwood and Sons, 1871; rpt. Westmead: Gregg International Publishers, 1972), 245–70; John Clive, *Scotch Reviewers: The Edinburgh Review, 1802–1815* (London: Faber and Faber, 1957), 186–97; Cockburn, *The Life of Lord Jeffrey*

with a Selection from His Correspondence (Philadelphia: J.B. Lippincott & Co., 1856), 100–11; Cockburn, *Memorials*, 159–63; Halpern, *Sydney Smith*, 29–33. The close association of the *Edinburgh* with its editor only strengthened with the years. The March 1818 issue of *Blackwood's* features a *faux* letter by J.G. Lockhart, writing in the guise of the Baron von Lauerwinkel, "On the Periodical Criticism of England." He concludes his description of Francis Jeffrey and "his Review" by noting, "I have spoken of Mr Jeffray [*sic*] as if he were the sole conductor and animating spirit of this Review." Lockhart, "Remarks on the Periodical Criticism of England – in a Letter to a Friend," *Blackwood's Edinburgh Magazine* 12/2 (March 1818), 677, 678. For a consideration of the extent of Jeffrey's editorial control of the *Edinburgh Review*, see Clive, *Scotch Reviewers*, 42–70.

7. Jon P. Klancher, *The Making of English Reading Audiences, 1790–1832* (Madison, WI: University of Wisconsin Press, 1987).

8. Actually, Opie had published another novel before *The Father and Daughter: The Dangers of Coquetry* (1790).

9. Francis Jeffrey, "1. *Records of Woman: with other Poems*. By Felicia Hemans ... 2. *The Forest Sanctuary: with other Poems*. By Felicia Hemans," *Edinburgh Review* 50/99 (Oct. 1829), 32–47.

10. The adjective is surely a pun on Opie's married surname.

11. Schoenfield, "Regulating Standards," 149.

12. Thomas Brown (1778–1820) was a member of the Academy of Physics (f.1797) in Edinburgh, whose members included Jeffrey, Smith, Brougham, and Horner. A metaphysician who succeeded Dugald Stewart as lecturer in moral philosophy, Brown also produced collections of poetry with titles not unlike those of Amelia Opie (*Paradise of Coquettes* [1814]; *The Wanderer in Norway* [1815]; *The Warfiend* [1815]; *The Bower of Spring* [1817]; *Agnes* [1818]; and *Emily* [1819]). Identified by Jeffrey's early biographer, Lord Cockburn, as an esteemed friend, Brown nevertheless left the *Edinburgh Review* after the second number, having taken offense at some editorial intervention (Cockburn, *Life*, 110, 115). On the evidence of Brown's withdrawal from the enterprise upon editorial disagreement, his assessment of Opie's *Poems* in the inaugural number must, then, represent a view consonant with the editors' own. For more on Thomas Brown and his involvement with the early *Edinburgh Review*, see Clive, *Scotch Reviewers*, 21, 188–9, 195–6; Halpern, *Sydney Smith*, 30; and David Welsh, *Account of the Life and Writings of Thomas Brown, MD* (Edinburgh: Tait, 1825).

13. Mark Parker, *Literary Magazines and British Romanticism* (Cambridge: Cambridge University Press, 2000), 12–16.

14. Francis Jeffrey, *Contributions to the* Edinburgh Review (Philadelphia, PA: Carey and Hart, 1846).

15. On the question of the *Edinburgh Review* and labor, see Schoenfield, "Regulating Standards:" "the periodicals do no work, but replace the labor of others with their own representations of that labor; simultaneously, their judgment erases the labor of the reader, or limits it to conforming to the *Edinburgh*'s program" (148).

16. Francis Jeffrey, "*The Excursion, being a portion of the Recluse, a Poem*. By William Wordsworth," *Edinburgh Review* 24/47 (Nov. 1814), 1–30. *The Excursion* provides Jeffrey with the perfect target for his group/individual attack, for Wordsworth has committed the fatal sin of individual valuation – writing as if he does not read the *Edinburgh Review*: "if Mr Wordsworth ... had condescended to mingle a little more with the people that were to read and judge of [*The Excursion*], we cannot help thinking, that its texture would have been considerably improved" (24/47 [Nov. 1814], 3–4).

17. Francis Jeffrey, "*De L'Influence attribuée aux Philosophes, aux Francs-Maçons, et aux Illuminés, sur la Revolution de France*. Par J.J. Mounier," *Edinburgh Review* 1/1 (Oct. 1802), 1–18. Jeffrey rejects conspiracy theory in the Mounier article, however, only to endorse it in his review of *Thalaba*. For more on the *Edinburgh*'s reading of Mounier, see Jerome Christensen, "The Detection of the Romantic Conspiracy in Britain," *South Atlantic Quarterly* 95/3 (1996), 605–8. On the periodical's usage of conspiratorial rhetoric to further Whig interests, see also Kim Wheatley, *Shelley and His Readers: Beyond Paranoid Politics* (Columbia, MO: University of Missouri Press, 1999), 34.

18. On the notion of groups and literary production in the Romantic era, see Jeffrey N. Cox, *Poetry and Politics in the Cockney School: Keats, Shelley, Hunt and their Circle* (Cambridge: Cambridge University Press, 1998), 1–15.

19. When he finally gets around to critiquing the poem, Jeffrey identifies a kind of willful presentation of individuality, all the more contemptible and dangerous because Southey's stance of defiant originality actually occludes his indebtedness to a group of like-minded literary models. "The productions of [Southey's] school," Jeffrey sneers, insisting upon Southey's membership in a group, "are so far from being entitled to the praise of originality, that they cannot be better characterised, than by an enumeration of the sources from which their materials have been derived" (1/1, 64). Instead of creating his own poetical corruptions, which would at least have the distinction of invention, Southey has merely *copied* his disgusting imaginings from others. The suggestion of copying here anticipates Jeffrey's later review of Opie's *Simple Tales* which have similarly failed to "copy" the dictates of masculine reason; as a female poet, however, Opie does well to copy, while Southey, a male poet, ought to aim for invention and so deserves scorn for his failure either to create anew or to copy pleasingly. Jeffrey finds an imbalance between individual and group presentation in Southey's *Thalaba* similar to that which Brown identifies in Opie's *Poems*: "There is little of human character in the poem, indeed; because Thalaba is a solitary wanderer from the solitary tent of his protector: But the home-group, in which his infancy was spent, is pleasingly delineated" (1/1, 80).

20. Opie's most celebrated novel, *Adeline Mowbray* (1804), which the periodical's second review of her work mentions, models its heroine on Mary Wollstonecraft. The erasure of Opie's radical connections may provide an example of the *Edinburgh*'s investment in eliminating the radicals from its desired political dynamic, making the Whigs the only and natural opposition to the Tories with the *Edinburgh* playing authoritative moderator.

21. Andrea Henderson, *Romantic Identities: Varieties of Subjectivity, 1774–1830* (Cambridge: Cambridge University Press, 1996).

22. Ibid., 7.

23. Christensen, "Detection," 616.

24. Recall the "softness and delicacy of hand" which Jeffrey describes, in his review of Felicia Hemans, as "characterising the purer specimens of female art" (50/99 [Oct. 1829], 34).

25. In addition to the binary of natural versus unnatural, that with which Brown begins the review – feeling versus reason – raises the difficult matter of the *Edinburgh*'s aesthetic principles, codes of reading and reviewing whose Augustan tendencies seem vexed by more Romantic currents of taste. Especially in the later numbers, one cannot easily separate the periodical's aesthetics from those of its editor, Francis Jeffrey. Denounced by his contemporaries and later critics with charges of insincerity, political maneuvering, and financial manipulation (especially in relation to his reviews of Wordsworth and the Lake Poets), Jeffrey nevertheless maintained poetic precepts that were genuinely complex and often contradictory. Even in the first numbers of the *Edinburgh*, as the Opie review indicates, one finds tensions between an Augustan adherence to poetic principles and a Romantic response in feeling and taste (Jeffrey's review of Southey's *Thalaba* in the first issue provides an admirable instance of this strain). For more on the vacillating aesthetic practices of Jeffrey's *Edinburgh Review*, see J.H. Alexander, "Edinburgh Reviewers and the English Tradition," *Two Studies in Romantic Reviewing*, Vol.1 (Salzburg: Institut für Englische Sprache und Literatur, 1976), 103–90; Clive, *Scotch Reviewers*, 151–65; James A. Greig, *Francis Jeffrey of* The Edinburgh Review (Edinburgh: Oliver and Boyd, 1948); and Russell Noyes, *Wordsworth and Jeffrey in Controversy* (Bloomington, IN: Indiana University Publications, 1941).

26. This essentialist take on naturalism in poetry might be considered in light of Henderson's descriptions of the Romantic era's competing models of subjectivity: the canonical model favored by the *Edinburgh* might argue for the naturalness of innate characteristics, common to general and universal nature, while the context-based model of identity, propounded by Godwin and, at least initially, by Opie, might resist the very notion of an essential or determinable nature.

27. Francis Jeffrey, "*Epistles, Odes, and other Poems*. By Thomas Moore, Esq.," *Edinburgh Review* 8/16 (July 1806), 456–65.

28. Jeffrey's account of Moore's poetic crimes resulted in his own nearly criminal activity. Moore issued a challenge to Jeffrey for his scathing *Edinburgh* review and the two duly met in the summer of 1806 at Chalk Farm in London. Fortunately, "neither party [was] very sanguine," as Philip Flynn remarks (Philip Flynn, *Francis Jeffrey* [Newark, DE: University of Delaware Press, 1978], 82). The police arrived in time to intervene, and the two were taken to Bow Street Station, where they struck up a literary conversation while awaiting bail. The potentially fatal confrontation produced not further enmity but a remarkable friendship between the two men, an unlooked-for but successful instance of the *Edinburgh*'s mission to co-opt its resisting readers.

29. "The life and conversation of our sex, we are afraid, is seldom so pure as to leave them much to learn from publications of this description; and they commonly know enough of the reality, to be aware of the absurd illusions and exaggerations of such poetical voluptuaries" (8/16 [July 1806], 458).

30. In addition to "attaint" and "pollution," such loaded words as "contamination," "corruption," and "stain" (8/16, 460–61) mark the discourse of Jeffrey's attack on Moore's verse. This language of infection recalls that employed by Jeffrey in his review of Southey's *Thalaba* and anticipates the character of his condemnatory remarks on Wordsworth's *Excursion*. Mixing the metaphors of biology and economy, Jeffrey proposes to cure or at least retard the progress of literary diseases by bringing sick specimens within the healthy circulation of the *Edinburgh*'s own critical bloodflow. As David Bromwich notes, Jeffrey's critical mission has the healing qualities of an "antidote" (David Bromwich, "Romantic Poetry and the *Edinburgh* Ordinances," *Yearbook of English Studies* 16 [1986], 5). In his reviews of both Southey and (later) Opie, Jeffrey aims to match corruption with amputation, contamination with purgation. Both poets' "affectations," whether of simplicity, originality, or pathos, carry the taint of illness, but Jeffrey the physician-critic means to eradicate the disease by judicious application of his analytical powers. While Jeffrey knows he cannot "cure" the dangerous maladies of such poets as Wordsworth and Moore, and so resorts to language hyperbolic in its critiques, he may have a shot at restoring and shaping the poetical powers of other poets like Southey, Pratt, Hemans, and Opie, and so employs a discourse more subtle in its contours but no less ambitious in its aims.

31. On the use of sarcasm within the *Edinburgh Review*, see Christensen, "Detection," 608–10.

32. Recall, too, Jeffrey's denunciation of the Southey School's refusal to make distinctions, particularly among speech and class.

33. Bromwich, "Romantic Poetry," 15.

34. The *Edinburgh* aimed to organize and contain the spectrum of cultural production not only by praise but also by silence. On the periodical's exclusionary practices, see Marilyn Butler, "Culture's Medium: The Role of the Review," *The Cambridge Companion to British Romanticism*, ed. Stuart Curran (Cambridge: Cambridge University Press, 1993), 138–9.

Novel Marriages, Romantic Labor, and the Quarterly Press

MARK SCHOENFIELD

> The sly humour is so nicely, and almost imperceptibly, mingled with worldly wisdom ... nothing affected, sickly or sentimental – but common sense arrayed by the garb of fancy. The vivid exhibition of scenes of domestic life; the opposition of motives and passions ... The curtain seems lifted on an elegant drama of manners; husbands and wives quarrel and recriminate in dialogue almost as graceful as Sheridan's; youths of fortune become the prey of rustic lasses in spite of obdurate fathers; and good moral better enforced than most stage conclusions, dismisses the parties and charms the audience.

Given the tendency of Romantic-era reviewers to use legal and theatrical metaphors, this passage could easily be describing the domestic novels of Maria Edgeworth, Frances Burney, or Jane Austen. It is, however, the *Quarterly Review*'s Victorian assessment of the collected judgments of William Scott, Lord Stowell (1745–1836), whose rulings in the consistory court were the most significant force in shaping marriage law during the careers of those writers.[1] This quotation neatly signals that, from the perspective of the periodical press, the ideological work performed by the court not only resembled that achieved by the novel, but was grounded in the same dual axis of judgment – moral and aesthetic. Scott's stylistics, and the Tory *Quarterly*'s emphasis on them, recognize that it is not the law that enforces itself, but the habits of mind or, in polite terms, manners that disseminated both respect for the law and the naturalization of specific laws so that they were experienced not as something imposed upon a society, but as that society's rational expression of its own best self. Demonstrating awareness that such rational expression was amenable to novelistic presentation, the *Quarterly* reviewer reminisces that William Scott "once said he could furnish a series of stories from the annals of Doctor's Commons which should rival the Waverley Novels in interest; and we wish he had tried it!" (*QR* 75 [Dec. 1844], 49).

More than Sir Walter Scott's historical fiction, however, the novel of manners was positioned to express and regulate the ordinary. Reviewers emphasized this project as an aesthetic norm of the genre, counterbalanced yet occasionally interpenetrated by the Gothic as a genre of excess and spectacle.[2] An anonymous notice in the *Monthly Review* recommends *Emma* especially for those "who seek for harmless amusement, rather than deep pathos or appalling horrors," while another one in the *British Critic* distinguishes it from "fanatical novels and fanatical authoresses [of whom] we are already sick." In differentiating *Emma* from Gothic novels, reviews emphasized the everydayness not only of its characters and their local community, but of its literary goals; the *Gentleman's Magazine* notes that *Emma* "delineates with great accuracy the habits and manners of a middle class of gentry; and of the inhabitants of a country village at one degree of rank and gentility beneath them."[3] In his more substantial review of *Emma*, Sir Walter Scott praises Jane Austen's early novels as "belong[ing] to a class of fictions which has arisen almost in our own times, and which draws the characters and incidents introduced more immediately from the current of ordinary life than was permitted by the former rules of the novel."[4] Paradoxically, such praise intends to render the novel passive for the reader who is figured as a "youthful wanderer" that can "return from his promenade to the ordinary business of life, without any chance of having his head turned by the recollection of the scene through which he has been wandering" (*QR* 14, 200). Yet the work of Austen, Frances Burney, and Maria Edgeworth, rather than only celebrating, also criticizes the ordinary. Insisting on the political and historical ramifications of the lives of women, their novels disrupt the easy return to the "ordinary business" that Scott highlights. This disruption, as Claudia Johnson has pointed out with regard to "social criticism" more generally, required female authors "to develop strategies of subversion and indirection which would enable them to use the polemical tradition without being used completely by it;"[5] however, subtlety and satire were novelistic techniques that reviewers could strategically misread and misrepresent.

This essay explores the responses that Frances Burney's *The Wanderer* (1814) and Maria Edgeworth's *Patronage* (1814) provoked in the two major quarterly Reviews. The *Edinburgh Review* (founded 1802) followed by the *Quarterly Review* (founded 1809) dominated the periodical market from nearly the inception of the *Edinburgh* until the late 1810s, when *Blackwood's Magazine*, soon joined by the *London Magazine* and other monthlies, deliberately represented themselves as an option to their monopoly.[6] Gary Dyer notes that Thomas Love Peacock focuses considerable satire on how the Romantic public sphere "is exemplified by the quarterlies:" "Peacock's characters quote the *Edinburgh Review* numerous times, the *Quarterly* even more. He reproduces these forums as microcosms of the public sphere in order to burlesque the public sphere itself, and the celebration of it."[7] Even at the height of their popularity, these quarterlies were reinforced, challenged, imitated, and even ignored (albeit necessarily *studiously*) by other periodical productions across a political and aesthetic spectrum[8] and certain cultural sites remained indifferent to them. Nonetheless, their eminence and sophisticated generic maturity by 1814 compels the question of how their attention to the novels of Burney and Edgeworth intersects with their more overt political and economic arguments.[9]

Claudia Johnson notes that "By 1814, the climate had changed for women writers" from the 1790s when magazines "treat[ed] female and male writers as menaces or allies of comparable magnitude" and, consequently, *The Wanderer* "was stridently denounced by J.W. Croker [Secretary of the Admiralty and deeply engaged with the *Quarterly Review*] as the work of a shriveling hag:" Johnson's focus on the mid-1810s as a turning point in the aesthetical norms imposed upon women novelists corresponds to the collision between Burney and Edgeworth on the one side and the *Quarterly* and *Edinburgh* on the other, as the acknowledged champions of their respective literary industries.[10] A resonant aspect of this collision is that intrinsic to their literary judgments is an attempt by the periodicals to recoup and to professionalize patriarchy in the midst of a reconfiguration of marriage integral to developing economic imperatives. Marital union provides the impetus and the psychological bulwark for commercial risk; as Leonore Davidoff and Catherine Hall put it, "Family, hearth and home were both rationale and setting for the business enterprise while domestic ideals increasingly set the terms for economic activity." This new economy deployed a rhetoric of partnership in which, as Hudson and Lee note, "affective individualism replaced family [that is, parental] decisions about love and marriage."[11]

In its hyperbolic assertions, William Hazlitt's critique of Burney's *The Wanderer*, to which I will return in more detail later, reflects a number of the key features and anxieties of the quarterlies' encounter with powerful and popular women writers. Hazlitt distinguishes men from women through a kind of literary physiognomy intended to render feminine literary labor as a natural, nearly compulsive, extension of their sex, and so in distinct opposition to the professional labor of the male periodical writer:

> The surface of their minds, like that of their bodies, seems of a finer texture than ours; more soft, and susceptible of immediate impression. They have less muscular power, – less power of continued voluntary attention, – of reason – passion and imagination: But they are more impressed with whatever appeals to their senses or habitual prejudices ... They learn the idiom of character and manner, as they acquire that of language.[12]

The echo of "impression" with "more impressed" in this quotation establishes female authors as translators of everyday experience, as much written upon as writing. Burney's strength, it follows, should consist in relaying "immediate observation," except that her novel is predicated upon an artificial elegance shared equally by the author and the heroine:

> Because a vulgar country Miss would answer "yes" to a proposal of marriage in the first page, Mad. D'Arblay makes it a proof of excessive refinement, and an indispensable point of etiquette in her young ladies, to postpone the answer for five volumes [*ER* 48, 337].

This ability to choose with regard to marriage produces a paralysis of decision-making that defies verisimilitude, an aesthetic blunder. Hazlitt's reading arises from the conjunction between the modern perception of marriage, in which a "Miss" could solve everything on the first page – or at least could speak "yes" in her own voice – and the sufficient reminders of earlier (and sometimes exaggerated) patriarchy that occasioned considerable distress about the new marital formations. This anxiety is both displayed and neutralized in the novel of manners, and the reviews of *Patronage* and *The Wanderer*, despite the lukewarmly positive assessment of the former and the decidedly hostile response to the latter, refashioned both of these novels to highlight the affinities between contemporary marriage economics and a more traditional patriarchic hierarchy. A language of aesthetic judgment was employed to achieve this effect, by locating the authors within the narrowed realm of "female novelist." Although the *Quarterly* and the *Edinburgh* are politically, and often aesthetically, oppositional, their editorial agreement about these works suggests the periodical industry's investment in controlling the form. Their similar responses do not reflect collusion, but clarify an aspect of their competitive relationship, as each seeks to reify literary masculinity and femininity, in accord with their respective social visions. For each, the desire to regulate feminine manners through the adjudication of feminine literary forms – both the Gothic and novel of manners – stems from their recognition of the juridical significance of manners themselves as a quasi-legal formation that Edmund Burke, David Hume, and William Blackstone had acknowledged as necessarily aesthetic.[13]

II

The construction of the genre of the novel of manners as a particularly feminine form provided a central mechanism of the endeavor to regulate the female novelist. Hazlitt wrote of Burney, "her *forte* is in describing the absurdities and affections of external behavior, or *the manners of people in company*" (*ER* 48 [Feb. 1815], 336); considering *Patronage* for the

Quarterly, John William Ward accounts for the improvement in novels in recent years by noting that it has fallen "very much into the hands of the other sex," who "appear particularly well qualified" because they "are, generally speaking, gifted with a nice perception of the various shades of character and manners."[14] In some respects, these novels, and the public careers of their authors, were amenable to redactions that signaled an obedience to patriarchy as a correlative to their interest in manners and marriage; *Patronage* begins with Edgeworth's father's "paternal *imprimatur*" and, in his own words, "the sanction which she requires."[15] But it is the erasure, or disempowerment, of the resistances to such constructions that occupied the reviews. For both these novels, that resistance is most evident in scenes of feminine labor that expose the economic systems restraining it, and so reviewers disable such scenes by delineating them as either affected or merely natural.

In the inaugural issue of the *Edinburgh Review*, Thomas Brown presents a dynamic of family economy operating in the literary world of feminine authorship. His critique of Mrs Opie's *Poems* acknowledges her established popularity, derived from work in the 1790s and – although the review does not specify the link – associated with the radical politics of Wollstonecraft and Godwin, but then announces that on Opie's second outing, she must expect that she "has exhausted the indulgence" of the critic who now "expects to applaud, rather than to forgive" ("Article XVII," *ER* 1 [Oct. 1802], 113). *Poems*, however, was hardly her second appearance in print, as she had already published several volumes and a variety of songs. The operative distinction that the *Edinburgh* reviewer displaces onto Opie's misrepresented career was between a literary terrain of unprofessional reviewers and that of the newly founded *Edinburgh*, determined to construct itself as the universal (and profitable) bar of public opinion.[16] As Andrea Bradley observes in the previous essay in this collection, Opie's popularity provides at once the rationale for reviewing her work and the anxiety that shapes the condescending tone of the review. Noting Opie's deftness with small poems – opuscular verse, as he fashions it – the *Edinburgh* reviewer asserts her ineptitude with anything grander:

> She has *attempted* blank verse, but with the real music of blank verse is wholly unacquainted … the regular heroic couplet she has also *attempted*; but a line of ten syllables is too large for the grasp of her delicate fingers [*ER* 1, 115].

The reviewer continues in this gendering vein, until announcing, in the final paragraph, that the problem of her having chosen inappropriate subjects and forms has most likely been solved by her recent "marriage with a celebrated artist," whereby:

she may be said to have united, in conjugal rivalry, two of the most elegant arts; and if, as we trust, she will submit to abandon all idle decoration, and to give her whole fancy to simplicity and tenderness, though the pencil of her competitor should even increase in power, "ut pictura poesis" will be a compliment, not of flattery, but of truth.[17]

This review derives from the cultural objectives of the *Edinburgh*, as it seeks to distinguish its own commentary as "truth" from the "flattery" of both earlier and competing periodical and serial productions. To do so, it reflects the ideology of marital partnership as at once economic and aesthetic, and gives to that ideology a characteristic narrative shape: a young woman of untested talent arrives of age in the world of letters with little to distress or to vex her, attracts considerable attention with her native charms, and consequently stumbles into a series of generic social blunders until she happens into a match with a man of suitable aesthetic fortune. In short, a novel of manners, a strategy of control.

About a year prior to the inaugural *Edinburgh Review*, William Scott preached to a woman seeking a divorce for cruelty: "Having assumed the relationship of a wife, she is bound to execute the duties that that relation imposes; and particularly to abstain in future from inordinate pretensions and exaggerated complaints" (*Oliver* v. *Oliver*, 1801).[18] This call to relative silence within the household is offered as an implicit term in a contract willingly chosen, and so reaffirms a male-dominated hierarchy refigured in commercial terms. To complain is to be "inordinate," to violate both the holy vows of ordination that marriage imposes, and its legal complement of ordinates that proscribe behavior. Scott is insisting that, precisely because she has freely chosen her position as wife, she is under particular obligation to regulate her speech and, avoiding exaggeration, to measure it by patriarchic expectations.[19] The new familial space did not displace patriarchal hegemony but restructured its processes. The increased freedom of women to choose their own partners – once a threat to patriarchy – became part of the mechanisms of gender control and the central plot of the novel of manners as the reviews represented them.

Frances Burney's final novel, *The Wanderer: or, Female Difficulties*, is, in one sense, a traditional novel of manners illustrating that a single man in possession of a good fortune, must be in want of a wife. Although the character of Harleigh bears out this proposition, *The Wanderer* is also an anti-marriage novel, its narrative propelled by a secret, coercive marriage that overshadows the heroine Juliet's struggles. She takes on a series of different identities and disguises (many involving covering her head and face); her name is reduced to the initials L.S. and then reconstituted under the pseudonym Ellis (with the mixed-language embedded pun on "Elle-es" that positions her as "every woman," a position with which Hazlitt cannily concurred in order to trivialize both her and the novel). As her economic position deteriorates and that deterioration makes her less willing to accept economic aid, Juliet embodies a grotesque caricature of the *feme covert*, whose identity is dissolved, if not in this case exactly into her husband's, then because of it. After a series of escapes, she is finally overtaken by her husband (a French commissary who blackmailed her into marriage to gain her dowry of £6,000) in the presence of her lover, and an exchange between the men ensues. Ostensibly, the discussion concerns legal rights, and especially those rights to the body and knowledge of a woman, but the disabling effect of both men – hero and villain – on Juliet is registered in the gothicized language of the scene:

> The man roughly gave her a push; seeming to enjoy, with a coarse laugh, the pleasure of driving her on before him.
>
> Harleigh, who saw that her face was convulsed with horrour, fiercely planted himself in the midst of the passage, vehemently exclaiming, "Infernal monster, by what right do you act?"
>
> *"By what right do you enquire?"* cried the man; who appeared perfectly to understand English.
>
> "By the rights of humanity" replied Harleigh: "and you shall answer me by the rights of justice! One claim alone can annul my interference. Are you her father?"
>
> *"No,"* he answered, with a laugh of scorn; *"but there are other rights."*
>
> "There are none!" cried Harleigh, "to which you can pretend. None."
>
> *"How so? Is she not my wife? Am I not her husband?"*
>
> "No!" cried Harleigh, "no!" with the fury of a man seized with sudden delirium, "I deny it! – 'tis false! and neither you nor all the fiends of hell shall make me believe it!"[20]

There is no dispute here on the significance of marriage; if they are married, the commissary acquires the rights of the father over the body of the daughter. The parallel structure of the Frenchman's questions – "Is she not my wife? Am I not her husband?" – invokes a rhetoric of mutuality, but one immediately contested by Gothic phrases such as "infernal monster" and "fiends of hell." On the question of her being married, Juliet herself is resolutely silent, a silence inaugurated at the wedding ceremony itself, in which she answers nothing to the presiding official; throughout is the fear that should she speak, she might, despite her intentions, authorize the marriage. Juliet's silence and her uncertainty as to whether she is married constitutes a shrewder understanding of the law than the quick certainty of various

Englishmen. Both characters and reviewers asserted the belief that, because the marriage would not have been valid if performed under English law, it would not be valid in England; to the contrary, in *Dalrymple* v. *Dalrymple* (1811), William Scott found that the validity of a marriage was determined – by English law – by reference to the law where the marriage occurred.[21]

Hazlitt, reviewing the novel, converts this genuine legal conundrum into a false delicacy; Burney's "ladies stand so much upon the order of their going, that they do not go at all" (*ER* 24, 337). Reconfiguring a question of law and institutional power as one of manners and feminine attributes, Hazlitt justifies this claim with examples out of context and completely negates the economic distresses caused by the strictures limiting female labor within the novel. He observes that "a lady appears regularly every ten pages, to get a lesson in music for nothing" (*ER* 24, 336); rather than recognizing this regularity as indicative of the repetitive economic deprivation in which Juliet must survive, and acknowledging the significance of an art form – music here, but other ones throughout the novel – that contributes to maintaining a disabling discourse of female amateur accomplishments, Hazlitt puns on "for nothing," converting its meaning from "without pay" within the novel to "for no reason" as a critique of the novel. Commenting on the scene in which Juliet faces her putative husband in the presence of Harleigh, Hazlitt – ignoring the legal complexity – asserts that "she runs from her honourable lover into the power of a ruffian and an assassin, who claims a right over her person by a forced marriage;"[22] the *Quarterly* describes the "commissary, who pretended to be married to her" as "pursu[ing] his alleged wife" ("Article IX," *QR* 11 [April 1814], 128). A novel about getting Juliet unmarried, *The Wanderer*'s narrative sequence en route to a formally happy ending requires her husband's death, which precludes either a legal battle or paying him off (an act implying a validity to his claim), and the recovery of a codicil to her father's will. The same court that protects Juliet's rights by its assumed willingness to enforce the codicil granting her an independent fortune is also the site of danger in which her marriage may be validated. As in *Patronage*, the heroine's freedom to choose her own spouse becomes a trial of her loyalties and obedience to a patriarchic system which she has thoroughly internalized. In part because of her experiences with the chaos of the "dire reign of the terrific Robespierre," this internalization is marked by a paranoia indistinguishable from her material fears; by satirizing these fears as "obstacles, lighter than 'the gossamer that idles in the wanton summer air,'" raised "into insurmountable difficulties" (*ER* 24, 338), Hazlitt insists on the impossibility of a political reading. The *Quarterly* criticizes the novel for a "surprising view of the state of religion, manners, and society in England" and, similar to Hazlitt, dismisses moments of economic or political pressure as:

troublesome intricacies in which [the characters] had been so long, without any visible cause, involved and perplexed, like the persons of the fairy tale, who were fettered by invisible chains, and placed in ridiculous and unnatural attitudes, till the sleeping beauty should be awakened to life and a husband [*QR* 11,127–8].

In this rhetoric, the *Quarterly* maintains that this is a bad novel of manners, rather than an exploration of the conditions that polite manners perpetuate.

Edgeworth's *Patronage*, like *The Wanderer*, turns on a scrap of legal writing, a deed which insures a patriarchal lineage. Because it is temporarily lost, however, the proper family to inherit, the Percys, can demonstrate their worthiness through labor. The Falconers, their foil, make their way by patronage into jobs they cannot sustain, homes and social classes for which their taste is deficient, and marriages that are not happy. For the Falconers, marriage is subsumed into patronage, and the novel – to the extent it links patronage with benevolent (or not) father-figures – displays the failure of patriarchy. But for the Percys, the daughters have the liberty of choosing by their own heart. In a passage quoted in the *Edinburgh* as representative of their characters, the two daughters discuss marriage in the presence of their mother. The lengthy excerpt ends with Caroline's appeal to her mother and sister:

> "Mother!" continued Caroline, turning eagerly, and seizing her mother's hand – "My guide, my guardian, whenever you see in me any, the slightest inclination, to coquetry, warn me … as you wish to save me from that which I should most dread, the reproaches of my own conscience … in the first, the very first instance, reprove me, mother, if you can … with severity. – And you, my sister, my bosom friend, do not use your influence to soften, to open my mind to love; but if ever you perceive me yielding my heart to the first tenderness of the passion, watch over me, if the object be not every way worthy of me, my equal, my superior. … Oh! as you would wish to snatch me from the grave, rouse me from the delusion – save me from disappointment, regret, remorse, which I know that I could not bear, and live –."[23]

These exclamations are what she is supposed to say, not only for her family, but for the reviewer, Sydney Smith.[24] Caroline understands her freedom from her father's control as a test of her own ability to choose as he would. For her husband to be her equal, he must be her superior, and the call for her mother and sister's aid with this test enacts the process of internalizing the ethic of proper marriage as the feminine equivalent to the masculine work ethic of making one's way in the professions and the working classes – by labor and merit, not patronage. In the denouement, merited forms of patronage become necessary – Caroline's brother attracts the notice of his superiors in his law firm, and Caroline eventually earns a Count, partly by her declining to dance with someone less worthy and less stationed; the *Edinburgh* reviewer uses this last point to argue that "Miss Edgeworth, we are afraid, is somewhat enamoured of *high station*," and suggests that the sections of the novel concerned with royalty smack of another hand (*ER* 22, 432). This joke, leveled at her father's strong influence over her ("surely some heavy spirit has occasionally guided her pen"), deconstructs the binary of patronage and friends that Richard Edgeworth's Preface maintains. But what appears in this context as a criticism of the novel actually borrows one of its fundamental themes, as becomes apparent in the novel's complex overlay between the international economies and the marriage market. From the reviewer's perspective, the weakness of the book comes from Edgeworth's own internalization of the patronage system; yet the *Edinburgh* recognized that Edgeworth's critique of patronage implicated its own reviewing strategy. Acknowledging that Edgeworth's remark, "if productions have any real merit, they will make their way on their own," also "applies to literary merit," they offer a long string of patronage systems: "Ministers – Mecaenas's – mistresses – patrons at court – in the church – and in the drawing room – all cashiered and depreciated" (*ER* 22, 417–18). Conspicuously absent are the periodicals, though the novel itself had noted the importance of the periodical press to the performance of patronage: "Dr Frumpton's name, and Dr Frumpton's wonderful cures, were in every newspaper, and in every shop window. – No man ever puffed himself better even in this puffing age" (*Patronage*, 1:186). Sydney Smith may have felt personally implicated in this dynamic which his review suppresses since, as Marilyn Butler has documented, he apparently agreed with the widely held (though erroneous) assumption that he was the model for Buckhurst Falconer.[25] Though primarily satirized as a dissipated cleric, Falconer is explicitly connected, simultaneously, to social ambitions and the periodical press; Alfred Percy writes his mother that:

> I know no more of what is going on in this great metropolis, than if I were at Tobolski. Buckhurst Falconer used to be my newspaper, but since he has given up all hopes of Caroline, he seldom comes near me. I have lost in him my fashionable *Daily Advertiser*, my *Belle Assemblée*, and tête a tête magazine [*Patronage*, 2:174–5].

In the reviews of both these novels, the policing of literary strategies is linked to the construction of modern gender. In explaining why the Greeks were incapable of writing novels, J.W. Ward, the reviewer of *Patronage* for the *Quarterly*, does not turn to ancient aesthetic theory, but situates the question within the material conditions:

> Slavery spread a gloomy uniformity over three-fourths of the
> population of Greece and Rome. The free citizens were devoted
> chiefly to public affairs, and their private life exhibited nothing but a
> stern unsocial strictness on the one hand, or a disgusting shameless
> profligacy on the other. To them that steady settled influence of
> women upon society was utterly unknown, which in modern times has
> given grace, variety, and interest to private life, and rendered the
> delineation of it one of the most entertaining and one of the most
> instructive forms of composition [*QR* 10 (Jan. 1814), 301].

This mythology of the modern invention of the private sphere locates
women within two productions – first, the creation of a private space and,
second, the means of its representation, as a mode of self-fulfilling
instruction. In reading a novel, a woman can imagine her own household
transformed with "variety" and "grace" – she becomes a locus of
consumption through this production. In Greece, the opposition was
between slaves and free citizens; now, it is between free citizens (male) and
women, whose influence is "steady" and "settled," that is, conservative,
rather than reforming. This description excludes women such as Mary
Wollstonecraft (and her literary counterpart in *The Wanderer*, Elinor
Joddrell[26]) from the category of woman as aggressively as it excludes
homoerotic practice – here conjured as "shameless profligacy" – from the
activities of the contemporary "free citizen." This doubling functions both
to focus the forms of desire in (and onto) marriage, and to delineate that
marriage as a particular kind of economic partnership. The glorification of
the role of the novel of manners in this mythology encourages readings and
valuation of the novel and of one's own life along specific cultural
parameters. The *Quarterly* review of *Patronage* postulates that the novel's
popularity derives from the "charm in the description of scenes which every
one has witnessed, and of feelings with which every heart sympathizes"
(*QR* 10, 302). This conjunction is rhetorically deft, since many readers are
reading about scenes they have not witnessed: the joyful reunion with the
long-lost, and invariably wealthy, paternal figure; the rediscovery of
codicils that render all safe for marriage, and so on. In compensation for our
individual lack of experience with such scenes, our sympathy must be
universal – we applaud the woman who waits on her parent's permission of
marriage even as, or especially because, she asserts her own right to marry
as she chooses.

   In the *Quarterly*, the pointed survey of the history of the novel serves to
introduce Maria Edgeworth who, along with Frances Burney, is taken as the
premiere novelist of manners. Her particular skill lies in delineating the
good that comes of virtue – only in the private sphere:

> She has, doubtless, observed that this mode of instruction is not
> adapted to those cases in which to deviate from virtue is palpably a
> crime. It is to the Decalogue, and to the terrors of the law that we are
> to look for the prevention of these graver and more striking offenses
> [*QR* 10, 305].

Edgeworth's moral instruction operates circumscribed within a wider
sphere of juridical power. The reviewer, nonetheless, soon complains that
the law intrudes into the text; his task is to make that presence an aesthetic
error rather than a social critique. Edgeworth can inculcate the habits of
mind to "controul our passions and to exert our faculties" and emphasize the
lesson that all good comes of "labour – severe and continued labour,"
whether it is masculine industry or feminine reproduction and domesticity.
But she cannot – in the reviewer's representation – insist on a political
relation between these forms of labor.

In the next paragraph, the reviewer insists on the aesthetic virtue of
Edgeworth's productions – by making it mirror the scene of labor he has just
described. Most writers, he contends, use "dazzling characters" stuffed with
"rash courage, inconsiderable generosity, love ardent and irresistible at first
sight" – traits the public habitually finds pleasurable. Edgeworth uses more
ordinary characters, and so, by additional labor, she must overcome readerly
expectations and, as a consequence, can teach readers more about their own
lives. In this view, the reviewer encourages a reader to understand her own
function in society, and in marriage, through the lens of Edgeworth's novel;
this means to build one's hopes on the market's valuing of labor as a
commodity. Yet the commodified value of a woman depends on her
eschewing the marketing of that value, through codes of politeness,
obedience, and taste. Further, the reading submerges the running critique in
the novel about the habit of reading novels, especially as that habit is
implicated in the wider distribution methods of the publishing industry;
Miss Hauten, showing considerable skepticism about the claims of novelists
to understand the human heart, adds that:

> Some of these novels are sad trash – I hope Mr Godfrey Percy will not
> judge of my taste by them. That would be condemning me for the
> crimes of my bookseller, who will send us down every thing new that
> comes out [*Patronage* 1:148].

Against the reviewer's praise comes his criticism that Edgeworth's morality
is too visible, that the signs of her labor are too evident: "We know how
necessary the square and the rule are to the architect, but we do not like to
see the chalk-marks upon the building" (*QR* 10, 307–8). This objection
privatizes feminine labor, insisting its marks not show on the outside of the

house. Similarly, the reviewers of Burney's *Wanderer* trivialize female labor (both in producing material objects such as cloth and cultural artifacts such as plays, music, and novels) not because it is unnecessary, but because the novel refuses to take it for granted and render it charmingly invisible. To not see labor is to not pay for it, and so the *Quarterly* review of Edgeworth at once acknowledges the role of women in the formulation of a market society, but then, using standards of decorum and grace, erases that role or, more precisely, asks that women erase it themselves. Their labor, like Edgeworth's learning, ought to be inconspicuous. Though nearly contradicting the earlier praise of Edgeworth's additional labor in choosing ordinary subjects, this view is consonant with a liberal ideology in which wives are taken to have chosen their own lives, to have married of their free will, but in doing so have expended that will by dedicating it to the role of wife, of *feme covert*.

The claim that Edgeworth's strengths are in her moral representations of events that fall beneath the law's notice is reinforced by critique of moments when her work discusses legal issues or presents political scenes. Edgeworth "should carefully avoid employing her popularity and influence to create a belief in such [evils] as are purely imaginary," specifically "the right of impressments," which "under proper management might one day ... become the parent of as numerous a progeny of patriots as the *borough-mongering system* itself" (*QR* 10, 312). By corollary, a reader should not value those portions of the book that challenge the system of the ministry:

> The character of lord Oldborough, though distorted, ... is much the most interesting in the book. We are inclined, however, to doubt the propriety of introducing ministers of state among the "dramatis personae" in a novel. Not indeed from any undue reverence or admiration for that order of men, but from reasons purely literary [*QR* 10, 312].

These purely literary reasons, however, are derived precisely from a consideration of "that order of men:" "This mixture of reality with fiction spoils both. ... All readers of taste are shocked by the combination." This aesthetic judgment derives from the *Quarterly*'s maintenance of its own political representational power; the reviewer recommends that should Edgeworth wish to present another "unfavourable representation of the king, or a vehement panegyric on one of his law officers, to choose for them a more suitable vehicle than the pages of a romance." The reviewer's anxiety about Edgeworth's representations is evident in that he had earlier distinguished her novel from romance, but he hopes to control what can be said about the government by controlling what genres are available to potential criticizers. At the same time, the review reifies the position of women as the authors of novels; they become metaphorically *feme covert*, having – in being novelists – put themselves under the governance of the periodicals.

John Wilson Croker, writing the *Quarterly Review*'s assessment of *The Wanderer*, picks up on the theme of an anti-marriage as a way to attack Burney, but also to reinforce the identity shift entailed in a woman's marriage:

> If we had not been assured in the title-page that this work had been produced by the same pen as Cecilia, we should have pronounced Madame D'Arblay to be a feeble imitator of the style and manner of Miss Burney ["Article IX," QR 11 (April 1814), 124].

This raillery takes for granted the power of marriage to transform, and that the mark of that transformation is implied in the woman's new name; the reviewer has repeated the joke of his opening sentence: "none of our female novelists (not even Miss Edgeworth) ever attained so early and so high a reputation as Miss Burney, or, as we must now call her, Madame D'Arblay." The shift from "Miss Burney" to "Madame D'Arblay" corresponds to a shift from the reviewer owning her as the best of "our female novelists" to her coming under another, foreign power, whose force reverberates to the review itself that "*must* now call her" by the French surname (*QR* 11, 123). That such a dynamic replays the crucial scene in the novel, when Harleigh confronts – and then yields to – Juliet's putative French husband, underscores the *Quarterly*'s investment in the clear delineation of the feminine realm. Despite lamenting her changed state, the review, seemingly contradictorily, argues that all of Burney's novels, including *The Wanderer*, are indistinguishable; the reviewer quotes a criticism by Inchbald regarding *Evelina* and challenges the reader to determine for which of Burney's novels it was meant. *The Wanderer*, then, is a failure because it is too much like Burney's other novels, and yet, for that very reason, too different from them: "The Wanderer has the identical features of Evelina – but of Evelina grown old" (*QR* 11, 125). Marriage is the condition of being both oneself and another, of being Juliet/Ellis, but it is crucial to the *Quarterly* that this condition is presented as both a legal disempowerment and purification of feminine nature, not as subversion of masculine law. Among its errors in reporting the novel's plot is the claim that Juliet divorces her husband – a divorce implies a legal marriage and a legal tribunal and Juliet's need for precisely the protection which she demonstrates strength by refusing. The accounts of both Burney's and Edgeworth's early reputations – narratives repeated by both the *Edinburgh* and *Quarterly* – locate them in the period of amateur reviewing, allowing the reviewers to transform those reputations through its new professionalized criticism; concurrent with this development is the production of the female novelist as the graceful observer of the inevitable. *The Wanderer*, Croker writes:

cannot, in our judgment, claim any very decided superiority over the thousand-and-one volumes with which the Minerva Press inundates the shelves of circulating libraries, and increases, instead of diverting, the ennui of the loungers at watering places [*QR* 11, 124].

Initially, her works form a decided whole, and stand in relationship to one another, as she forms her own literary identity through the expectations of the reviews. But *The Wanderer* reduces her to the namelessness of a mythicized press that overproduces volumes that hamper the economy of the circulating libraries, and mar the restorative functions of places like Bath, where, traditionally, the novel was given freer reign.

The periodicals sought to contain the possibilities of these novels, especially as they threatened patriarchy with the subversive possibilities of the *feme covert*, and in doing so developed a structure of genre and aesthetic judgment, one also linked to their own organizational structure. The world implied in "The firm of Wife, Children, and Friends" is one in which the periodicals were deeply invested.[27] The various publishers – themselves often family-owned firms – depended for their success on a corporate literary identity. In the dialogue of masculinized periodical and feminized novel, the dynamics of husband and *feme covert* were both displayed and enacted, and their concern with policing this representation of marriage, and its implications about personal identity, sheds light on the disciplinary practices of the periodicals and the commercial society they sought to represent; to define the novelistic genre was not just to limit ideological possibilities, but to construct the periodical's own masculinized potential. Because the marriage debate hung uneasily between the private and the public, the old patriarchy and the new economy, the reviewers were anxious to mark out their own contribution. In his 1809 review of Edgeworth's *Tales of Fashionable Life*, Francis Jeffrey opens with an unusual confession:

> If it were possible for reviewers to *envy* the authors who are brought before them, we rather think we should be tempted to envy Miss Edgeworth; – not [for her literary talents but] for the delightful consciousness of having done more good than any other writer, male or female, of her generation ["Article VII," *ER* 14 (July 1809), 375–6].

The continual qualifications of this comment – "if," "rather," "tempted," "her generation" pitted against the generationless "we" of the *Edinburgh* reviewer – betrays its anxious significance. The rhetoric of romanticized rapture becomes a courting ritual in which, finally, Edgeworth is admonished to recognize her limitations with regard to that public political realm the *Edinburgh* is engaged in shaping. *Patronage* and *The Wanderer* refuse this admonishment, and the reviews of those novels are correspondingly disciplinary.

To conclude, I want to glance at the political utility of this disciplinary construction for containing the writings of women in other fields. By constructing rules of genre as aesthetic and reflective of the natural condition of gender, critics could deploy their judgments as if equally natural, neutral, unbiased, and masquerade interventionist readings as descriptive or evaluative. Maria Graham's *Journal of a Residence in India* (1812) touched on questions that continuously concerned the *Quarterly Review* from its inception to well into the Victorian period – namely, the economic, social, and political relationships between India and both Europe and England. The reviewer, probably John Barrow,[28] begins by offering a plot to the journal:

> "The Journal of a Residence in India" by a young lady who, probably, went thither, like most young ladies, to procure a husband instead of information, is a literary curiosity which we are not disposed to overlook ["Article VIII," *QR* 8 (Dec. 1812), 406].

Inserting into the book a marriage plot that the author does not acknowledge recasts the commentary on Indian culture as incidental, the observations picked up by the way, since her primary attention would be directed towards the British men.[29] To further insist on the centrality of Graham's sex to her project and its merits as a "literary curiosity," the first paragraph contrasts her work to the writings of various men: governor-generals' letters on finance, reports of committees on affairs civil, military, and commercial; Mr Colebrook's reasonings, and Captain Wilford's reveries, an abundance of learned disquisitions on language (*QR* 8, 406–7). This list simultaneously maps out the public world and marks the differences in the various men – Mr, Captain, governor-general – who take up these topics as against the relative uniformity of the category "young ladies." What is missing, the reviewer continues, from the work of the men is a "popular and comprehensive view of the manners, customs, and conditions" of India. As Edgeworth is praised for her keen view of English manners but rebuked for drawing political implications from it, Graham addresses a subject not quite worth the more precious labor of men, for which she is suited by her ability not to analyze, but to "observe" and "view," both verbs recurring through the review. Again, as I argued with the reviews of Edgeworth and Burney, although the book is amenable to such a reading, it is not reducible to it as the *Quarterly* insists. The reviewer notes that Graham claims the journal was written "for the amusement of an intimate friend," a framing device common for epistolary novels. But the reviewer adds to this remark that "we are ready to believe [it], and think not the worse of [the journal] for that." That is, as a literary curiosity, it is no less, or more, than it should be.

Her descriptions, the reviewer remarks, as far as Graham had the opportunity to observe, are correct. As the review develops, however, her limitations stem not from the extent of her view, but rather from her abilities to reason; the reviewer uses this limitation as a justification for glossing and correcting her text, and thereby encourages a reading style that depoliticizes Graham's observations. By contrast, in reviewing David Macpherson's *History of European Commerce with India* (1812), George Ellis highlights the author's expertise, and positions the reader as student ("Article VII," *QR* 8 [Sept. 1812], 114–44). Macpherson's underlying theme is not the narrative of the marriage plot, but rather the problem of how to trade with India. In his narrative, descriptions of food become commentaries on trade potential; in Graham's, similar descriptions are lessons in domesticity. The topics that Graham's memoirs are said *not* to be about – the public ones – are persistently visible in the narrative. The reviewer, however, blocks their recognition by the readerly lens suggested by a marriage plot in which the implicit hero is the British soldier, and in which the natives remain exotic. The longest quotation in the review is of Graham's visit to "a greater curiosity," the same word which the reviewer uses to characterize the book itself. That curiosity is the harem, and the description of it, we are told by the *Quarterly*, is amusing. In it, Graham ascends into "the women's apartment" by a ladder "which is removed when not in immediate use, to prevent the ladies from escaping." Few of the women can read or write and the quotation ends with an assertion of the mundanity of their life: "They thread beads, sleep, quarrel, make pastry, in the same daily round; and it is only at a death, a birth, or a marriage, that the monotony of their life is ever interrupted" (*QR* 8 [Dec. 1812], 411–12). The description of the harem, which Graham called shocking, not amusing, with its regulated monotony, might pressure the cycle of the novel of manners, its powers to organize daily life around rituals, and its teleology of marriage. But by insisting that Graham's observations are distinct from political commentary, the reviewer forestalls this possibility, and the review can continue on through India as Graham silently, already covert, searches for a husband, a desire nowhere named in her text but implicit in her being.

Noticing Anna Letitia Barbauld's *Eighteen Hundred and Eleven* in the issue just prior to the review of Graham, the *Quarterly Review* exclaims: "We had hoped, indeed, that the empire might have been saved without the intervention of a lady-author" ("Article VI," *QR* 7 [June 1812], 309).[30] By limiting the novel of manners, the Quarterly reviewer and its brethren – precursors to the "bachelors" of *Blackwood's Maga* that Lisa Niles discusses in this collection – hoped, rather, to avoid imagining what an empire saved by the intervention of a lady-author might look like. In an odd echo of Graham's conjectural quest for a husband as the impetus for her text in the *Quarterly*, Francis Jeffrey makes a gossipy cameo appearance in a letter of Maria Edgeworth (the bulk of which discusses female authors), in which his rumored quest for a spouse is rendered as distinctly economic, not only severed from his writing but secondary to it:

> Have you heard that Jeffrey, the reviewer, is gone to America in pursuit of a lady, or, as some say, to take possession of an estate left him by an uncle? He is to be back in time for the "Edinburgh Review" in September! ["To Mrs Buxton," 9 Aug. 1813, *Life and Letters*, 231–2]

Attuned to the masculine space of the periodicals, Edgeworth registers the irony that such space depends upon women – women to marry and women to review.

NOTES

1. "Article II – *Cases Argued and Determined in the Consistory Court of London …*," *Quarterly Review* 75 (Dec. 1844), 49. Citations in the text to periodicals will be by volume and page.
2. For one account of the periodical reviews' engagement with the Gothic genre, see Michael Gamer, *Romanticism and the Gothic: Genre, Reception, and Canon Formation* (New York: Cambridge University Press, 2000), especially Ch.2. Discussing Sir Walter Scott's 1810 review of Charles Maturin's *The Fatal Revenge*, Gamer suggests that "Scott's Dantesque descent to that lowest circle of literary hell – gothic fiction – shows him participating unproblematically within the conventions of periodical reviewing, whose task he sees as one of confirming existing literary hierarchies and enforcing unchanging standards of taste" (34).
3. *Monthly Review* 80 (July 1816), 320; *British Critic* n.s. 6 (July 1816), 98; *Gentleman's Magazine* 86 (Sept. 1816), 248–9. All of these are reprinted in Ian Littlewood (ed.), *Jane Austen: Critical Assessments*, 4 Vols. (East Sussex: Helm Information, 1998), 1:304–8.
4. "Article IX," *QR* 14 (Oct. 1815), 189. Summarizing the plot of *Emma*, Scott remarks that "all these entanglements bring on only a train of mistakes and embarrassing situations, and dialogues at balls and parties of pleasure, in which the author displays her peculiar powers of humour and knowledge of human life" (196).
5. Claudia Johnson, *Jane Austen: Women, Politics, and the Novel* (Chicago, IL: University of Chicago Press, 1988), 19.
6. Despite the presence of other periodicals, Scott – in contemplating the founding of the *Quarterly* in a letter to its eventual editor, William Gifford – suggests that the huge popularity of the *Edinburgh* stemmed from "its being the only respectable and independent publication of the kind." *The Letters of Walter Scott*, ed. H.J.C. Grierson, 12 Vols. (London: Constable & Co., 1932), 2:105. In the popular perception, the *Quarterly* did not so much break this monopoly as join it; writing as the German correspondent Baron von Lauerwinkel reporting on his journey through London, John Gibson Lockhart declared that "those strange *Reviews* … at present rule the authors and readers of the freest country in Europe, with as arbitrary and merciless a sway as was ever exerted over the civil and political world by a sportive Nero, or a gloomy Tiberius." *Blackwood's Magazine* 2 (March 1818), 670. With more economics and less humor, James Mill repeats the charge in the 1824 inaugural issue of the *Westminster Review*. Jon Klancher notes that by 1819, "the *Edinburgh Review*'s own confidence in the English audience seemed shaken" in the face of Cobbett's new two-pence *Political Register* and *Blackwood's Magazine*, both emblems of what Jeffrey described as "the unhappy estrangement between the two grand divisions" of the English population, the "upper and middle classes and the lower classes." Klancher, *The Making of English Reading*

Audiences, 1790–1832 (Madison, WI: University of Wisconsin, 1987), 48–9, quoting *Edinburgh Review* 32 (Oct. 1819), 294. The centrality of the professional reviewers of the *Edinburgh* and *Quarterly*, tied respectively to the dominating political parties of Whigs and Tories, has an eighteenth-century prehistory in the formation of the specific public sphere "first emerging out of the coffeehouses, club, and newspapers in early-eighteenth-century England," as Erin Mackie points out. Drawing on Habermas, Mackie shows that "largely through publications like the *Tatler* and the *Spectator*, the public sphere becomes the place where an encompassing set of cultural and social norms are formulated for polite modernity." Erin Mackie, *Marker à la Mode* (Baltimore, MD: Johns Hopkins University Press, 1997), 18. Such a formulation depends less on a distinction between private and public spheres than on acknowledging the private sphere as a particular enactment of public-sphere values, and in this regard Mackie's study, focusing on fashion, establishes the *Spectator* as a particularly salient precursor to the *Edinburgh*.

7. Gary Dyer, *British Satire and the Politics of Style, 1789–1832* (Cambridge: Cambridge University Press, 1997), 121. In his unfinished "Essay on Fashionable Literature," Peacock "criticizes the conformity of the major periodicals" (Dyer, *British Satire*, 121).

8. Radical voices that challenged the quarterlies' hegemony prior to the monthlies have been explored by Kevin Gilmartin in *Print Politics: The Press and Radical Opposition in Early Nineteenth Century England* (Cambridge: Cambridge University Press, 1996), and Marcus Wood, *Radical Satire and Print Culture: 1790–1822* (Oxford: Clarendon Press, 1994).

9. Philip Connell has articulated one salient connection between the *Edinburgh*'s Whig politics and its literary aesthetics in terms of a sense of a developing "fragmentation of learning into a confusing multitude of superficial literary forms united only by their transient mediocrity," a worry presented at length in Jeffrey's 1813 review of Madame de Staël. Jeffrey saw this disintegration, operating simultaneously on readers and writers, as implicating the "refined, commercial state of society" that the *Edinburgh* itself had helped produce. Connell, *Romanticism, Economics and the Question of "Culture"* (New York: Oxford University Press, 2001), 94–5.

10. Johnson, *Jane Austen*, xv. Johnson schematizes a reification in the gendering of authorship: "While the novel had proved especially attractive to eighteenth-century women writers precisely because it was not already the territory of men, starting from as early as around 1815, reviewers insist on a fairly rigid distinction between the 'male' and the 'female' novel" (xiv).

11. Leonore Davidoff and Catherine Hall, *Family Fortunes: Men and Women of the English Middle Class, 1780–1850* (Chicago, IL: University of Chicago Press, 1987), 195; P. Hudson and W.R. Lee, "Introduction," in *Woman's Work and the Family Economy in Historical Perspective*, ed. P. Hudson and W.R. Lee (New York: Manchester University Press, 1993), 20. Although beyond my explicit analysis, this literary quarrel occurs within a wider transformation of the economic role of marriage and family. The author of the anonymous 1777 *Laws Respecting Women* locates marriage as the origins of both economic desire and its apparatus: "Indeed marriage seems to have been at first instituted as necessary to the very being of human society: for without the distinction of families there can be no encouragement to industry, nor any foundation for the care in acquiring riches." Anon., *The Laws Respecting Women, as they regard their Natural Rights* (London: Johnson, 1777), 23. Thus, an important corollary to the introduction of commercial language into the marital contract was the inculcation into the domestic sphere of an ideology of individualism as understood within the classical liberal economy. See also David Levine, *Family Formation in an Age of Nascent Capitalism* (New York: Harcourt Brace Jovanovich, 1977). Levine notes "Insofar as earnings, not property, became the pre-requisite for family formation and marriage, a family economy emerged" (120). E.J. Hobsbawm contends that, "the obvious way of industrial expansion in the eighteenth century was not to construct factories, but to extend the so-called domestic system." Hobsbawm, *Age of Revolution: 1798–1848* (New York: New American Library, 1962), 36. Much work has been done both emphasizing continuities and shifts of family economics, stemming from Lawrence Stone's *The Family, Sex, and Marriage in England 1500–1800* (New York: Harper and Row, 1977), and a good summary of some of it in relation to its implications for the property classes appears in "Theories of the Family," Ch.6 of Eileen Spring, *Law, Land, and Family: Aristocratic*

Inheritance in England, 1300 to 1800 (Chapel Hill, NC: University of North Carolina Press, 1993).

12. "Article III," *Edinburgh Review* 48 (Feb. 1815), 337. Although titled "Article III: *The Wanderer*," the article's structure – it does not turn to Burney until more than halfway through – is more accurately reflected in the running head, "Standard Novels and Romances."

13. For a discussion detailing these positions in relation to the literary implications for Austen, see David Kaufmann, "Law and Propriety, *Sense and Sensibility*: Austen on the Cusp of Modernity," *ELH* 59 (1992), especially 386–91. On the juridical status of the aesthetic in the late eighteenth century, which provided a common intellectual inheritance for the *Edinburgh* and *Quarterly*, see Terry Eagleton, *The Ideology of the Aesthetic* (Cambridge, MA: Basil Blackwell, 1990), especially Ch.2: "The Law of the Heart: Shaftesbury, Hume, Burke."

14. "Article I," *Quarterly Review* 10 (Jan. 1814), 303. John William Ward (1781–1833), eventually made Lord Dudley and Canning's Foreign Secretary in 1827, survives in literary history mainly in Byron's satiric passing reference (in a 21 Aug. 1817 letter) to the literary clutter in John Murray's quarters: "The room's so full of wits and bards, / Crabbes, Campbells, Crokers, Freres and Wards." George Gordon Byron, "Dear Doctor, I Have Read Your Play," (pub. 1830), in *Letters and Journals of Lord Byron*, ed. Leslie Marchand, 12 Vols., Vol.5: *So Late into the Night 1816–1817* (Cambridge, MA: Harvard University Press, 1976), 260. Although I have identified the authors of the various reviews, I have in general represented the corporate entities of the Edinburgh and Quarterly Reviewers as the producers of the reviews, to emphasize the dependence on the review's meaning on its situation within the specific periodical; I have made an exception of Hazlitt, as his review exists within literary history as part of his own canon.

15. Maria Edgeworth, *Patronage*, 4 Vols. (London: Johnson and Co., 1814), 1:ii. Edgeworth's father summarizes both moral and plot: "To excite the rising generation to depend upon their own exertions for success in life, is surely a laudable endeavour; but while the young mind is cautioned against dependence on the patronage of the great, and of office, it is encouraged to rely upon such friends, as may be acquired by personal merit, good manners, and good conduct." Burney's dedicatory letter to her father ends in a paternal encomium: "Will the public be offended, if here, as in private, I conclude my letter with a prayer for my dearest Father's benediction and preservation? No! the public voice, and the voice of his family, is one, in reverencing his virtues, admiring his attainments [etc.]." Frances Burney, *The Wanderer; or Female Difficulties* (London, 1814), ed. Margaret Anne Doody, Robert Mack, and Peter Sabor (New York: Oxford University Press, 1991), 10.

16. The review of Opie's *Poems* is framed by two brief notices, the only ones in the volume shorter than a page. Each savages its chosen book by deploying a parodic representation of the periodical press's own social function. The review following that of *Poems* attacks *Public Characters of 1801–02*, the latest in a successful series that presented contemporary biographies of individuals and served to register their public fame. The series, as the guarantor of renown, occupied a discursive space coveted by the Edinburgh Reviewer, which announces that the "design of the book appeared to us so extremely reprehensible" that it was the "fair object of the literary police," but on closer perusal, the book turns out to be merely inept – harmless and ungrammatical (*ER* 1, 122). The prior review attacks *Anniversary Sermon of the Royal Humane Society*, a regular publication which, according to the narrative of the review, puts its reader into such a "most profound sleep" that he could only be revived by "flinging in the smoke of tobacco, applying hot flannels, and carefully removing the discourse itself to a great distance" (*ER* 1, 113). Both these reviews deploy common tropes – of physician and police – for the critic, but turn out not to be reviews, but rather explanations of why these works are beneath the notice of the Edinburgh Reviewer and, by extension, of its readership. By this strategy, the *Edinburgh Review* seeks to disable potential competitors for the serial productions of both fame and value. For more on Thomas Brown, the author of the review on Opie, see Andrea Bradley's essay, n.12.

17. *ER* 1, 121. As Bradley notes, the fact that Opie's marriage occurred four years prior to the review (and the publication of *Poems*) emphasizes the rhetorical element of invoking the marriage as a solution to her failings.

18. 1 *Haggard Consistory Reports* 361; 161 *English Reports* 581. William Scott noted, by
    contrast, that the courts could provide no redress for language, unless it had the import of
    "actual danger of bodily harm:" "Of words, it is sufficient to say, that, if they are words of
    mere present irritation, however reproachful, they will not enable this court to pronounce a
    sentence of separation … the most innocent and deserving woman will sue, in vain, for its
    interference for words of *mere* insult, however galling" (emphasis added). Like Austen in
    Emma, both Edgeworth and Burney contest the notion that "insult" is ever a "mere insult"
    and without material consequences, because words are not "mere present irritations," but
    constitutive of future material conditions; these are the grounds upon which Knightley
    rebukes Emma for insulting Miss Bates who, he reminds Emma, "has sunk from the comforts
    she was born to; and, if she live to old age, must probably sink more." Jane Austen, *Emma*
    [1816], ed. James Kinsley (New York: Oxford University Press, 1995), 339.

19. An executor of Samuel Johnson's estate, the elder brother of Lord Eldon, and identified by
    Holdsworth as both the most influential and most literary of the Civilian judges, William
    Scott eventually became Lord Stowell, his sole speech before the Lords being on the 1822
    Marriage Act. In an earlier case, *Evans* v. *Evans*, one singled out by the *Quarterly Review*
    (75 [Dec. 1844], 47–9), Scott explained that the court's insistence on the rigid enforcement
    of the marital contract was required for "the greater and more general good" (1 *Haggard
    Consistory Reports* 35): "[Spouses] become good husbands and good wives, from the
    necessity of remaining husbands and wives; for is a powerful master in teaching the duties
    which it imposes." The law here coerces manners, or at least the appearance of manners.
    Since cases of this sort that came before Scott were generally wives suing for a separation
    from an abusive husband, the symmetry of this argument (slightly belied by the
    uncharacteristic representation of "necessity" as male) conceals a dynamics of power under
    a rhetoric of equality. During the years of some of his harshest judgments, he was estranged
    from his second wife; perhaps too generously, James Hammerton follows Scott's friendly
    biographers in calling this a "nice historical irony." Hammerton, *Cruelty and
    Companionship: Conflict in Nineteenth-Century Married Life* (New York: Routledge, 1992),
    122.

20. The italicized portions appear originally in French on the text, and are translated in footnotes
    by Burney; *Wanderer*, 726–7.

21. 2 *Haggard Consistory Reports* 54–70. Scott wrote: "The only principle applicable to such a
    case by the law of England is, that the validity of Miss Gordon's marriage rights must be tried
    by reference to the law of the country, where, if they existed at all, they had their origins"
    (58).

22. *ER* 48 (Feb. 1815), 338. Like Hazlitt, the *Quarterly Review* disavows any potential political
    reading of *The Wanderer*, and accounts for the historically-charged Preface as mere posing:
    "Madame D'Arblay is not likely to continue to flatter [Napoleon], when her flattery can no
    longer conduce to her personal convenience. Hereafter, therefore, we shall be prepared to
    find, instead of 'this alludes to the days of Robespierre,' 'this alludes to the days of
    Bonaparte.'"

23. "Article X," *ER* 22 (Jan. 1814), 421; *Patronage*, 1:368–9. Edgeworth herself had declined a
    marriage proposal in 1803, about which her stepmother wrote: "Maria was mistaken as to her
    own feelings. She refused M. Edelcrantz, but she felt much more for him than esteem and
    admiration; she was exceedingly in love with him. Mr Edgeworth left her to decide for
    herself; but she saw too plainly what it would be to us to lose her, and what she would feel
    at parting from us. She decided rightly for her own future happiness and for that of her
    family." Quoted in Grace Oliver, *A Study of Maria Edgeworth with Notices of Her Father
    and Friends* (Boston, MA: A. Williams and Co., 1882), 175.

24. Although Sydney Smith, a cofounder of the *Edinburgh*, wrote the review of *Patronage*,
    Francis Jeffrey reviewed most of Edgeworth's earlier works and Smith consciously links his
    review as by the same corporate pen, reminding readers of the "ardent admiration with which
    we greeted the first steps of this distinguished lady" and asserting "the eagerness with which
    we turn to every new production of Miss Edgeworth's pen." *ER* 22 (Jan. 1814), 416.

25. Marilyn Butler, *Maria Edgeworth: A Literary Biography* (Oxford: Clarendon Press, 1972),
    257. Smith wrote Lady Holland that if Edgeworth "has put into her Novels people who fed

her and her odious father, she is not Trustworthy," although Butler has shown that the composition dates of the novel mean that Buckhurst "could not have been directly based on Smith" (257–8).

26. The *Quarterly* sums up her career: "after appearing as a gay, trifling pleasant sort of young gentlewoman," she "breaks out, of a sudden, as a Jacobin, philosopher and atheist, runs away from her family, disguises herself as a man, wears a mask and dagger" until she is "persuaded" by Harleigh "to abandon her mask and dagger, and to give over the practice, to which she was greatly addicted, of cutting her own throat" (*QR* 11, 129). Overextending Joddrell's cross-dressed disguise, the *Quarterly* aligns her return to sanity with a return to gender and, perforce, an end of politics.

27. A Wolverhampton salesman offered a poem to his betrothed that declared "the heart is given bills which are never protested / When drawn on the firm of *Wife Children and Friends*." Quoted in Catherine Hall, "Strains in the 'Firm of Wife, Children and Friends'? Middle-Class Women and Employment in Early Nineteenth-Century England," in Hudson and Lee (ed.), *Woman's Work*, 117.

28. John Barrow, a prolific contributor to the *Quarterly*, was also Second Secretary to the Admiralty. According to the *Quarterly Review Project Website*: "[Barrow's] *Quarterly Review* geographical and exploration articles were widely believed (in the United States for instance) to reflect, if not official policy, certainly policy under official consideration. Barrow's writings, and the Royal Geographical Society, of which he was the chief founder, played a significant part in creating the nineteenth-century mania for exploration literature and, indeed, popular and official interest in exploration itself." Jonathan Cutmore (ed.), "Biographical Encyclopedia," *Quarterly Review Project 1808–1824* (2000), 30 Aug. 2002: http://www.dreamwater.com/edu/earlyqr/encycolopB.htm#sectB.

29. Maria Edgeworth wrote, "We have had great delight in Mrs Graham's 'India,' – a charming woman, writing, speaking, thinking, or feeling." "To Mrs Buxton," 19 Nov. 1813, in *The Life and Letters of Maria Edgeworth*, ed. Augustus J.C. Hare, 2 Vols. (Boston, MA: Houghton, Mifflin, and Co., 1895), I:233.

30. The review opens: "Our old acquaintance Mrs Barbauld turned satirist! The last thing we should have expected, and, now that we have seen her satire, the last thing we could have desired …"

Reading the Rhetoric of Resistance in William Cobbett's Two-Penny Trash

BONNIE J. GUNZENHAUSER

When I ask my students what they read for pleasure, about two-thirds of them typically answer that they gravitate toward magazines. When I ask why, their answers point toward what Margaret Beetham calls the "openness" of the periodical form – the fact that magazines allow them to fit small slices of reading into busy lives because such texts need not be read from cover to cover, unappealing articles may be skipped over, and readerly choice, rather than the necessity of narrative logic, governs the reading experience.[1]

That readers have long craved "openness" in their reading is evidenced by the fact that a number of early nineteenth-century periodicals explicitly made such openness part of their aim. The *Penny Magazine*, for instance, marketed itself to readers who might not be willing or able to read the text from start to finish but who nevertheless "were desirous to snatch a little time from the duties of each day for the pleasure and real advantage of acquiring some knowledge."[2] Similarly, women's magazines of the period offered what Sonia Hofkosh describes as a "heteroglossia" in which "high art consorts with commerce" in their attempts to draw in the widest possible array of readers.[3] While these magazines made the promise of piecemeal consumption central to their marketing strategies, some journalists roundly rejected this kind of reading practise as an acceptable *modus operandi* for early nineteenth-century periodical readers. In the introduction to the 1830 revival of his *Two-Penny Trash*, for example, the political journalist William Cobbett insists that readers must read his periodicals from start to finish if they are to cultivate either new knowledge or readerly discipline. In fact, Cobbett notes, his principal writerly strength lies in the fact that while his periodicals cover "a great variety of subjects, and all of them *very dry*; nevertheless the manner of treating them is, in general, such as to induce the reader to *go through the book*, when he has once begun it."[4]

It would be easy to dismiss Cobbett's self-description as simply an alternative marketing strategy, a claim that serious readers should adopt his model of reading and buy the periodical that would help them to practice it. But to view Cobbett's claim in this way would be to overlook the fact that he explicitly addresses this call for serious reading of "very dry" material to an audience that included a substantial number of lower-class readers, whose reading practices were typically dismissed by the early nineteenth-century cultural elite as superficial, caught up in what William Hazlitt called "the dust and smoke and noise" of the moment.[5] When Cobbett refuses to position his readers simply as casual consumers of small-scale textual commodities, and suggests instead that both the style and the content of his *Two-Penny Trash* will transform them into serious thinkers with a "taste for study,"[6] the claim that at first looks like an alternative marketing strategy in fact emerges as a key point of intellectual and political opposition to commodity culture. A number of recent studies acknowledge this oppositional strain in Cobbett's writings, and rightly point out that it escalates after his self-described "conversion" in 1816, when he became convinced that direct address to the lower classes – "The Journeymen and Labourers of England, Wales, Scotland, and Ireland" – was the only viable way to accomplish the social and political change he sought.[7] Kevin Gilmartin argues for the self-consuming nature of Cobbett's oppositional discourse, asserting that its ultimate goal is to render political struggle unnecessary by establishing the grounds for return to a non-political, agrarian past; Cobbett's aim, according to Gilmartin, is "to restore a world in which they [such writings] had no place."[8] Leonora Nattrass also reads Cobbett as looking backward for a solution to Britain's early nineteenth-century political turmoil. In Nattrass' estimation, Cobbett invokes not an ideal pre-political past, but an ideal political one, in the form of the Ancient Constitution. Like other radicals, Nattrass argues, Cobbett "identif[ied] the Norman Conquest as the political Fall, when power relations first went hopelessly askew," and his writings posit a reassertion of "the Common Law of England, as [something] both native to the British Isles and immemorial" to be the only real solution.[9]

While I think Gilmartin and Nattrass are correct in seeing history as the wellspring of Cobbett's political inspiration, I would suggest that in his post-1816 periodical writings Cobbett draws on an even older model of political organization for the solution to Britain's social and political ills: that of classical antiquity, in which, as Jane Tompkins puts it, "the reader … is seen as a citizen of the state, the author as a shaper of civic morality, and the critic as a guardian of the public interest."[10] In the post-1816 *Political Register*, Cobbett consistently envisions periodical discourse not as a commodity to be consumed for enjoyment or even self-cultivation, but rather as a dialogic practice through which he and his readers must forge discursive partnerships in order to generate social and political change. At a time when the periodical was increasingly focused on superintending polite letters and instantiating class distinctions,[11] Cobbett kept his *Weekly Political Register* unflinchingly focused on political initiatives and

injustices, repeatedly figuring the *Register* as a battlefield and his readers as
soldiers fighting the good fight for political justice. If we take Cobbett's
texts and his metaphors seriously, it becomes clear that the post-1816
Political Register – also called the *Two-Penny Trash* because of Cobbett's
populist pricing scheme – does much to reanimate ancient republican ideas
of both literacy and citizenship during a moment when both were in danger
of disappearing.[12] In the *Two-Penny Trash*, Cobbett makes republican ideals
of reading and writing accessible to a broad readership because he links
these ideals not to classical texts,[13] but to the contemporary literary
discourse of sympathy – a discourse that offered common ground on which
Cobbett's socially divergent readership could meet and from which they
could be persuaded to become activist citizens rather than consuming
subjects. Through his appropriation of sympathy in the *Two-Penny Trash*,
Cobbett constructs a readerly campaign of discursive resistance that
ultimately challenges both the periodical and the political culture of early
nineteenth-century Britain.

While it is difficult, as Marilyn Butler notes, to "isolat[e] the general
characteristics and impact of so large a body of writing" as that of early
nineteenth-century periodical literature,[14] the reviewer and essayist Hazlitt
undertook precisely such a synoptic assessment of the periodical press in an
1823 article for the *Edinburgh Review*. One key feature of the genre,
according to Hazlitt, is its insistence that politics must be tempered with
literary and belletristic topics if the periodical is to be marketable. In the
early nineteenth-century periodical:

> It is necessary to insert politics in a sort of sandwich of literature, in
> order to make them at all palatable to the ordinary taste. The war of
> political pamphlets, of virulent pasquinades, has ceased, and the ghosts
> of Junius and Cato, of Gracchius and Cincinnatus, no longer "squeak
> and gibber" in our modern streets. ... Mere politics ... will not go
> down without an infusion of the Belles-Lettres and the Fine Arts.[15]

That civic matters must be mitigated by cultural ones is not entirely
surprising because, as the political historian J.G.A. Pocock points out, early
nineteenth-century Britain saw politics becoming decentralized not just in
periodicals but in the culture at large. The eighteenth-century growth of
commerce and diffusion of political power meant that, by the early
nineteenth century, the possibilities for political identity had changed
dramatically. Individuals who had previously been able to see themselves as
part of "the farmer-warrior world of ancient citizenship" now found
themselves in what Pocock calls "an increasingly transactional universe of
'commerce and the arts'" – a universe in which "the activity of ruling and
being ruled" was supplanted by "commerce, leisure, and cultivation."[16] And

while the virtue-based world of "ancient citizenship" had been restricted to Britain's ruling elite, Pocock notes that this new situation encompassed a much broader cross-section of the population, one that included all who participated in Britain's commercial culture.[17]

Several recent critics have convincingly argued that the novelistic discourse of sympathy played a key role in acculturating Britons to the demands of this increasingly commercial society. Nancy Armstrong suggests that "the prominence of domestic fiction" signals Britain's turn from civic life to commercial culture. By "suggest[ing] the degree to which … power did not in fact rely on overtly juridical or economic means so much as on … the polite use of language, the regulation of leisure time, and all those microtechniques that constitute the modern subject,"[18] she argues, the novel put culture rather than *civitas* foremost in the minds of its readers. In a similar vein, Catherine Gallagher suggests that the novel's

> release into the culture of strongly marked overtly suppositional identities, belonging to nobody and hence temporarily appropriate to anybody … should be seen as one among many modes of facilitating property exchange and investment in the period, of creating the speculative, commercial, and sentimental subject.[19]

Deidre Lynch puts the acculturating force of the early nineteenth-century novel perhaps most succinctly when she claims that the process of confronting and interpreting the behavior of fictional characters accustomed novel-readers to "the social struggles that effected the transition from gentry to middle-class hegemony."[20] In each of these accounts, the novel succeeds as an acculturating tool because of its characters: readers identify, learn provisional sympathy, and so become more adept at negotiating what Pocock calls the "multiplying relationships, both with things and persons" that lie at the heart of commercial humanist culture.[21] Furthermore, those whom the novel was meant to acculturate came from a wide cross-section of early nineteenth-century British society. Novels, as Gary Kelly puts it, were "the most widely read form of imaginative writing" in the period, and as such "could be made to address the various classes comprising the 'nation,' as poetry, belles-lettres, and even drama, popular as it was, could not."[22]

Despite the broad social appeal of the novel, the idea that fictional characters should be the focus of readerly sympathy and identification was neither uncontroversial nor universally accepted. Socially, the ideology of sympathy created considerable anxiety because readers from all social registers were meant to feel similarly,[23] and because, as Barbara Benedict puts it, this sympathy was usually "felt for socially or morally marginal characters, those society has rejected."[24] Some writers of the period also attacked the discourse of sympathy on moral grounds, arguing that sympathetic identification drained readers of the capacity to respond effectively to real-world situations that might require sympathy and understanding. Cobbett and Wordsworth are two such: Wordsworth's jeremiad against "frantic novels" that will "blunt the discriminating powers of the mind" and "reduce it to a state of almost savage torpor" is well known,[25] and Cobbett seemingly echoes these sentiments 19 years later, when he cautions that novel-reading may result in a dehumanizing schizophrenia. The readers of sentimental fiction may "weep over the tale of woe in a novel," he asserts, "but 'round their 'decent fire-side,' never was compassion felt for a real sufferer, or indignation at the acts of a powerful tyrant."[26] Despite these critiques of sympathy, neither writer wants to abandon the discourse altogether. Rather, each reformulates it – and these reformulations show how Cobbett alone uses sympathy to move readers toward a more classical and activist kind of literacy.

In his reformulation of sympathy, Wordsworth targets the middle-class readers of *Lyrical Ballads*, and takes as his goal the improvement of their "taste."[27] He assumes that these readers will identify with his notion that poets – and other selected writers of imaginative literature – are *the* proper guides to understanding "moral relations."[28] And the means through which these "moral relations" will be made clear – the object of readerly sympathy and identification, in other words – is poetry. That Wordsworth substitutes poetry for the hyper-sentimentalized characters of eighteenth-century fiction is made strikingly apparent in one of the Preface's more bizarre metaphors, in which he personifies poetry and then casts it in a role almost identical to that of an eighteenth-century heroine:

> Poetry sheds no tears "such as angels weep," but natural and human tears; she can boast of no celestial Ichor that distinguishes her vital juices from those of prose; the same human blood circulates through the veins of them both.[29]

With this insistence on poetry as a living, breathing thing with which readers may identify in very human terms, Wordsworth retains the idea that sympathy's proper objects are found in imaginative literature; he simply relocates those objects from prose to poetry. But this reformulated discourse of sympathy leaves Wordsworth entrenched within the confines of commercial culture: his redirected readerly sympathy remains focused on a textual commodity (poetry), and his reader's role remains that of consumer. Wordsworth concedes that an imagined *future* audience might be able to join him in an activist reforming partnership stimulated by poetry, but he remains convinced that contemporary readers must focus simply on developing "taste" – again, an appetitive word connoting not activism, but consumerism.[30]

In his *Two-Penny Trash* reformulation of sympathy, Cobbett directs readerly attention away from aesthetic matters and toward civic ones. The discourse of sympathy is potentially useful, Cobbett suggests, not because it can refine individual "taste," but because it can generate such productive social emotions as "indignation" or "compassion." Even when Cobbett praises literary figures, he does so in spite of their literary merits rather than because of them; writing of Pope (one of his heroes), Cobbett "beseech[es]" his readers "to abstract themselves from the poetry and the wit, and fix their attention wholly upon his *reasoning*."[31] Why is Cobbett – a writer who was not without rhetorical flair himself – so insistent that his readers not get caught up in the stylistic dimension of Pope's writing? Because the primary reason for reading Pope, in Cobbett's estimation, is no different from the primary reason for reading the *Political Register*, or for reading about Malthus, or Blackstone, or Locke: namely, to learn how to recognize "Corruption," and to acquire the means to resist it. Invoking classical ideals of citizenship, Cobbett enlists all readers in this superintendence of Britain's public good: "Let free discussion take its course," Cobbett argues, "and as you proceed, abuses and corruption are done away, redress from time to time, is obtained."[32] Reading, in other words, is not about refining individual psychology through identification. Rather, as Cobbett sees it, reading is about facilitating communal improvement through rooting out corruption and directing readerly sympathy toward its proper objects: citizens like "the Journeymen and Labourers of England, Wales, Scotland, and Ireland" who are perhaps most subject to "abuses and corruption" and most in need of "redress." Cobbett thus reformulates the discourse of sympathy far more dramatically than does Wordsworth, because Cobbett removes himself from the sympathy loop altogether; rather than asking readers to identify with the writer or even with the genre that excites these emotions, Cobbett asks readers to feel sympathy by focusing directly on the plight of those who most deserve it. Consider, for instance, the salutation and opening from this 1831 *Two-Penny Trash* "Letter to the Working People:"

> My friends,
> You, who do all the bodily labour, who make to come all the food, all the drink, all the clothing, all the houses, all the horses and carriages; you, without whose help those who do not work would be starved to death, or would die with cold; you, who are at once the only source of the country's wealth, and the only means of its security; to you I now address myself.[33]

The anaphora – in both form and content very typical of Cobbett's *Two-Penny Trash* open letters[34] – ensures that even the most rudimentary readers will understand whom Cobbett posits as the proper objects of their sympathy: hard-working but unappreciated laborers like themselves. But Cobbett does not position his readers as objects of sympathy merely to incite their righteous indignation. The arrangement of the passage, with its final emphasis on the *active* role these laborer-readers play (they are "the only means of [the nation's] security") makes clear that Cobbett reformulates the discourse of sympathy to push readers beyond anger or self-pity to action; these readers must accept responsibility and become political *actors* if Britain's current situation is to be improved.

But what sort of agency does Cobbett imagine for these readers? Certainly literacy is a crucial precondition. A virulent opponent of religious reformers like Hannah More, Cobbett decried the religious and moral tracts such reformers produced, insisting that "stories like these are not sufficient to fill the minds of the working classes of the people. They want something more solid."[35] And in his *Two-Penny Trash*, the autodidact Cobbett gives his readers more "solid" material, offering them lengthy extracts from Blackstone,[36] précis of Malthus,[37] tutorials on the Lockean notion of private property,[38] and numerous reprinted speeches, letters, and bills from contemporary political discourse. Nattrass sees the heteroglossia of the *Two-Penny Trash* as the key to Cobbett's political project, suggesting that:

> Cobbett pits one discourse against another, brings oppositions into unexpected congruities, and addresses normally polarized audiences within a single text, in order to *subvert* as well as to resist encroaching social polarization and to oppose the devaluing of the working class.[39]

But to see Cobbett's *Two-Penny Trash* in Nattrass' terms is to classify Cobbett as a full participant in a Habermasian public sphere, in which the chief "civic task of a society" is to "engage in critical public debate."[40] And Cobbett repeatedly insists that debate is not enough. Even in his initial 1816 letter "To the Journeymen and Labourers," Cobbett advocates readerly activism, telling his readers that "petition," rather than just communal discussion or education or complaint, "is the channel for your sentiments."[41] This demand that his readers move beyond debate to action signals Cobbett's awareness that the commercialized public sphere of early nineteenth-century Britain might generate inaction or apathy just as easily as change,[42] and it marks a key step toward his reactivation of an ancient notion of the public sphere in which, as Habermas says, "a citizenry acting in common" assumed authority over political tasks.[43]

Cobbett reinforces the classical ideal of an activist citizenry – and the notion that the discursive arena is the proper originary site for such activism – by repeatedly framing discursive resistance in martial terms. Summoning his readers to petition for parliamentary reform, Cobbett warns them to "prepare for a *long war* against [Corruption]. If she out-live us, let us arm our children for the contest; let us give them those most powerful and most durable of all arms, the arms of the *mind*."[44] With this rhetoric, Cobbett casts his lower-class readers as citizens of a republic – as stakeholders prepared to do battle for the principles in which they believe. Such a characterization carries a strong political valence, as Pocock notes; the language of republican citizenship had a long tradition in Britain, and clearly signified "a devotion to the public good; … the practice, or the preconditions of the practice, of relations of equality between citizens engaged in ruling and being ruled; and … a mode of action and of practicing the active life."[45] By positing a situation in which his readers are citizens devoted to the common good, Cobbett frames them as reasonable people whose grounds of resistance to the issues at hand are neither irrational nor personal – a point reinforced when Cobbett exhorts his readers to "subdue in us anything like a *spirit of revenge*" and to "enter upon … discussion with minds unheated by anything that has recently transpired."[46] This point about "discussion" is crucial, because it reinforces the transactional nature of the discursive practice Cobbett advocates. His readers cannot be content with what Paolo Freire has called "the nutritionist concept of knowledge" – the simple absorption of information.[47] These readers must also be able to write properly so that they may "assert with effect the rights and liberties of [their] country."[48] In Cobbett's system,[49] literacy is not simply the individual "acquirement [*sic*] of knowledge;" rather, it is "the capacity of *communicating that knowledge to others*."[50]

The immediate communicative task in which Cobbett enlists his readers is that of petition. From November 1816 to April 1817, Cobbett acted as a general in the war for parliamentary reform, using his *Two-Penny Trash* to issue weekly updates and directives to his citizen-readers about the roles they should play in the great struggle to establish annual elections for representatives to the House of Commons and secure the franchise for those members of the lower classes who paid direct taxes.[51] The discursive offensive mounted by Cobbett and his readers was large in scope – the 15 February 1817 issue of the *Two-Penny Trash* reports that "more than thirty thousand of us" unanimously agreed to and "not fewer than *five thousand people* actually *signed*" a petition for parliamentary reform at Portsdown on 10 February[52] – and it generated a correspondingly large number of counterattacks from the conservative press. Almost to a number, these counterattacks adopt Cobbett's format, impersonating his authorial persona and blending lengthy political articles with items of material and cultural interest to lower-class readers (recipes for soup, new lyrics for traditional ballads, price comparisons for bread).[53] Perhaps most closely paralleling Cobbett's form – and most strenuously working to demobilize his readers – was the *Anti-Cobbett: or, the Weekly Patriotic Register*, which ran in weekly numbers responding directly to Cobbett's latest offensives. Its initial number, which appeared on the very day that Cobbett claimed 5,000 signatures on his petition for parliamentary reform, warns Cobbett's readers that their general is merely a pretender to knowledge and is thus leading them astray. The *Anti-Cobbett* acknowledges that Cobbett "has talked very confidently, and very fluently about a number of words ... such as *Finance*, *System*, *Parliamentary Reform*, *Universal Suffrage*, and many others," but his talk, they argue, is devoid of meaning. Its editors pledge that, "by and by [we shall] convince you, that he really knows little or nothing."[54]

Even more sympathetic contemporaries of Cobbett were disinclined to see him as capable of leading a clear, consistent, principled offensive. William Hazlitt, for instance, praises Cobbett's "vast industry, vast information, and the utmost power of making what he says intelligible," but fears that Cobbett is doomed to play the perpetual antagonist, because his nature "only finds itself at ease in systematic opposition."[55] It is certainly the case that Cobbett articulated an astonishing array of political convictions during his 35-year public career, many of them absolutely contradictory. However, Cobbett's most intensive attempt to build a discursive community of "Journeymen and Labourers" occupied only four months (November 1816 to March 1817), and during this period Cobbett displayed such remarkable consistency that the *Anti-Cobbett*'s attempts to attack him as an incendiary purveyor of empty rhetoric proved ineffective. In the November 1816–March 1817 editions of the *Two-Penny Trash*, Cobbett recognized his readers' potential unfamiliarity with the abstractions of political discourse and took great pains to make these abstractions concrete, consistently using his weekly open letters to address new audiences and in each case illustrating how the terms of reform would affect "the particular scene before us."[56] Cobbett pushed his readers to translate their understanding into action, advocating public meetings and marches on London in addition to petition – and these calls to action incited the *Anti-Cobbett*'s most serious counteroffensive. In response to a *Two-Penny Trash* request that readers send their petitions to Parliament, the 15 March 1817 *Anti-Cobbett* adopts a divide-and-conquer strategy with these would-be petitioners:

> Pray let me ask you candidly and fairly, what necessity there can possibly be for them [the petitions]? You are taught to believe that the Prince Regent knows nothing about State affairs. A very reasonable notion, to be sure! But what do you know of them, and where do you get your knowledge? Now let us speak plainly. You get all your supposed knowledge from reading Cobbett: and so you are to tell the Prince Regent what is to be learnt out of Cobbett's Two-Penny Pamphlet. Would it not be a shorter way, think you, to send one of

Cobbett's Pamphlets to the Prince Regent or his Ministers, and let it speak for itself?[57]

As Michel Foucault points out, isolating the enemy is a key strategy in discursive warfare. Reducing the *"half a million of men"* who signed petitions for parliamentary reform to the person of a single author transforms a powerful grassroots political movement into an individual act easily rendered "subject to punishment."[58] In this battle, the *Anti-Cobbett* strategy would appear to have worked. Fearing arrest, Cobbett fled to America in March 1817, and the *Anti-Cobbett* declared victory, asserting that "this publication has certainly answered its end, in a very striking degree."[59]

But the *Anti-Cobbett* undercuts its victory with this self-congratulatory assertion. By acknowledging that its influence stems from circulation – the editors claim to have "opened the eyes of many thousands, in all parts of the kingdom" – the *Anti-Cobbett* locates itself in a classical field of discourse in which the periodical is no longer conceived as a commodity but as an *act*.[60] When periodical discourse is framed in these transactional terms, the idea of an originary author – the very idea the *Anti-Cobbett* invoked to countermand Cobbett's petitioning – becomes virtually meaningless. The author-function, as Foucault tells us, is intimately linked to conceiving of texts as commodities: only when "strict rules concerning author's rights, author–publisher relations, rights of reproduction, and related matters were enacted – at the end of the eighteenth and the beginning of the nineteenth century" did the idea of the author become a cultural necessity.[61] In their counterattack, then, the editors of the *Anti-Cobbett* defeat their own purpose by trying to have it both ways. They use the author-function to assign accountability to Cobbett, thereby making him singularly responsible and denying agency to his readers. But they simultaneously reject the author-function in their own text, thereby downplaying their own authorial role and making circulation and readerly discernment central to their text's efficacy.

The irony here is that circulation and readerly discernment are precisely the strategies Cobbett uses to diffuse his authority and continue the collective discursive struggle even from America. From the moment of his "conversion" in 1816, Cobbett subordinated authorial interests to the need for wide circulation of his writings, offering "any of [his] countrymen" the right to reprint and distribute his works.[62] And in the 26 March 1817 issue of the *Two-Penny Trash* – his last before he emigrated to America – Cobbett effaces his status as individual author almost completely by claiming indissoluble unity with his readers. Writing of his opposition, Cobbett asks his readers: "Do they imagine … that the people who read my Register, will not in this case, regard any attack upon me, as an attack upon themselves?" Is it possible, he continues, "that millions of men, all united in petitioning," will simply be silenced?[63] They will not, Cobbett insists, and in explaining why Cobbett not only intensifies his martial rhetoric by describing himself as a fallen "General" and his opposition as "the enemy in the field;"[64] he also redefines the classical republican ideal by insisting that his lower-class readers are citizens whose "attachment ... to the place of their birth" justifies their civic activity just as surely as an aristocrat's landed property justifies his.[65] When Cobbett thus locates citizenship in what Ian Dyck calls "a vertical configuration of countrymen – including landlord, farmer, labourer and village tradesman" who are linked not by "relationships with the means of production but [by] rural residence, a love of the land,"[66] he develops an image of republicanism that (Hazlitt notwithstanding) he maintains throughout his career. An 1831 *Political Register* article in which he plays on the fluidity of meaning between "country" and the emergent concept of "nation" makes this clear: "Why, the land is the *country*, is it not?" Cobbett writes. "It *is the people of the country* [who are vital to the civic good]; for though there are great numbers of manufacturers, what are they compared with the whole of those who own, who occupy, who till the land?"[67] But Cobbett recognizes that republican idealism also requires concrete skills, and to ensure that his countrymen would not be silenced, he produced his *Grammar of the English Language* in America the year after he emigrated, 1818. Aimed chiefly at the newly literate, Cobbett explains that this text – which Gilmartin aptly calls a "grammar of resistance" – will "qualify [his readers] to write correctly" and will thus arm them with the "weapons of the mind" called for in the ongoing fight against corruption.[68]

Jon Klancher argues that Cobbett's November 1816–March 1817 discursive battle ensured that "to middle-class writers and readers, William Cobbett became the very emblem of an English radical public."[69] But Cobbett consistently defies emblematic status.[70] In addition to blurring the lines between himself and his readers ("any attack upon me, [i]s an attack upon themselves") and empowering his readers to "*write on!*" in the fight against corruption,[71] Cobbett takes care to ensure that his program for discursive resistance will outlive him. His first step is to give the *Two-Penny Trash* a life of its own, personifying both the 1816–19 version – "Thou hast acted thy part in this grand drama. Ten thousand wagon-loads of the volumes that fill the libraries and booksellers' shops have never caused a thousandth part of the thinking, nor a millionth part of the stir, that thou hast caused" – and the revival in 1830: "TWO-PENNY TRASH is now again come to life."[72] By positioning the *Two-Penny Trash* as an agent in its own right, Cobbett establishes the periodical, rather than himself, as the central identifiable force in the ongoing discursive war against corruption. To use Foucault's terms, Cobbett makes "*Two-Penny Trash*," rather than "William Cobbett," the brand name for "a certain mode of being of discourse" – namely, the discourse of radical reform.[73] This explicit subordination of writer to text allowed Cobbett's son James to continue publishing the *Political Register* after Cobbett's death in 1835, secure in the "kn[owledge] that, determining to pursue the precise same course with my honoured father ... the support of his respected readers would be continued *to this work*."[74] The clearly demarcated tiers of authority here confirm the primacy of readers in the radical fight for reform: James Cobbett's identity is subordinate to that of the "work," which is in turn subordinate to the work's "respected readers." In this ongoing discursive battle for reform, readers remain paramount.

One might argue that this authorial self-effacement implicates Cobbett in the very commercial economy that, I am suggesting, he actively resists. Such self-effacement is central to the profile Mary Poovey establishes for the commercialized nineteenth-century author, for instance, according to which "the writer was constructed not as an individual, much less a 'genius,' but ... just one instance of labor, an interchangeable part."[75] But industrial commercialism is not the only realm in which interchangeability of individuals is crucial; armies also rely on the principle that any one soldier may be replaced by another without detriment to the cause. So when Cobbett downplays his singularity, I would argue that he does so to reinforce the martial rhetoric of the citizen-soldier that runs throughout his *Two-Penny Trash*. This rhetoric is crucial to his cause, because it allows Cobbett to create an alternative model of political identity for readers typically dismissed as irrational "deluded people."[76] By insisting on his readers' rationality (they have "a competent knowledge of public matters" and "understand well what they read") and on their deep organic attachment to their native soil,[77] Cobbett positions them as citizens fully capable of and justified in republican resistance. Transformed by knowledge and discursive ability, they are prepared for a republican citizenship that allows them, as Pocock puts it, to "join with others to form a political body whose soul [i]s collective intelligence."[78]

The dilemma that such a "political body" presents, of course, is this: to what extent can and does discursive political resistance translate into action and, perhaps, concrete change? I have been emphasizing the extent to which Cobbett's *Two-Penny Trash* was seen – both by himself and by such opponents as the editors of the *Anti-Cobbett* – as an active force in the battle for reform. Certainly I am not alone in seeing the early nineteenth-century periodical as a socially constitutive kind of speech act. Paul Thomas Murphy, for example, argues that early nineteenth-century working-class periodicals were instrumental in establishing "a working-class canon of 'great' literature,"[79] while Mark Parker sees literary magazines in the period, because of their efforts to define and create "taste," as "entangled in the struggle for gentility that is characteristic of the middle class."[80] But the speech acts in which these periodicals engage remain *within* the discursive sphere; canons and taste are registers of social circumstances, to be sure, but they are still chiefly *discursive*, even literary, categories. Even Jon Klancher, who ascribes a broader range of social effects to early nineteenth-century periodical discourse, translates social reality into semiotic terms to describe the periodical's social influence. For example, while he identifies class struggle as a key issue in early nineteenth-century periodical discourse, he suggests that this struggle is epitomized less by concrete events such as Peterloo than by *representations* of those events: central to his analysis are the ways in which periodical discourse "interpret[ed], constitut[ed], and struggl[ed] over signs."[81] But Cobbett, as Gilmartin has convincingly shown, consistently uses periodical discourse to point beyond signs to the world of *things*: loads of wheat, taxes, livestock, and paper money all have a place in his *Two-Penny Trash* calls for reform, because these things illustrate that "reform" is not a discursive abstraction, but a concrete, situationally-specific material necessity. The *Two-Penny Trash*'s insistent emphasis on what Gilmartin calls "the material dimensions of cultural processes" reinforces for readers the practical ameliorative aims of their discursive struggle,[82] and thus offers both these readers and ourselves a way to see their discursive battles as tangible analogues to republican battles of old: as struggles conducted by citizens fighting for the future of their nation.

There is also clear anecdotal evidence to suggest that the *Two-Penny Trash* had remarkable material effects. Numerous working-class autobiographies, for instance, document Cobbett's influence. One radical weaver, looking back on the November 1816–March 1817 discursive struggle, wrote in his autobiography that:

> at this time the writings of William Cobbett suddenly became of great authority … they were read on nearly every cottage hearth in the manufacturing districts … riots soon became scarce … The Labourers … soon became deliberate and systematic in their proceedings.[83]

But beyond such anecdotal accounts, Cobbett's reformulation of the discourse of sympathy provides additional compelling reason to see the *Two-Penny Trash* as a text that forged a more-than-virtual community. Often criticized for positioning himself as a community of one in his prose, Cobbett's so-called "egotism" is still, as Hazlitt explains, curiously without vanity: "He [Cobbett] does not talk of himself for lack of something to write about," Hazlitt notes, "but because some circumstance that has happened to him is the best possible illustration of the subject … [he] places us in the same situation with himself, and makes us see all that he does."[84] In other words, Cobbett talks about himself to establish an identity, a community, even an interchangeability, between writer and reader. Cobbett thus creates a community – what Friedrich Kittler calls a "discourse network" – in which sympathy is neither consistently produced by nor consistently directed toward any particular individual, but rather circulates among a host of possible objects: journeymen and laborers, to be sure, but also any person or group whom those journeymen and laborers might identify as worthy of sympathy. By refusing to reduce the possibilities for sympathy to a particular individual, Cobbett implicitly embraces Kittler's claim that "the manifest secret of a discourse network that places ultimate value in the individual is never to inscribe the individual."[85] In this community, any individual member could (and did) cross the boundary between reader and writer; many of Cobbett's readers produced petitions, letters, and radical journalism of their own, and Cobbett routinely reserved space in his *Political Register* for "whatever may be sent to me in the way of answer [to my writings], … thus securing to truth the fairest possible chance of success."[86] Through his writings, then, Cobbett transformed readers into writers who with their discursive work "modif[ied]," as Pocock puts it, "the things that could be said and done" in print.[87] Because these reader-writers shifted the ground of what counted as political discourse in early nineteenth-century England, they surely emerge as more than an imagined community, and through them Cobbett and his *Two-Penny Trash* surely did much to alter both lower-class political identity and periodical discourse in early nineteenth-century England.

NOTES

1. Margaret Beetham, "Open and Closed: The Periodical as a Publishing Genre," *Victorian Periodicals Review* 22 (1989), 96–100. Mark Parker also has a helpful discussion of the concept in *Literary Magazines and British Romanticism* (Cambridge: Cambridge University Press, 2000), 15.
2. Quoted in Scott Bennett, "The Editorial Character and Readership of *The Penny Magazine*: An Analysis," *Victorian Periodicals Review* 17 (1984), 128.
3. Sonia Hofkosh, "Commodities Among Themselves: Reading/Desire in Early Women's Magazines," *Essays and Studies* 51 (1998), 88.
4. William Cobbett, *Cobbett's Two-Penny Trash; or, Politics for the Poor* (Wm. Cobbett, Johnson's Court, Fleet-street, 1831), I:1. Cobbett refers to his periodical as a "book" here because, as he explains, "The twelve Numbers [of the *Two-Penny Trash*] will make a volume of 288 pages, costing *two shillings and six-pence*, and another *six-pence, for binding*, makes a *neat little book* of it, to be kept and read, I hope, for a century to come" (I:7). That Cobbett imagines the periodical not just as ephemeral but as a text with lasting value is a fact worthy of study in its own right, because such a self-conception pushes him even further from those who see periodicals as the quintessential to-the-moment genre.
5. William Hazlitt, "On Reading Old Books" [1821], in *Selected Writings of William Hazlitt*, ed. Duncan Wu (London: Pickering & Chatto, 1998), VIII:206. Cobbett's 1816 "conversion" and his subsequent price reduction for the *Register* combined to generate a huge increase in the number of his lower-class readers. Richard Altick notes that "within a few months the circulation of the twopenny *Register* leaped to forty or fifty thousand, thus completely eclipsing every other journal of the day." See Altick, *The English Common Reader: A Social History of the Mass Reading Public, 1800–1900* (Chicago, IL: University of Chicago Press,

1957), 325. But Cobbett did not write exclusively for a working-class audience. Leonora Nattrass notes that his beginnings as a "mainstream, respectable journalist" meant that he had "gained a solid readership for his *Weekly Political Register*" long before 1816 and, she argues, this readership did not disappear when he added these new lower-class readers. See Nattrass, *William Cobbett: The Politics of Style* (Cambridge: Cambridge University Press, 1995), 3, 109.

6. Cobbett, *Cobbett's Two-Penny Trash*, I:3.
7. *Political Register* (2 Nov. 1816), 434 and *passim*.
8. Kevin Gilmartin, *Print Politics: The Press and Radical Opposition in Early Nineteenth-Century England* (Cambridge: Cambridge University Press, 1997), 190.
9. Nattrass, *William Cobbett*, 21, 23.
10. Jane Tompkins, "The Reader in History," in *Reader-Response Criticism: From Formalism to Post-Structuralism*, ed. Jane P. Tompkins (Baltimore, MD: Johns Hopkins University Press, 1980), 204.
11. Several recent works on Romantic-era periodicals identify the supervisory and stratifying functions as central to the genre. See Marilyn Butler, "Culture's Medium: The Role of the Review," in *The Cambridge Companion to Romanticism*, ed. Stuart Curran (Cambridge: Cambridge University Press, 1993), 120–47, *passim*; Jon Klancher, *The Making of English Reading Audiences, 1790–1832* (Madison, WI: University of Wisconsin Press, 1987), 15–17; Parker, *Literary Magazines*, 17–20.
12. Cobbett explains his pricing plan – publishing the *Political Register* in "open sheets" that "require no stamp, and may be circulated and sold without any" for "about *two-pence halfpenny* for each of them." *Political Register* (26 Oct. 1816), 410. I will be referring to the post-1816 *Political Register* as the *Two-Penny Trash* throughout the text of my essay, since Cobbett himself argues for the power of that name when he resurrects the format in 1831. (See Cobbett, *Cobbett's Two-Penny Trash*, I:5–7.) However, when Cobbett collected the 1816–19 issues of his *Two-Penny Trash*, he bound them as *Weekly Political Register*; therefore, in my citations I will refer to the texts as *Political Register*.
13. Indeed, Hazlitt comments on Cobbett's hostility toward classical texts in his 1817 volume *The Round Table*, noting that "a celebrated political writer of the present day … is a great enemy to classical education." Hazlitt, *The Round Table: A Collection of Essays on Literature, Men, and Manners* (London: George Bell and Sons, 1881), 7.
14. Butler, "Culture's Medium," 127.
15. William Hazlitt, "The Periodical Press," *Edinburgh Review* 38 (May 1823), 359.
16. J.G.A. Pocock, *Virtue, Commerce, and History: Essays on Political Thought and History, Chiefly in the Eighteenth Century* (Cambridge: Cambridge University Press, 1985), 48.
17. Ibid., 50.
18. Nancy Armstrong, *Desire and Domestic Fiction: A Political History of the Novel* (New York: Oxford University Press, 1987), 201.
19. Catherine Gallagher, *Nobody's Story: The Vanishing Acts of Women Writers in the Marketplace, 1670–1820* (Berkeley, CA: University of California Press, 1994), 194.
20. Deidre Shauna Lynch, *The Economy of Character: Novels, Market Culture, and the Business of Inner Meaning* (Chicago, IL: University of Chicago Press, 1998), 133.
21. Pocock, *Virtue, Commerce, and History*, 49.
22. Gary Kelly, "Romantic Fiction," in *The Cambridge Companion to British Romanticism*, ed. Stuart Curran (Cambridge: Cambridge University Press, 1993), 197.
23. That this was a controversial idea in the period is clear from Francis Jeffrey's *Edinburgh Review* piece on Robert Southey's "Thalaba," in which Jeffrey attacks Southey and the Lake Poets for their focus on lower-class subjects. The problem with using rustic language for poetry, Jeffrey asserts, is that "the different classes of society have each of them a distinct character, as well as a separate idiom; and the names of the various passions to which they are subject respectively, have a signification that varies essentially, according to the conditions of the persons to whom they are applied. The love, or grief, or indignation of an enlightened and refined character, is not only expressed in a different language, but is in itself a different emotion from the love, or grief, or anger, of a clown, a tradesman, or a market-wench." *Edinburgh Review* 1 (Oct. 1802), 156. Novels that assume commonality of feeling

across social registers obviously pose a significant challenge to a position like the one Jeffrey articulates here.

24. Barbara Benedict, *Framing Feeling: Sentiment and Style in English Prose Fiction, 1745–1800* (New York: AMS Press, 1994), 9.

25. William Wordsworth, Preface to *Lyrical Ballads,* in *The Oxford Authors: William Wordsworth,* ed. Stephen Gill (Oxford: Oxford University Press, 1984), 599. All future references to Wordsworth texts will be taken from *The Oxford Authors* edition.

26. *Political Register* (2 Nov. 1816), 461.

27. Wordsworth, Preface to *Lyrical Ballads,* 614.

28. Ibid., 595.

29. Ibid., 602.

30. Wordsworth develops these ideas in his 1815 *Essay, Supplementary to the Preface,* in which he makes a distinction between the contemporary reading "PUBLIC," among whom a poet has "the task of creating the taste by which he is to be enjoyed," and the "PEOPLE" – an imagined future audience no longer in need of tutelage, and instead capable of "extend[ing] the domain of sensibility for the delight, the honour, and the benefit of human nature" (657–8, 662).

31. *Political Register* (4 Feb. 1809), 187.

32. Ibid., 191.

33. *Two-Penny Trash* (Nov. 1831), 97.

34. Cobbett begins positioning the working classes as objects of sympathy from the opening salvo in his journalism for the lower classes, the 1816 "Letter to the Journeymen and Labourers," in which he tells them that "all these [advantages of British society] spring from *labour.* Without the Journeymen and the labourer none of them could exist." See *Political Register* (2 Nov. 1816), 433. Lynne Lemrow's thoroughgoing grammatical and rhetorical analysis of Cobbett's journalism for the lower classes indicates that anaphora is one of Cobbett's "most common schemes" to emphasize key points for lower-class readers. See Lemrow, "William Cobbett's Journalism for the Lower Orders," *Victorian Periodicals Review* 15 (Spring 1982), 15. Nattrass also discusses Cobbett's rhetorical strategies for lower-class readers; see Nattrass, *William Cobbett,* Ch.4.

35. *Political Register* (28 March 1817), 9.

36. *Political Register* (4 April 1818), *passim.*

37. *Two-Penny Trash* (1 July 1831), *passim.*

38. *Two-Penny Trash* (1 Nov. 1831), *passim.*

39. Nattrass, *William Cobbett,* 30.

40. Jürgen Habermas, *The Structural Transformation of the Public Sphere,* trans. T. Burger and F. Lawrence (Cambridge, MA: MIT Press, 1989), 52.

41. *Political Register* (2 Nov. 1816), 457.

42. Harry C. Boyte remarks on this danger in the Habermasian public sphere. "When common action is separated from public debate," Boyte argues, "the processes through which citizens learn crucial dimensions of public life are lost because reflective reason is separated from experience of the consequences of action." See Boyte, "The Pragmatic Ends of Popular Politics," in *Habermas and the Public Sphere,* ed. Craig Calhoun (Cambridge, MA: MIT Press, 1992), 345.

43. Habermas, *Structural Transformation,* 52.

44. *Political Register* (19 Sept. 1816), 1087.

45. Pocock, *Virtue, Commerce, and History,* 42.

46. *Political Register* (20 May 1809), 774.

47. Paolo Freire, *The Politics of Education: Culture, Power, and Liberation* (South Hadley, MA: Bergin and Garvey Publishers, 1985), 100.

48. William Cobbett, *Cobbett's English Grammar* (London: Henry Frowde, 1906), 11. While the work takes the form of letters to Cobbett's son, the subtitle indicates that it is intended "for the use of schools and young persons in general, but more especially for the use of soldiers, sailors, apprentices, and plough-boys."

49. Gilmartin points out Cobbett's obsession with the notion of a system of "CORRUPTION," arguing that "the *Political Register* was unapologetically didactic, a relentless and sometimes

violent initiation into the arcane causal mysteries of the system," and identifying the lessons Cobbett offers to his readers in the *Political Register* and elsewhere as a "countersystem" (*Print Politics*, 169).

50. *Political Register* (29 Nov. 1817), 1108.
51. Cobbett outlines this agenda in his very first conversion letter. See *Political Register* (2 Nov. 1816), 356.
52. *Political Register* (15 Feb. 1817), 193, 194.
53. Numerous anti-Cobbett pamphlets, papers, and tracts were published during this late-1816 to early-1817 period. Nearly all are anonymous, though many appear under such Cobbett-inspired pseudonyms as "A True Friend of the People," and still others are written by people who actually claim to *be* Cobbett. Cobbett warns his readers of these forgeries in the 20 March 1817 *Political Register*, noting that his impending American exile virtually ensures that "they will now play off this trick more than ever. But, the *matter* of their publications will soon undeceive you" (29). Two of the most interesting pamphlets, in addition to the *Anti-Cobbett*, are "An Address to the Men of Hampshire, intended as a Postscript to Cobbett's *Weekly Political Register* of the 15th of March," dated 26 March 1817, printed and sold by W. Jacob, Winchester, and *The Poor Man's Friend, or Companion for the Working Classes; Giving them Useful Information and Advice: Being the System of Moral and Political Philosophy Laid Down and Exemplified by William Cobbett* (London: H. Stemman, 1816).
54. *Anti-Cobbett: or, the Weekly Patriotic Register* (15 Feb. 1817), 4.
55. William Hazlitt, "Mr Cobbett," in *The Spirit of the Age* (London: J.M. Dent & Sons, 1910), 320.
56. *Political Register* (11 Jan. 1817), 44. Numerous Cobbett critics have commented on his skill in concretizing abstract ideas. Kevin Gilmartin writes eloquently of Cobbett's "fascination with the immediate and the material" (*Print Politics*, 177), Lynne Lemrow discusses these strategies throughout her article ("William Cobbett's Journalism"), and Ian Dyck argues that the *Political Register*'s "politicizing potential lay in its ability to rally traditional symbols and canons [of oral and rural life] on behalf of experienced injustice." See Dyck, *William Cobbett and Rural Popular Culture* (Cambridge: Cambridge University Press, 1992), 85.
57. *Anti-Cobbett* (15 March 1817), 136.
58. Cobbett gives the "half a million" statistic in *Political Register* (11 Jan. 1817), 39. Foucault discusses the accountability inherent in the author-function in "What is an Author?" See *The Foucault Reader*, ed. Paul Rabinow (New York: Pantheon Books, 1984), 101–20.
59. *Anti-Cobbett* (5 April 1817), 225.
60. Ibid., 225.
61. Foucault, "What is an Author?," 108.
62. *Political Register* (26 Oct. 1816), 408. Cobbett does ask that anyone who reprints his writings "publish, at one and the same time, the *whole* of any article, or letter" and "that they retain both the *date and the name*." While this second caveat may seem to indicate authorial vanity or proprietariness, Cobbett explains that he is chiefly concerned about "the *garbling* of what I write" – a particularly legitimate concern given the number of Cobbett forgeries that emerged in response to Cobbett's 1816–17 campaign.
63. *Political Register* (26 March 1817), 9.
64. Ibid., 9, 10.
65. Ibid., 16. Cobbett's insistence on his readers' necessary and organic connection to the land seems to me more than accidental; as Pocock points out, classical republican political formations held that "the individual whose sword was rooted in property was free from fortune to … join with others to form a political body whose soul was collective intelligence" (*Virtue, Commerce, and History*, 56).
66. Dyck, *William Cobbett and Rural Popular Culture*, 47.
67. *Political Register* (21 May 1831), 439.
68. Gilmartin, *Print Politics*, 172; *Political Register* (29 Nov. 1817), 1065–6.
69. Klancher, *The Making of English Reading Audiences*, 122.
70. Gilmartin comments on the difficulties Cobbett would have faced in seeing himself as an "emblem," noting that "the central standard-bearer of reform was himself radically decentered and displaced, an itinerant sign of the system's ravaging effects on its victims" (*Print Politics*, 167).

71. *Political Register* (26 March 1817), 23.

72. *Two-Penny Trash*, I:7.

73. Foucault, "What is an Author?," 107.

74. James Cobbett, *Renewal of Cobbett's Register: Address to the Readers of the Register, on the Reasons for Temporarily Discontinuing, and on the Plan to be Adopted on Renewing This Work* (1 Jan. 1836), 4 (emphasis added).

75. Mary Poovey, *Uneven Developments: The Ideological Work of Gender in Mid-Victorian England* (Chicago, IL: University of Chicago Press, 1988), 104.

76. *Political Register* (20 March 1817), 354.

77. *Political Register* (2 Nov. 1816), 457; *Political Register* (28 March 1817), 8.

78. Pocock, *Virtue, Commerce, and History*, 56.

79. Paul Thomas Murphy, *Toward a Working-Class Canon: Literary Criticism in British Working-Class Periodicals, 1816–1858* (Columbus, OH: Ohio State University Press, 1994), 3.

80. Parker, *Literary Magazines*, 20.

81. Klancher, *The Making of English Reading Audiences*, 7. Parker offers a trenchant appreciation and critique of Klancher's work; see especially *Literary Magazines*, 10.

82. Gilmartin, *Print Politics*, 172.

83. Quoted in Klancher, *The Making of English Reading Audiences*, 122. For more information about working-class autobiographies, and the influence ascribed to Cobbett in them, see also Jonathan Rose, *The Intellectual Life of the British Working Classes* (New Haven, CT: Yale University Press, 2001), 64.

84. Hazlitt, "Mr Cobbett," 318.

85. Friedrich Kittler, *Discourse Networks, 1800/1900*, trans. Michael Metteer (Stanford, CA: Stanford University Press, 1990), 119.

86. *Political Register* (8 April 1809), 773.

87. Pocock, *Virtue, Commerce, and History*, 18.

"May the married be single, and the single happy:" Blackwood's, *the* Maga *for the Single Man*

LISA NILES

"Then sent he for one cunning in sharp instruments and edged tools, even in razors; but he had taken unto himself a wife, and could not come."[1] These lines from "The Chaldee Manuscript," which appeared in the October 1817 issue of the refashioned *Blackwood's Edinburgh Magazine*, induct readers into the ways women are filtered through the lens of the masculinized, bachelor space of *Maga*, as it was affectionately known.[2] As the satirical narrative of the formation of the magazine, "The Chaldee Manuscript" brought condemnation, libel suits, and public outcry, and was quickly pulled from the issue.[3] Although the piece was objectionable because of its parodic biblical structure and its scurrilous attacks on *men* – rivals such as Francis Jeffrey of the *Edinburgh Review* and the now-despised former editors of *Blackwood's*, Thomas Pringle and James Cleghorn – the comic reference to wives as a barrier to participation in the periodical appears to have passed without notice. Yet this comic reference deserves notice as it puts a woman in the *middle* of men – in between a writer and his writing "instruments" – inviting a theoretical framework by which to read *Blackwood's* as a space of male homosociality.[4]

In *Literary Magazines and British Romanticism*, Mark Parker notes that *Blackwood's*, in particular among its competitors, traded in personalities while working under the veil of anonymity.[5] Not only did *Blackwood's* trade in personalities in terms of scurrilous personal attacks, it traded in personalities as easily identifiable types: types that embody a particular attitude; essays that foreground readers' expectancy when that type is invoked. Parker writes: "As one reads more numbers of a magazine, even in snatches, a set of expectations might take shape to give more determinate shape to response" (15). Playing on the stock familiarity of the bachelor writer, *Blackwood's* draws on its readers' expectations to give a new shape to this well-known type: one that by 1817 had become a trope for periodical culture itself.

In the first issue of the *Spectator* in 1711, Joseph Addison introduces Mr Spectator, a confirmed bachelor, who observes: "A Reader seldom peruses a Book with Pleasure 'till he knows whether the Writer of it be ... Married or a Batchelor."[6] Creating a community of bachelors through its club, the *Spectator* cemented an association of the periodical contributor with the bachelor, and a century later that association had gained a particular stature through continued emergence in places like Samuel Johnson's *Rambler* (1750–52) and James Hogg's *Spy* (1810–11).

Gestating in "The Chaldee Manuscript," the *Blackwood's* bachelor emerges fully-formed in the next issue with "Letters of an Old Bachelor" and flourishes in other early essays, including "Hint to the Ladies," "A Letter from a Young Fellow," and "Letters of Advice from a Lady of Distinction."[7] Framed within the larger events of 1817's "Chaldee" and 1822's inauguration of the *Noctes Ambrosianae* series, these four essays need not be viewed as discrete articles; rather, considering them in sequence allows for an interrogation into the broader schema of the representation and placement of women in *Blackwood's* during its early years. The compositions from the pens of "single" men – edifying letters-to-the-ladies and a review of a manual directed at a matrimonially-inclined female audience – draw upon a well-established tradition in eighteenth-century periodical culture. The male persona's didactic address to a female audience on everything from fashion to etiquette to education was a familiar forum; periodicals like the *Spectator* and the *Tatler* often weighed in on women's issues, attempting to shape gender-specific behavior through molding public opinion. For *Blackwood's*, the male periodical contributor's relationship to women is exemplified through the seemingly antithetical posture of the bachelor. It is in this space of antithetical construction that a more complicated picture of women emerges. Not one type among many, but a governing trope of typology itself in *Blackwood's*, the bachelor voices *Blackwood's* complicated and contradictory configurations of and responses to women, both as signifiers in male-authored essays penned by self-avowed bachelors and as material bodies in those women writers who appear within *Maga*'s pages.[8]

In 1817, the future home of George Eliot's fictional debut displayed an anxiety about the proliferation of women writers; in turn, a surprisingly low number of female authors appear in *Maga* during its early years. From 1817 to 1825, fewer than five percent of *Blackwood's* contributors were women.[9] Yet the many reviews of women's works during this time period and the many essays that focus on women's issues from a male perspective reveal *Blackwood's*' practice of using these gendered "issues" as a segue into the amalgam of topics in *Maga*'s volumes. The essays I analyze do not merely name and contain the feminine sphere. Rather, they utilize "feminine" topics – fashion, beauty, the marriage market, women's writing – as tropes to mediate the larger, masculinized concerns of the periodical project: professions, political economy, international affairs, marriage as anathema.

This redeployment of gendered concerns through figurative language evokes Gayle Rubin's thesis of women as a site of exchange in male bonding.[10] Drawing on Rubin's formulation of the interconnectedness between sex, gender, and social relations in "The Traffic in Women," I offer a slightly different term from her "traffic." In *Blackwood's*, women are figured into the relational dynamic of male bonding as a *displacement* – a site of comic relief, a site of disempowerment, a site of problematic nearness and distance. As textual presences in the pages of the periodical, women figure not as a medium of exchange, but as a locus of reflectivity (and ultimately reflexivity) for the male bachelor personas. These bachelors create and reinforce this displacement to explore concerns that resonate both inside and outside of the gendered framework of the essays' surface texts.[11]

While Rubin's argument is central to my understanding of women in patriarchy, her cultural and economic parameters limit the applicability of her thesis to early nineteenth-century periodical culture. To bring Rubin's argument under the rubric of the commodity pressures of the periodical as those pressures relate to women, Karl Polanyi's "ideological transformation," his "commodity fiction" wherein land, labor, and money become "commodities," can be extrapolated to *Blackwood's* deployment of women.[12] Femininity becomes commodified through a referential move that cites women as a signifier of the economic topoi of other essays in *Blackwood's*. Thus, the bachelor essays illuminate a heteroglossic production of meaning as women are repeatedly, yet differently, inscribed within *Maga*'s masculine space, affirming that the structure of desire in *Blackwood's* is negotiated not only in terms of gender but also in terms of broader social constructs.[13] The bachelor type, in an ideological relationship to *Blackwood's*, serves the editorial goal of the periodical in disseminating particularized, yet competing, views on issues ranging from domestic politics to economics to foreign policy. One way the bachelor names these larger issues as being *for men only* is through the triangulated structure of male homosociality; that is, through a woman.

Signed "Un Vieux Celibataire," Thomas Hamilton's "Letters of an Old Bachelor" (2/8, 192–4) ushers in *Blackwood's*' didactic model of the bachelor's letter-to-the-ladies format.[14] The essay's title, however, alludes to *Maga* as a space for the single man. "Letters of an Old Bachelor," listed in the table of contents and at the top of the page, is contradicted by the title at the beginning of the piece, which reads "Letters to an Old Bachelor." The discrepancy, although probably accidental, is a significant slippage as it specifies the reader as male and places him in the role of both consumer and producer of the text.[15] The title directed "to an Old Bachelor" implies that the reader occupies the same social position as the author "of" the letters, affirming *Blackwood's* as a periodical for the bachelor, and places the women he addresses in the essay as a necessary component for the bonding between a male reader and author. The reader, then, *is* the Old Bachelor and is written into the text not only as reader-consumer, but as identifying with the author-producer.

This reader is then drawn into a nostalgic rumination on England's former glory as the nation known for sending the wealthy, but insufferably provincial, traveler to the Continent. The "'Milord Anglais' of the old breed," the Englishman who "goes abroad with the determination of finding nothing to his taste," is "an animal now more rarely to be met with" (2/8, 192). Noting the disheartening reversal of the English traveler's financial superiority abroad, the Old Bachelor laments that foreigners are "now beginning to pay us off in our own coin" and "few of the French travellers who have lately visited our Isle appear to have been much gratified with their trip" (2/8, 192). Contemptuous of the "national partiality for roast beef and potatoes," disapproving the "fashion of wearing small hats," and complaining bitterly of "weak tea" and "exhorbitant charges" in English hotels, the French traveler becomes both consumer and critic of English culture (2/8, 192–3). On the pretext of defending his nation's honor, the Old Bachelor prepares a counteroffensive not against the criticisms leveled at high prices or port wine or weak tea, but against the criticisms directed at "English ladies" (2/8, 193).

Trusting that his "fair countrywomen" will "not suspect [him] of participating in the sentiments therein expressed," the Old Bachelor blurs the line he has drawn between himself and the French authors he wishes to refute not only by participating in but by reinforcing the disagreeable sentiments expressed through the "deliberate opinions" of the French travelers (2/8, 193). Citing "'Six Mois à Londres,' a work, [he] regret[s] to say, read with great avidity in Paris,"[16] Hamilton declares it "vile slander" that a Frenchman would criticize English women for wearing too many flowers or too many feathers. And yet, "candor obliges [him] to confess, that [he has] occasionally seen heads *covered* with flowers, and ladies wearing *quite as* many feathers as were becoming" (2/8, 193). Drawing attention to a "charge of *gluttony*" brought by the same author in "Quinze Jours à Londres," the Old Bachelor regrets that he is "incapable at the present moment of refuting this disagreeable charge" (2/8, 193). In fact, he is not incapable, but unwilling. So, when Hamilton signs his essay "Un Vieux Celibataire," identifying himself as "An Old Bachelor" in French, he offers a playful nod toward his identification with the opinions of these "foreigners." The French texts, which the Old Bachelor puts forth as needing refutation, become the sites through which he constructs a disparaging valuation of British women, and the distinction between two theoretically opposed views – French and English – collapses.

Drawing on other *Blackwood's* essays' economic motifs (an article on "New Gold Coinage" appears in the same issue),[17] the Old Bachelor mediates the critique against British women through the motif of international commodity exchange. Through tropes of circulation and valuation, he renders women's accomplishments a devalued commodity, one that only has value within the closed system of the private sphere. Economically infused terms – coin, credit, charge – provide the basis for reading women's beauty as an exportable commodity:

> Strange as it may seem, they all unite in allowing the British ladies but little credit, either in elegance or beauty. This appears to us poor natives the more surprising, as we have hitherto actually considered them (as I am sure they consider themselves) the very pink of elegance and refinement, and believed, most firmly, that their charms required only to be seen to be universally admired [2/8, 193].

The obvious economic pun – "allowing the British ladies but little credit" – needs to be read in light of the basis for extending that credit. "Elegance," "beauty," "refinement," and "charms" are intangibles – of little use-value – and are rendered valuable only through tacit agreement. These qualities, then, become akin to precious commodities having economic agency only insofar as consumers have a collective faith in their value. British women's "charms," thought to have potential on the international marketplace, are devalued through the French criticism. The Old Bachelor, having conditionally located his opinion in a time before British women had been assigned a value in this marketplace, raises the possibility through his word choice that he is now convinced of this negative assessment, thus situating the women he addresses not only in a male–male relational dynamic between himself and his readers, but in a relational dynamic with the French and English views that he alleges to be oppositional.

These surprising "sentiments of foreigners" on the subject of English ladies come not from Frenchmen who are "infamous and detestable," but from "much more sensible and trust-worthy authors, who in other respects have really formed a tolerably fair estimate of our character and habits" (2/8, 193). As the authors the Old Bachelor presents are "sensible" and "trust-worthy," the "fair" estimate they have made shows a freedom from bias – fairness expressed as a quality of masculine judgment. In the next sentence, he declares: "In order to show, therefore, the utter depravity of these gentlemen's taste, I have ventured to collect a few of the most objectionable passages from their works, which I now submit to the indignation of my fair countrywomen" (2/8, 193). Considering their sensible trustworthiness in assessing other aspects of British life, these French critics hardly appear disposed to "utter depravity" in their taste regarding women. The censorious tone regarding the "objectionable passages" rings hollow as a means to rouse British women to indignant fury. Further undercutting the possibility for indignation is the fact that the Old Bachelor's countrywomen are described in terms analogous to these very "foreigners." Also describing his countrywomen as "fair," the Old Bachelor charges the word "fair" itself with conflicting meanings that run along gendered lines. The adjective now becomes an assessment value in terms of beauty. As beauty has been commodified when applied to these countrywomen, this usage of "fair" draws the connection between beauty and its circulation in the essay as the only means of having (or not having) agency and power. Rather than an indicator of impartiality, the fairness of these countrywomen denies them full claim to the offer of rendering a judgment against their accusers.

Further displacing women from participation in the public sphere – which would represent an alternative mode of garnering economic agency – Hamilton prints what he considers the most objectionable passage in French:

> The next passage, I confess, I dare not translate, lest some female Lord Advocate should think proper to indict me for the propagation of a libel; and I fear, if tried by a jury of Belles, I should stand a poor chance of being acquitted [2/8, 193].[18]

Denying this fictive "jury of Belles" the opportunity to find him culpable through legal means, he instead displaces the responsibility for these sentiments onto the French critic, by giving up "my author," Abbé Vauxcelles (2/8, 193). By citing the passage in French and naming its author, the Old Bachelor simultaneously distances himself from and draws closer to the content of the passage. Refusing to translate this French text into English as he has done for other works, the Old Bachelor obscures his implicit agreement with what is apparently the most objectionable paragraph of all under the pretense of plausible deniability. It is not in his native language, nor in his own words; yet the Old Bachelor's assessments cannot seem to avoid humorously concurring with what he calls this "false and atrocious" calumny (2/8, 193).

In refuting Abbé Vauxcelles' untranslated text, the Old Bachelor renders beauty not as a commodity with intrinsic value, but as an attainment through simple economic exchange. Arguing against the charge of English women's "bad teeth," he describes with specificity how much a woman can pay – two guineas for a single tooth or a "trifling consideration" for a complete set (2/8, 193) – in order to possess that which should be natural: her beauty. He further devalues and demystifies women's physical charms by suggesting that women can hold their own against a standard of judgment used for horses: "If we judged of a lady's age as we do of a horse's, they would all be found to have the *mark in their mouths* at fourscore" (2/8, 193). Not only insulting in its comparison of women to horses, the bachelor's statement aligns women's attempts to soften the effects of aging with the unnatural. The false teeth, the "mark in [women's] mouths" that the bachelor mockingly endorses, would, through its very artificiality, decry a woman's age regardless of her care to conceal it. A lady's care for her appearance through choosing to avail herself of improved aesthetic technology becomes a perversity. Denigrated for perversity and unnaturalness, those "dowagers" who opt for "a complete set of the *most beautiful* teeth, made from the tusks of the *hippopotamus* or *river horse*" (2/8, 193) are further chastised for fueling the economic demand for an apparently endless supply of low-cost beauty-enhancing dental devices. Beauty, then, has become a function of a market economy where any woman may have it at a cheap price.[19] The focus on English women's paying, with "money" – which, in Polanyi's terms, becomes a commodity itself – for an item of both aesthetic and functional value, situates beauty more firmly in economic terms, and this availability reduces what should be a precious commodity to that of the common and easily obtained. In so doing, the Old Bachelor strips away the "beauty" women possess in a move reminiscent of Swift's "A Beautiful Young Nymph Going to Bed."[20] *Any* woman may now only appear to be "natural" and that priceless naturalness may be had at a fixed price. The primary difference in ironic devaluation between these two "fair" subjects is that of Swift's localized morality versus Hamilton's (and, by extension, *Blackwood's*') broader economic motif. The devalued "beauty" in "Letters of an Old Bachelor" is couched in economic terms both to displace women's value to domestic tasks and to inaugurate a commodification of femininity itself.

The Old Bachelor's final defense of English women is not invoked through the intangibles of "elegance" or "beauty," but rests in the concrete realm of accomplishments:

> What ladies of any other nation possess the same knowledge of languages, and play so charmingly on the piano-forte? What ladies can paint tables and fire-screens with such taste and delicacy of execution? In short, until our continental belles can excel us in these qualifications, we shall still retain the unshaken conviction, that in this island are to be found the most charming and *accomplished* women in the world [2/8, 194].

The claim that no other nation's ladies "possess the same knowledge of languages" becomes tenuous when considering John Lee's review of "Madame de Staël on the Usefulness of Translation," which appears in the same issue.[21] Placed only pages away from the very type of woman the Old Bachelor will attempt to edge out of material participation in the periodical's pages, De Staël's textual presence both undercuts the claim he makes for English women's linguistic accomplishments and challenges the sincerity with which the magazine as a whole puts that claim forward. All that is left for these "charming" women to defend, then, are domestic tasks: music and painting. Centered on courtship rituals, these occupations have little or no value outside of the sphere within which they are deployed.

Shifting outward to his constructed female audience, the Old Bachelor sounds the call for "some *Blue Stocking* lady to come forward and give these foreign calumniators *a complete set down*. Let them either speak now, or for ever after hold their tongues" (2/8, 194).[22] The call to women writers, through the figure of a Blue Stocking lady, to speak "now" or remain silent (one presumes on this or any other topic) proscribes, through an echo of the marriage vow, the proper sphere for women's writing as domestic. The ironic admission that the Old Bachelor himself is incapable of mounting a complete defense, and must leave it to women to write their own, divides writing itself along gendered lines. Women's duty in writing is to focus on the domestic; men's duty is to bring this topic to women's attention in order to situate women authors outside of intellectual discourse.

The Old Bachelor assures the economic success of such a venture, tying domestic writing to a specific publishing format:

> I am certain that Mr Blackwood, or any other of our bickering booksellers, will be happy to treat with any lady for two quarto volumes on the subject. There can be no doubt of such a work having *a great run*, particularly should some amateur adorn it with his etchings [2/8, 194].

The "great run" will occur not within the periodical's pages, but safely outside.[23] The Blue Stocking lady is directed to write her defense *not* as a letter to the magazine, but rather to seek her publishing venue outside the periodical, thus retaining *Blackwood's* as the space for the single man. The "Letters of an Old Bachelor" essay deploys domesticity through an economic value motif as it directs women writers to domestic topics – shifting even Blue Stocking ladies into the intellectually unsatisfactory realm of painted fire-screens and piano-fortes.

Yet the essay, with its invocation to Blue Stocking ladies to go and write elsewhere – thus maintaining *Blackwood's* as a space free from intellectually-minded women – is undercut by the presence of Blue Stocking writers in its pages, most notably Felicia Hemans. Her "On the Death of the Princess Charlotte" appears in the April 1818 issue, and Hemans was among *Blackwood's*' most favored women writers.[24] The Old Bachelor's attempt at derision fails. As he circulates the anachronistic and disparaging term Blue Stockings to move women writers outside *Maga*, he actually invokes those women writers who are materially, not just figuratively, participating in *Blackwood's*, further complicating the role women play in structuring male homosocial desire in the periodical.

Hamilton's "Un Vieux Celibataire," *Maga's* inaugural letter-writing bachelor, was quickly followed in January 1818 with a "Hint to the Ladies," signed by "An Old Fellow" (2/10, 377–8). This "Hint" elicits a rejoinder, with "A Young Fellow" penning an indignant response to the letter he observed "in [the] Magazine for last month" (2/11, 513). As both articles are unascribed and stylistically similar, raising the possibility of a single author, these heteroglossic companion pieces form a double-voiced rhetorical structure to critique women's fashion.

In a gesture harking back to the *Tatler* and the *Spectator*, the Old Fellow issues a didactic diatribe on women's dress,[25] pleading for his "fair country women" to "add an inch to the length of [their] petticoat, or a straw breadth to the hem of [their] tucker" (2/10, 377, 378). Yet the language in which this Old Fellow couches his descriptions of women's clothing is particularized in its masculinity. He situates women's fashion and their opportunities for marriage as does the Old Bachelor in November 1817's issue – as commodities:

> I beg my fair countrywomen to reflect on the sensations with which they have contemplated, in the month of June, a ribbon or a cap, if these unfortunate articles, no matter how pretty, had satiated the gaze of the multitude, from a haberdasher's window or on a milliner's tête, during the fashionable months of winter and spring; as, most certainly, something of a similar feeling arises in the minds of the men, when *they* contemplate charms that have been fully displayed in one season, and are still destined to remain on show, for the poor chance of meeting admirers in the next [2/10, 377–8].

Shifting from the commodity of beauty – which tests the fickle nature of "admirers" when choosing products that display one's "charms" – the Old Fellow invokes martial imagery to describe the marriage market, entreating "those ladies, who are now entering on their winter campaign, to consider whether, in the warfare they are about to wage, it may not be more advantageous to make their attacks by detachment, rather than by deploying the whole brigade" (2/10, 378). As Eve Sedgwick points out, militarism is a site of male homosocial bonding and that, coupled with the Old Fellow's calm assurance of assuming "that all the men are in favour of the position with which I set out" (2/10, 377), places women's fashion as it plays a role in courtship at the center of a strategic martial engagement. Men must figure the display of women's bodies as that figuration shapes the discussion of women in terms relevant to male power structures; they must lead the charge.

It is the Young Fellow's letter, however, when read against the Old Fellow's, that shifts fashion from a trope that signifies women's actual, material bodies to a trope of periodical criticism itself. The Young Fellow writes:

> I am willing to give your correspondent full credit for the motives of his letter, but I cannot overlook its tendency to throw an unnecessary reflexion on my fair country-women, and to cast a veil over the brightest ornaments of my native land [2/11, 513].

In this one line, "credit," "veil," and "ornaments" resonate with the traces of economic concerns, anonymous personalities, and the faint echo of Edmund Burke. Ostensibly about "fair country-women," the sentence envelops a concern about fashion criticism in the language of the periodical's more masculinized pursuits. The Young Fellow first notes that "at least since the time of the Guardian," periodical mandates on women's fashions have not achieved great success (2/11, 513). He then goes on to note that "prompted, no doubt, by some Old Fellow above stairs," ladies' dress is, indeed, becoming more modest (2/11, 513). The paradoxical question – is or is not periodical criticism effective in modifying people's behavior? – could be asked of a number of issues that figure in the pages of *Blackwood's*.

The Young Fellow's applause for the "persevering spirit" of those ladies who retain their "partiality ... to the short petticoats" begs the question as to whether it is "the gentlemen's business to object to that fashion" (2/11, 514). In bold language, he declares that were he "a despotic sovereign" or an "act of Parliament," he would "take 'a short way'" with those who would "presume to oppose the wishes of the more amiable half of our species, in a branch of legislation so peculiarly their own" (2/11, 514). This apparently liberal defense of women's peculiar "branch of legislation" simultaneously frees and binds women within the periodical's patriarchy. Under the guise of an indignant remonstrance, a brash youth takes on a wizened elder as he encourages marriage-minded maidens to entice altar-phobic bachelors by flaunting conventional modesty. Shorter hems are to be preferred over those where a lady's ankles "become enveloped in the cumbrous load of descending petticoats" (2/11, 513).

This clear division between the Young Fellow and the Old Fellow, between the reformer who fights against "antiquated notions" and the conservative who deplores the current state of "undress" in Edinburgh, begins to erode when reading the Old Fellow's signature (2/11, 514; 2/10, 377). He informs "the ladies, that [his advice] proceeds from one, who, though he admires the sex (whether clothed or not) with all his heart, is only AN OLD FELLOW" (2/10, 378). The Young Fellow's attempt to liberate women from a fashion despot such as this seems less crucial and more perfunctory upon this highly comic revelation. Both essays function merely to circumscribe women's concerns to that of fashion and to situate women as objects of an admiring male gaze. As women's behavior falls under the purview of discordant and competing, but always masculine, opinions, so do all topics in *Blackwood's*. The language of legal sanction, which permits the Young Fellow both to provide women freedom in their choice of "fashion" and delimit that freedom as being given only through a male hegemony, highlights the women's fashion under contention in these two essays as a substitute for *any* issue on which *Blackwood's* wishes to hold forth. These two "Fellows," both as competing and as co-extant voices, produce a heteroglossic meaning for "fashion" that goes beyond "fashion" to "fashioning" critical positions for the periodical. Professional women writers can appear in *Maga* while women can remain a non-threatening presence through the displacement of the "amiable half of [the] species" into comical figures concerned only with petticoats and tuckers.

These essays' exploration of "fashion" puts a term into play that ricochets with resonances far beyond regulating a woman's "ribbon" or "cap." Traversing and transgressing these essays are "Dampers," a term in the Old Fellow's "Hint to the Ladies" that is reprised to redirect the homosociality in *Blackwood's* toward ever-broader concerns. The Old Fellow describes Dampers initially in the framework of women policing other women; when putting down "superfluous pride or vanity," such "people may be distinguished by the appellation of *Dampers*" (2/10, 377). Yet these Dampers, gendered female in "Hint to the Ladies," are severed from their singular association in two later essays: "The Dampers" signed by an "Old Fellow" and "The Dampers" signed by "A Damper."[26] Dampers are now "compounded of male and female members" (2/11, 528). No longer confined to policing fashion and manners, the Dampers that comprise this fraternal order shower criticism over all the issues in *Blackwood's*. "A Damper" relates his pleasure at "damping" on various and sundry topics, including Scottish drama, the authenticity of Ossian's poems, the "surrender of Lord Cornwallis's army at York Town," the Peninsular War, and the "bullion business" (2/12, 628–30). He ends his reflections by offering his services to *Blackwood's* with a nationalistic fervor:

> I am very much at your devotion, Mr Editor, on terms consistent with the purity of patriotism, whenever you shall stand in need of the sly services of one who has so long discharged, and, I may say, fulfilled, all the duties of A DAMPER [2/12, 630].

Women are displaced as Dampers, moved out of the representational centrality of the earlier Old Fellow/Young Fellow debate. "A Damper" becomes the masculine signifier for the term, as it comes to represent not haughty women, but a *Blackwood's* periodical contributor, whose interests are any and all that fall within the reach of the periodical itself. Thus women, situated as the site of establishing a male homosocial bond through didactic formations of femininity, get materially written out of the triangulation and become simply signifiers of masculine space. Moved out of these later articles, women serve as an initial stimulation to, but only as signifiers for, the masculinized discourse.

This shift from a concern with women as material bodies to the erasure of materiality in favor of women as signifiers of masculinized discourse is reconfigured yet again through an unsigned review of a marriage advice manual written as a series of epistles, "Letters of Advice from a Lady of Distinction, To Her Friend The Duchess of ******," which appears in the July 1819 issue:

> We are not ourselves a married man, and are not without hopes of being permitted to remain a bachelor all the rest of our lives. A few months ago (we will not attempt to deny it) we had some thoughts of trying a wife, for we conjectured that we could support a small family in a flat, not uncomfortably, on the produce of our various periodical labours [5/28, 416].

Reading the opening lines as an eroticized triangle of desire, one notes the reviewer, referring to himself in the plural pronoun "we," immediately setting up the expectation that he, as "we," speaks for himself, other male personas in *Blackwood's*' pages, and, by extension, his male readership. This essay functions within the periodical in a larger sense through its self-reflexivity. Presenting himself as a writer who might consider marriage, this author figures not as a disinterested bachelor type, but as *the* bachelor type that upholds the magazine's construction of marriageable women as a threat. Having thoughts of "trying" a wife places the female figure not as priceless, but as a purchasable and refundable commodity. This bachelor's decision to "try" marriage is tied into his periodical contribution itself, both as "produce" and "labor." Drawing on these commodifications and the notion that, as a gentleman scholar, one must do one's research, the author sets about reviewing marriage manuals. These texts help him weigh the decision to share the produce of his labor with another: a woman whose labors are not productive, but reproductive. Upon reviewing these marriage advice manuals, he concurs that: "we would not be induced to marry, though offered twenty guineas per sheet" (5/28, 416).[27] The potentially procreative connection of masculine production to feminine reproduction is negated through a whimsical wordplay that puns on the "sheet" of periodical production as evocative of the "sheet" of reproduction: the marriage bed.

The essay, then, paradoxically appears to embrace a view of domesticity that delimits women's economic activity to reproduction, while denying the contribution of male economic productive labor necessary to support that domestic economy. Kurt Heinzelman notes that "The Cult of Domesticity" came into being after commodity production had been separated from the home as:

> a replacement for or sublimation of the family as a viable, self-sustaining economic entity; it thus depended upon a division of female and male labor in which commodity production came to be seen as the masculine activity while female economic activity was regarded as reproductive.[28]

This sexual division of labor, as envisioned by Malthus in his *Essay on the Principle of Population*, breeds conflict: "male and female labor are always at odds and will inevitably cancel each other out … For Malthus, the economy of the family household is directly opposed to the political economy of the state" (Heinzelman, "Cult," 58). The foolish economic optimism Malthus identifies in men – leading them to greater sexual reproduction which "will outpace production exponentially just as money outruns commodities" (Heinzelman, "Cult," 58–9) – is, in this author's case, stoutly denied. He will not become a Malthusian "economic man," but instead prefers to outpace reproduction through production. The possible "wife" in this productive–reproductive asymmetrical structure of desire, which is predicated on maintaining the author's bachelor connection to his readers, is displaced in favor of maintaining a male space of a different type of division of labor, one based on the intellectual specificity of competing voices within the magazine.[29]

This rejected "wife" emblematizes the materiality of the female body and its attendant anxieties for the male reviewer; yet this review is not wholly tied to a triangulated structure of desire based on competing ideas of productivity and labor but works to figure women on dual fronts: both as signifiers of the reproductive body and as signifiers of the suspect woman writer.[30] For there are two women in this essay: the potential "wife," eliminated out of economic and intellectual desire to maintain *Blackwood's* as a male space, and the "lady of distinction," about whose advice the reviewer declares "we have felt very uncomfortable during the last two hours in being obliged to think so much on so very painful a subject" (5/28, 420). In his review, he determines that the authoress of these letters is not "a lady of distinction," but "a gentleman of no distinction at all" (5/28, 416). Yet, "be the sex of this lady what it may" (5/28, 416), he reviews the work as that of a woman writer revealing women's inherent duplicity in courtship and marriage.[31] The necessary intervention of a woman to maintain the male–male bond is, in this article, reconfigured to a wholly fictive construction. The "lady" is no lady at all, but a "young gentleman sitting in cheap furnished lodgings, off the Strand somewhere" (5/28, 416). In an act of textual transvestism, the reviewer continues to refer to the author as "lady," "old dame," "dowager," "tough old dame," and "old lady" (5/28, 416–19): all denotations of "woman" rather than the "man" he proposes as this marital advice volume's originary author. Thus, the young lady who reads this manual and is instructed in "all the arts of hypocrisy, duplicity, cunning, and hocus-pocus" in order to "hum-bug her husband" (5/28, 416) has been instructed not by a lady, but by the signifier of "lady," a male author confirming misogynistic representations of women as scheming and false. As the writer of this essay is convinced to remain single based on one wo/man's view of women, only the signification of woman is necessary to maintain male homosociality. And the "Letters of Advice" under review, symbolic of women's participation in the book trade, is rendered problematically masculine. This "lady" is written out of material participation in the masculine realm of professionalized writing in a nimble move of resignification – one which maintains the "idea" of a woman to affirm the male space of this essay.[32]

Within three years of the essay on "Letters of Advice from a Lady of Distinction," which ends with the reviewer shuddering at the thought of *anyone* marrying at all – "so we conclude with a well known sentiment, 'may the married be single, and the single happy'" (5/28, 420) – *Blackwood's* would reveal the heights of its comic disdain for matrimony through the ultimate bachelor party, the *Noctes Ambrosianae*. The bachelor type, who first appeared in "The Chaldee Manuscript," with Blackwood, as "Ebony," being called upon to "gird up thy loins like a man, and call unto thee thy friends,"[33] flourishes in the *Noctes*, where those "friends" have blossomed into "personalities" – pseudonymic enforcers of a male homosocial space.[34] In the first *Noctes* installment, Odoherty has told the editorial persona Christopher North that he intends to be modest as to his "amours," to which North replies: "You had better not. The ladies won't buy if you do so."[35] In the May 1822 *Noctes* installment, Odoherty sings a witty epithalamion to Mr Tickler upon his marriage to Miss Amarantha Aloesbud: "Though, perhaps, now no more, shall our friend, as before, / Join his bachelor mates in their frolicsome knot."[36] Odoherty's mock modesty about affairs of the heart, North's witty quip, and the humorous refrain on marriage as an end to frolicsome fun define and contextualize women's space and purpose within *Blackwood's*. Women are actual consumers; they are comic signifiers. They are barriers to intellectual masculine pursuit; they are vital to that pursuit. Both Caroline Bowles Southey and Buller, a male persona in *Noctes*, invoke the same phrase in *Maga*'s pages.[37] I invoke it here as the phrase that seems to sum up *Blackwood's* attitude towards women: *Blackwood's* "hates you cordially:" oxymoronic, yet oddly sensical; desiring, yet resisting. *Blackwood's* invites women in, but carefully renders them *women* and constrains their participation – both figuratively and literally,[38] not only in terms of asymmetrically structuring male–male desire through heterosexual normativity, but also in terms of commodity. Women are both producers and consumers in periodical culture, and *Blackwood's* must embrace its dually gendered audience by invoking a multiplicity of femininities, while carefully maintaining the primacy of its masculinity. Thus women must be present to make *Blackwood's* the *Maga* for the single man.

NOTES

1. James Hogg *et al.*, "Translation From An Ancient Chaldee Manuscript," *Blackwood's Edinburgh Magazine* 2/7 (Oct. 1817), 89–97, rpt. in John Wilson *et al.*, *Noctes Ambrosianae*, ed. R. Shelton Mackenzie, Vol.1 (New York: Redfield, 1855), xxii. All works will be cited in the text after the initial reference. Regarding *Blackwood's*' essays, references are listed with the shortened title "*Blackwood's*," and authors' names are given when known. If essays are printed with a pseudonymous signature, that pseudonym is given as it appears in *Blackwood's* with the author's name in brackets immediately following, when known. If no pseudonymous signature or author is given, essay is cited by title. All authorial ascription information is from Alan Lang Strout, *A Bibliography of Articles in Blackwood's Magazine, 1817–1825* (Lubbock, TX: Texas Technological College Press, 1959).
2. Blackwood himself coined the term "Maga," but his reason for it is not known (Strout, *Bibliography*, 3).
3. R. Shelton Mackenzie notes that words "cannot adequately describe the dismay, astonishment, wrath and hatred which greeted the seventh number of *Blackwood*" ("History of *Blackwood's Edinburgh Magazine*," in *Noctes Ambrosianae*, ix). With only 200 numbers of the magazine containing "The Chaldee Manuscript," Blackwood pulled the issue and replaced the piece with two articles: "A Curious Old Song" and "Strictures on the *Edinburgh Review*." Though issued in such limited numbers, "The Chaldee Manuscript" made a lasting impression. Ian Jack describes it as ushering in "a high circulation and a bad name in literary history" for *Blackwood's*. Ian Jack, *English Literature 1815–1832*, The Oxford History of English Literature, Vol.10 (Oxford: Clarendon Press, 1963), 18. Robert Morrison asserts that critical focus on the notoriety of *Blackwood's*' "bad name" obscures "how innovative and impressive" the issues under Blackwood's tenure as editor are. Robert Morrison, "*Blackwood's* Under William Blackwood," *Scottish Literary Journal* 22 (1995), 61. Alvin Sullivan and J.H. Alexander also call attention to the complexities, rather than the notoriety, of these early issues. Alvin Sullivan (ed.), *British Literary Magazines*, Vol.2, *The Romantic Age, 1789–1832* (Westport, CT: Greenwood Press, 1983), 47; and J.H. Alexander, "*Blackwood's*: Magazine as Romantic Form," *Wordsworth Circle* 15/2 (1984), 57–68.
4. Male homosociality, as I am using it, is drawn from Eve Kosofsky Sedgwick's *Between Men: English Literature and Male Homosocial Desire* (New York: Columbia University Press, 1985). Sedgwick defines male homosociality through a triangulated structure – one that utilizes women to enforce the bonds of masculine homosocial desire. Sedgwick writes of the shifting structural continuum of that desire: "the emerging pattern of male friendship, mentorship, entitlement, rivalry, and hetero- and homosexuality was in an intimate and shifting relation to class; and … no element of that pattern can be understood outside of its relation to women and the gender system as a whole" (1). This desire is the "affective or social force, the glue" (2) that shapes relationships; and Sedgwick's identification of

homosociality's function within a "heterosexualized" canon is particularly useful against the picture of *Blackwood's* as a public, heterosexual, and socially informative vehicle. While limited in terms of generic application to the diachronic nature of periodicals (*Between Men* does not address serialized works), Sedgwick's identification of "historically variable power asymmetries" (7) may help to trace the variable shifts in male homosociality I identify across essays in *Blackwood's*.

5. Mark Parker, *Literary Magazines and British Romanticism*, Cambridge Studies in Romanticism 45 (Cambridge: Cambridge University Press, 2000), 4.

6. Joseph Addison, "No.1," *The Spectator* (1 March 1711), rpt. in *The Spectator*, ed. Donald F. Bond, Vol.1 (Oxford: Clarendon Press, 1965), 1.

7. Un Vieux Celibataire [Thomas Hamilton], "Letters of an Old Bachelor. No.I," *Blackwood's* 2/8 (Nov. 1817), 192–4; An Old Fellow, "Hint to the Ladies," *Blackwood's* 2/10 (Jan. 1818), 377–8; A Young Fellow, "Letter from a Young Fellow," *Blackwood's* 2/11 (Feb. 1818), 513–14; "Letters of Advice from a Lady of Distinction," *Blackwood's* 5/28 (July 1819), 416–20. By examining this type through these four essays, I plan to gesture towards what Parker desires for critical work on periodicals: the analysis of the "dynamic relation among contributions" as that relation "informs and creates meaning" (*Literary Magazines*, 3). Parker's notion of a "run" fits with the recurring figure of the bachelor as that figure appears in various essays with multiple authors; this familiarity with an editorial ideological posture shapes audience expectations and responses in a similar manner. For example, the "Letters of an Old Bachelor" title is subtitled "No.I," implying that this will be a series. Although unfinished series were common in *Blackwood's* and Hamilton did not write any more "Letters" signed by an Old Bachelor, the continuation of the bachelor type who writes letters about "ladies" in later issues implies that the type and the format have the possibility to shape reader expectations.

8. That both William Blackwood and John Wilson, the primary editorial forces behind *Blackwood's*, were married men by the time *Maga* was formed supports the idea that the "bachelor type" is an ideologically necessary fiction used to promote the larger concerns of the periodical both with respect to women themselves and with respect to women as signifiers of male relational dynamics. The "bachelor" type allows for varied renegotiations of women as binding agents in male homosociality that a "married man" type would foreclose. One could read the bachelor type itself as a palimpsestic trope; superimposed on *Blackwood's* "personalities," the "type" invokes and connects the disparate opinions and attacks expressed through those personalities as a unifying figure of identification. For Blackwood's and Wilson's marriages, see Margaret Oliphant, *Annals of a Publishing House: William Blackwood and His Sons, Their Magazine and Friends*, Vol.1 (New York: Scribner, 1897), 14–19; and Mary Wilson Gordon, *"Christopher North:" A Memoir of John Wilson*, Vol.1 (Edinburgh: Edmonston & Douglas, 1862), 161–3. Addison, as the originator of the bachelor type in periodical culture, actually was a bachelor when the *Spectator* began, as was Hogg when he published the *Spy*. Johnson, on the other hand, was married when the *Rambler* essays were published.

9. My calculation of *Maga*'s women writers is based on Strout's authorial ascriptions. While the extent of female readers of the novel has been given a great deal of attention since Ian Watt's *The Rise of the Novel* (*The Rise of the Novel: Studies in Defoe, Richardson, and Fielding* [Berkeley, CA: University of California Press, 1957]), less attention has been paid to the Romantic-era periodical's readership. Jan Fergus, in "Women Readers: A Case Study," points to the difficulties of determining the extent of women's consumption of magazines in England. Married women are unaccounted for if their husbands hold the subscription; taking a subscription in no way guarantees reading; and one subscription can be shared among several readers (in *Women and Literature in Britain: 1700–1800*, ed. Vivien Jones [Cambridge: Cambridge University Press, 2000], 159–60). While earlier than *Blackwood's'* time frame, Fergus' case study of two booksellers in provincial England is useful for its notation that by 1780, women subscribers to magazines comprised 16 percent of the readership (174, n.10).

10. Gayle Rubin, "The Traffic in Women: Notes on the 'Political Economy' of Sex," in *Toward an Anthropology of Women*, ed. Rayna R. Reiter (New York: Monthly Review Press, 1975), 157–210.

11. This apparent use and "misuse" of women's concerns ties back to Sedgwick's argument: "on the one hand that there are many and thorough asymmetries between the sexual continuums of women and men, between female and male sexuality and homosociality, and most pointedly between homosocial and heterosocial object choices for males; and on the other hand that the status of women, and the whole question of arrangements between genders, is deeply and inescapably inscribed in the structure even of relationships that seem to exclude women – even in male homosocial/homosexual relationships" (*Between Men*, 25).

12. Karl Polanyi, *The Great Transformation* [1957] (New York: Octagon, 1980), 73.

13. In "Voices Together: Lamb, Hazlitt, and the *London*," Mark Schoenfield applies Bakhtin's notion of heteroglossia to periodicals "not only in the juxtaposition of discrete phrases, but in the simultaneous production of various voices within one unit of text, whether that unit is a single word, an article, or the confederation of articles which appear in one issue of a magazine." *Studies in Romanticism* 29 (1990), 258. The "production of meaning" I am suggesting is structured through reading a typology across several issues of a magazine and is complicated by differing views on who makes up the Romantic periodical's readership and what *Blackwood's*' impact on that readership is. In "Impersonation and Authorship in Romantic Britain," Peter T. Murphy writes of *Blackwood's* readers: "The reader is sent out through his or her world, looking for knowledge, for connection, or … for scandal about a neighbor. In any case, readers are made to feel their place in society. They are also prodded into a social speculation that seems always about to end in clarity, in knowledge of who is who. But the reader always falls short, running into the surprisingly dark veil over the truth, or into the durably confusing lack of identity and purpose." *ELH* 59/3 (1992), 644. I would suggest that there is not a confusing lack in purpose or identity, but a competition between various identities and purposes that serve to embrace a heterogeneous audience under the organizing principle of a homogeneity of type. For more on *Blackwood's*' readership and construction of audience, see Richard D. Altick, *The English Common Reader: A Social History of the Mass Reading Public 1800–1900* (Chicago, IL: University of Chicago Press, 1957) and Jon P. Klancher, *The Making of English Reading Audiences, 1790–1832* (Madison, WI: University of Wisconsin Press, 1987).

14. Hamilton was an early and prolific contributor to *Blackwood's*. Not only a periodical contributor, but novelist – author of *Cyril Thornton* (1827) and *Men and Manners in America* (1833) – Hamilton participated in forming the *Noctes* personas, sometimes writing under the name of Odoherty; Mr Odoherty [Thomas Hamilton], "Inconstancy; a Song to Mrs M'Whirter," *Blackwood's* 5/30 (Sept. 1819), 715–16. His periodical contributions range from reviews of books on cookery, to poems with a military theme, to discussions of historic military campaigns.

15. Although running titles were often shortened and even altered to reflect the content of the essay, the type of slippage I identify in this essay – shifting the preposition – appears to be atypical in the early issues.

16. *Blackwood's* 2/8 (Nov. 1817), 193. A.J.B. Defauconpret authored two of the works Hamilton discusses, *Quinze Jours à Londres à La Fin De 1815* and *Six Mois à Londres en 1816*, published anonymously with the pseudonym "M. ***" on the title page. They were printed together as *Londres Et Ses Habitans, Ou Quinze Jours à Londres à La Fin De 1815, Et Six Mois à Londres En 1816* (Paris: A La Librairie d'Alexis Eymery, 1817). These works were popular enough to be translated and printed in Milan and Weimer; *Quindici Giorni in Londra Alla Fine Del 1815, Del Sig* (Milano: Presso Batelli e Fanfani, 1818), and *London Und Seine Bewohner* (Weimar: Landes-Industrie-Comptoirs, 1818). As the English language edition did not come out until 1818, the Old Bachelor's readers would not have been able to compare his paraphrasing of the objectionable passage without a reading knowledge of French. Although neither of these works were listed in *Blackwood's*' "Monthly List of New Publications," another of Defauconpret's works is listed as "Observations sur l'Ouvrage intitulé 'La France, par Lady Morgan;' par l'auteur de Quinze jours et de Six mois à Londres, 8vo," *Blackwood's* 1/5 (Aug. 1817), 530. This notice hints at the possibility that *Blackwood's* readers would already have a familiarity with *Quinze Jours à Londres à La Fin De 1815* and *Six Mois à Londres en 1816* by the time "Letters of an Old Bachelor" went to press.

17. "M.," "New Gold Coinage," *Blackwood's* 2/8 (Nov. 1817), 169.

18. The objectionable passage is: "'*Pendant les trois premiers jours, on les trouve toutes jolies; après cela on s'apperçoit* [sic] *qu'elles ont la plupart, la marche niaise, le bras gros, le pied mal fait, les dents laides, la tête baissée, l'œil dur, des corsets mal taillés, des cheveux gras, à force d'en vouloir montrer la couleur naturelle,'* &c" (2/8, 193; emphasis added). During the first three days, one finds them all pretty; after that, one notices that most of them have a silly walk, fat arms, poorly formed feet, ugly teeth, a lowered head, a harsh eye, ill-made corsets, oily hair, by dint of wanting to show its [their hair's] natural color, etc. Translation mine.

19. The reference to women's teeth in commodity terms can be pressed further through Kurt Heinzelman's story of Marcel Duchamp in *The Economics of the Imagination* (Amherst, MA: University of Massachusetts Press, 1980), 5. Heinzelman, relating Duchamp's drawing a check on a sketch pad to pay for dental work then seeing the "check" take on actual value, interrogates the relationship between actual and fictive values with respect to commodities. Heinzelman points out that, in this case, dental work has both an actual and a fictive value, as does any business transaction.

20. Jonathan Swift, "A Beautiful Young Nymph Going to Bed," in *The Complete Poems*, ed. Pat Rogers (London: Penguin, 1983), 453–5. Swift's poem, "Written for the honour of the fair sex," satirically depicts a "lovely goddess" prostitute, who has a complete set of teeth that mark her not as beautiful, but as horrific: "Now dexterously her plumpers draws, / That serve to fill her hollow jaws. / Untwists a wire; and from her gums / A set of teeth completely comes" (lines 23; 17–20).

21. "T." [John Lee?], "Madame de Staël on the Usefulness of Translation," *Blackwood's* 2/8 (Nov. 1817), 145–9.

22. Hamilton invokes Blue Stockings again by disparagingly referring to women who dabble in "physic" as "culinary Blue Stockings." "B.P." [Thomas Hamilton], "Remarks on Cookery," *Blackwood's* 2/9 (Dec. 1817), 304.

23. Of course, the relationship between periodical publishers and book publishers is a complex one, as is evidenced through *Blackwood's* itself. For example, Susan Ferrier's novel, *Marriage*, was both published by Blackwoods and reviewed in *Blackwood's*.

24. F[elicia] D[orothea] H[emans], "On the Death of the Princess Charlotte," *Blackwood's* 3/13 (April 1818), 5–8. Not most favored in all literary circles, Hemans was criticized by Byron for her work. In a letter to John Murray, Byron declared that he did "not despise Mrs Heman[s]," but suggested that "if [she] knit blue stockings instead of wearing them it would be better." See George Gordon Byron, "Letter to John Murray," 28 Sept. 1820, in *"Between Two Worlds:" Byron's Letters and Journals – 1820*, ed. Leslie A. Marchand, Vol.7 (Cambridge, MA: Belknap Press of Harvard University, 1977), 182. Byron's denigration and the current critical recognition of Hemans' poetic intellectual subversion notwithstanding, many of Hemans' contemporaries did not consider her poetry subversive, but rather domestic, which problematizes the intended meaning of Blue Stockings. Stuart Curran notes that for the 1820s and 1830s reading public, Hemans' name was "synonymous with the notion of a poetess, celebrating hearth and home, God and country in mellifluous verse that relished the sentimental and seldom teased anyone into thought." Curran, "Romantic Poetry: The I Altered," in *Romanticism and Feminism*, ed. Anne K. Mellor (Bloomington, IN: Indiana University Press, 1988), 189. Hemans represents one of the few moments of agreement between *Blackwood's* and the *Edinburgh Review*. Francis Jeffrey writes of Hemans that her poetry is "a fine exemplification of Female Poetry," that which is delicate, charming, sensitive, beautiful, fine; in other words, poetry that is non-threatening or domestic. Jeffrey, "Felicia Hemans," *Edinburgh Review* 50/99 (Oct. 1829), 34. In light of Hemans' contradictory position situated between domestic poetess and Blue Stocking, making definitive claims about the function of women in *Blackwood's* is a dangerous business: women can be at once both "inside" as the domestic writer and "outside" as the Blue Stocking.

25. William Hazlitt's "On Fashion," published in *Edinburgh Magazine* in Sept. 1818, also invokes women's fashion as a vehicle for social criticism on a larger scale; rpt. in *The Complete Works of William Hazlitt*, ed. P.P. Howe, Vol.17 (New York: AMS Press, 1967), 51–6. Hazlitt apparently agrees with *Blackwood's* Old Fellow, noting: "Our belles formerly

overloaded themselves with dress: of late years, they have affected to go almost naked" (54). Yet Hazlitt's example need not be read as mere commentary on fashion, but can be extrapolated to broader social concerns. Fashion can refigure, mask over, replicate the "seeming" of appearance: "The only difference between the woman of fashion and the woman of pleasure is, that the one *is* what the other only *seems to be*" (56). This ambiguity resonates with the simultaneous distinguishability and indistinguishability between the Old Fellow and the Young Fellow of the *Blackwood's* essays: they are both cloaked in the trope of fashion from apparently opposite positions, yet their differences begin to collapse through the invocation of that trope.

26. An Old Fellow, "The Dampers," *Blackwood's* 2/11 (Feb. 1818), 528–30; A Damper, "The Dampers," *Blackwood's* 2/12 (March 1818), 628–30. The article signed by the Old Fellow appears in the same issue as the "Letter from a Young Fellow," which would support reading heteroglossic meaning as produced through articles in the same issue.

27. Mark Parker suggests that references to the periodical's "mode of production," which "has been, in the terminology of economists, rationalized," is commonplace in the 1820s; this seemingly standardized mode of production "is not occluded, as is often the case in later novels produced under the commodity system ... there is little space for the high-flown rhetoric of aesthetic idealism in the working world of magazines and reviews" (*Literary Magazines*, 12–13). While I would agree that *Blackwood's* rarely prints the "high-flown rhetoric of aesthetic idealism," I would suggest that the references to the essay's mode of production align that mode specifically with the typology of bachelorhood and its attendant ideological implications. This rhetorical move couples economic success of the periodical contributor with a resistance to the benefits of that success, marriage, thus creating a singularly male space. Jon P. Klancher draws the connection between the payment system for periodical contributors and its impact on readers: "From *The Edinburgh Review* on, public knowledge of ample payments to contributors signalled the distancing of the audience. No longer a society of readers and writers, the journal represented itself as an institution blending writer, editor, and publisher in what could only appear to be an essentially authorless text" (*The Making of English Reading Audiences*, 51). This essay invokes a separation of the editor and author function: "We were instructed by our mysterious Editor, not to suffer this article, on any account whatever, to exceed four pages" (5/28, 420). Yet that separation, with the editor as "mysterious," cannot penetrate the inscrutability of those functions, and this elision of specificity in authorship places the unidentifiable writer ever more firmly in the position of a bachelor Everyman, a representation of *Blackwood's* desire.

28. Kurt Heinzelman, "The Cult of Domesticity: Dorothy and William Wordsworth at Grasmere," in *Romanticism and Feminism*, ed. Anne K. Mellor (Bloomington, IN: Indiana University Press, 1988), 53.

29. Mark Parker notes that "the division of intellectual labor nevertheless sets up its own internal dynamic among the competing languages of middle-class Britain – the languages of aesthetics, of religious life, of economic life, or of the leisured gentleman. This struggle, recorded vividly in magazines, insures that a magazine carries a great variety of potential meanings, none of which can be said to be dominant" (*Literary Magazines*, 15). The author's decision not to marry is not necessarily dominant for the whole of *Blackwood's*, but resonates when read with similarly voiced opinions of other "leisured gentlemen" in the form of bachelor personas.

30. Peter T. Murphy sees *Blackwood's* as a language-experiment that negotiates pure linguistic freedom and the constraint of the materiality of the body ("Impersonation and Authorship," 629). This negotiation can be seen, in part, through the "lady of distinction" in this essay.

31. In an interesting juxtaposition, the reviewer of "Letters of Advice" would appear to be engaging Judith Butler's idea of performativity of gender in *Gender Trouble: Feminism and the Subversion of Identity* (New York: Routledge, 1999). Butler establishes that it is the performance of gender, the enaction of gendered attributes, which constitutes "the identity they are said to express or reveal" (180). Thus, the reviewer, although mockingly, accepts the constitution of a female identity in a male author.

32. The "idea" of woman also plays out in reviews of anonymously published, female-authored texts. In an unsigned review of "*Marriage*, A Novel," appearing one year earlier in the June

1818 issue, the reviewer detects a "female hand" behind this work. *Blackwood's* 3/15 (June 1818), 286. Peter T. Murphy notes that *Blackwood's* exhibits "a nearly obsessive interest in the interaction, attachment and slippage between authors (published names) and persons (bodies indicated by names)" ("Impersonation and Authorship," 626). This simultaneous slippage between and blending of body to author "is in itself criticism, a refusal to let writing escape and be judged on what would have been called literary grounds" ("Impersonation and Authorship," 628). The blending of materiality to language in this essay is an affirmation of male homosociality and a reversal of what occurs in "Letters of Advice from a Lady of Distinction." The "female hand" behind this text is, indeed, materially female; it is Susan Ferrier. Yet women (both actual and fictive) are distinguished by their gendered writing style; a style that is necessarily subordinate to the masculine mode of the *Blackwood's* reviewer. This subordination is borne out by *Marriage*'s reviewer, who writes: "The merits of those female authors who have written English novels are, we think, praised with more ardour than judiciousness" (*Blackwood's* 3/15, 286).

33. Quoted in Mackenzie, *Noctes Ambrosianae*, xx.

34. One authorial presence behind this type is James Hogg, whose pen contributed both to "Chaldee" and to *Noctes*. While Hogg's relationship to *Blackwood's* is a maelstrom of contribution, renunciation, feuds, and reconciliations, what figures in terms of *Blackwood's* and homosociality is what Hogg writes both inside and outside of *Maga*'s pages: *The Private Memoirs and Confessions of a Justified Sinner*. Appearing in *Blackwood's* in August 1823 at a time when Hogg's own "personality" was being caricatured by Wilson in *Noctes*, "A Scots Mummy" is Hogg's letter to Christopher North detailing the discovery of a body, which is then excerpted in the conclusion of the "Editor's Narrative" in *Confessions*. Hogg, "A Scots Mummy," *Blackwood's* 14/79 (Aug. 1823), 188–90; Hogg, *The Private Memoirs and Confessions of a Justified Sinner* (Oxford: Oxford University Press, 1999), 240–45. My connection of this periodical letter to the resulting novel and the issue of bachelor typology draws upon Eve Sedgwick's reading of *Confessions* (*Between Men*, 97–117). Sedgwick asserts that one of the structuring elements in *Confessions*' male homosocial desire is homophobia, demonstrated through Robert Wringhim's feminization and repression. The bachelor type drawn in Robert Wringhim and his doppelganger, Gil-Martin, no longer adheres to the fiction of desiring women to maintain homosociality, but instead resorts to violence and murder. This rage with its undercurrent of homosexual desire in tension with homophobia produces a radically different "bachelor" from that of the *Blackwood's* type, to which Hogg contributed. Within the pages of *Blackwood's*, the "bachelor" shapes audience expectations to read male heterosexuality as normatively based on the comic desiring and displacement of women, rather than a hostile resistance to them. I would suggest that this negotiation ties into *Blackwood's*' project of balancing a heterogeneous readership, so that the enforcement of male homosocial space must be done through the tropes of femininity and must signify a woman in a triangulated structure of desire. Thus an aversion to marriage pervades the "bachelor" identity in *Blackwood's* through comic renunciation.

35. John G. Lockhart, "Noctes Ambrosianae. No.I," *Blackwood's* 11/62 (March 1822), 374.

36. John G. Lockhart, "Noctes Ambrosianae. No.III," *Blackwood's* 11/64 (May 1822), 606.

37. "M.G." [Caroline Bowles Southey], "Thoughts on Letter-Writing," *Blackwood's* 11/62 (March 1822), 304; "Buller" [John Wilson], "Noctes Ambrosianae. No.II," *Blackwood's* 11/63 (April 1822), 480.

38. M. Munday notes that "although women like Maria Edgeworth and Joanna Baillie are given credit [in *Blackwood's*], they are praised as *women* writers. It is an important distinction." Munday, "Jane Austen, Women Writers, and *Blackwood's Magazine*," *Notes and Queries* 20 (1973), 290.

Blackwood's Edinburgh Magazine *and the Construction of Wordsworth's Genius*

DAVID HIGGINS

In an essay published in 1835, Thomas De Quincey argued that his "appreciation of Wordsworth" as a young man had put him 30 years in advance of his contemporaries. Although now, he claimed, magazines "habitually speak of Mr Wordsworth as *a* great if not *the* great poet of the age," during the first quarter of the nineteenth century, "language was exhausted, ingenuity was put on the rack, in the search after images and expressions vile enough – insolent enough – to convey the unutterable contempt avowed for all that he had written by the fashionable critics." According to De Quincey, for many years only one periodical supported the poet:

> *Blackwood's Magazine* (1817) first accustomed the public ear to the language of admiration coupled with the name of Wordsworth. This began with Professor Wilson; and well I remember – nay, the proofs are still easy to hunt up – that, for eight or ten years, this singularity of opinion, having no countenance from other journals, was treated as a whim, a paradox, a bold extravagance of the *Blackwood* critics ... In short, up to 1820, the name of Wordsworth was trampled under foot; from 1820 to 1830 it was militant; from 1830 to 1835 it has been triumphant.[1]

This account of *Blackwood's* as a lone voice crying in the critical wilderness is inaccurate, but the magazine was notable for its campaign to improve Wordsworth's reputation in the period from 1818 to 1822. The aim of this essay is to examine how and why it represented him as a great genius at a time when his position in literary culture was uncertain. I focus in particular on the third of John Wilson's "Letters from the Lakes" (March 1819), a panegyrical account of Wordsworth as a private man that foreshadows the widespread lionization of the poet in the 1830s and 1840s.

While it is no doubt true that, as Ashley Cross has recently put it, the "romantic myth of the Genius Author ... rose to obscure the reality of the literary marketplace," in the early nineteenth century attributions and assertions of genius also played an important role in the way in which that marketplace operated.[2] The essence of genius is, supposedly, that it is distinctive – it stands out from the crowd – and it was offered to consumers by publishers, critics, and authors as a mark of quality at a time of rapidly burgeoning literary production. Contemporary writers often distinguished between ephemeral popularity and the lasting glory with which true genius would be rewarded, but in reality it was the idea of genius that made it possible for certain creative artists, notably Lord Byron, to become popular celebrities whose private lives and personalities were an integral part of the marketing and sale of their works.[3] Such an emphasis was placed on the individual consciousness behind aesthetic creation that readers and critics were encouraged to consider writers' personal characters and life histories to be as interesting and important as their works, and this contributed to an explosion of literary biography in the 1820s and 1830s.

Much of this writing appeared in magazines, which tended to use representations of genius as a means of articulating their own ideological positions, and to distinguish themselves from their competitors. Yet at the same time, genius was often put forward as the only force that could unify a fragmenting public sphere: a form of pure subjectivity that transcended the realms of politics and economics.[4] The tension between the claims made about genius and its use in commercial and political conflicts was heightened and complicated by personal tensions between magazine writers and their "genial" subjects, and generic competition between periodical writing and more prestigious forms of literature. Those who wrote for the magazines often did so out of financial necessity and this sometimes lent a certain bitterness or anxiety to their accounts of more fortunate and famous authors. Furthermore, it was frequently argued that the rise of newspapers and magazines was the reason for the apparent dearth of poets and dramatists of the first rank. Original genius, it was claimed, was being swallowed up or stifled by the anonymous, teeming mass of periodical writing.

Modern critics, notably Jon Klancher, have emphasized the "transauthorial" discourse produced by periodicals, and, to some extent, this further problematized their accounts of autonomous genius.[5] For there was clearly a tension in the way in which unsigned biographical or critical articles effaced the identity of their own authors while simultaneously exploring and celebrating that of their subjects.[6] But the interplay of authorial agency, anonymity, pseudonymity, and public identity that we find in the literary magazines of the early nineteenth century was rather more complex than Klancher suggests.[7] In an important essay, Peter Murphy has examined *Blackwood's* "obsessive interest in the interaction, attachment and slippage between authors (published names) and persons (bodies indicated by names)."[8] He shows that its writers constructed an abstract written world that effaced individual personality through the use of a variety of pseudonyms that could not easily be related to the real authors of the magazine. Paradoxically, this destabilization of public identity by sundering it from the private realm was accompanied by a controversial form of criticism that sought "to punish written egotism by a fierce obtrusion of the bodily into the written," that is, through references to the appearances and private lives of the magazine's victims.[9] In this essay, I show that *Blackwood's'* notorious interest in "personality" both underpinned and ironized its account of Wordsworth as a transcendent genius. For although this account was based, in part, on representations of him as a private man, the very existence of those representations in the pages of the magazine complicated its claim that he stood above the literary marketplace.

Blackwood's succeeded in convincingly interpreting aspects of Wordsworth's life and work which had previously been put forward as reasons for his artistic "failure" – for example, his isolated existence in the Lake District – as evidence of his greatness.[10] In doing so, it helped to popularize what we would now identify as a typically Romantic model of cultural production: a model that emphasizes the importance of originality, individuality, and the transcendence of worldly concerns. Wordsworth's reputation, which had sunk very low after the critical and commercial failure of the *Poems* of 1807, was actually slowly recovering before William Blackwood started publishing his magazine in 1817. However, *Blackwood's* and, to a lesser extent, other new periodicals like the *London Magazine* and the *New Monthly Magazine* played an important role in the steady rise in the poet's cultural status during the 1820s and 1830s. In the latter period of his life, as well as being treated with much more deference by the critics, he attracted numerous visitors to Rydal Mount, his sales gradually increased, and he received a number of public honors culminating in the Laureateship in 1843.[11] The growing interest in Wordsworth around 1820 is apparent not only in reviews of his new volumes, but also in the appearance of a number of articles that offered general assessments of his work and "genius."[12] Although, as one might expect, these sometimes crossed the thin line between discussing his particular strengths and weaknesses as a poet, and describing his personality and private life, at that time it was only *Blackwood's* that published a directly personal, anecdotal account of the poet, in the form of the "Letters from the Lakes."

The magazine's approach to Wordsworth was initially rather inconsistent. In an article published in 1934, Alan Lang Strout shows that three anonymous letters on the poet's *Letter to a Friend of Robert Burns* (1816) which appeared in *Blackwood's* in June, October, and November 1817 were all written by Wordsworth's friend John Wilson, who was himself seen as a member of the "Lake School."[13] The first attacked Wordsworth and defended Francis Jeffrey, the editor of the *Edinburgh Review*, from the poet's criticisms. The second was a vindication of the poet, and the third was another attack. Strout argues that these articles were as much a reflection of Wilson's "extraordinary volatility" as a publicity stunt on behalf of a fledgling publication.[14] Yet they must also be read in the context of the magazine's explicit disdain for "unity of mind" and its capacity to contain conflicting arguments and opinions, a discursive heterogeneity apparent most strongly in the *Noctes Ambrosianae*.[15] As we shall see, Wilson certainly did have mixed feelings about his friend, but in the 1817 articles he was also, in a crude way, exploring different perspectives on Wordsworth and acting out the ongoing controversy surrounding the poet's merits. This combination of personal and structural ambivalence also led, I think, to the *Noctes Ambrosianae* of September 1825, in which Christopher North, the fictional editor of the magazine and Wilson's principal *Blackwood's* persona, stated that Wordsworth was "a good man, and a bad poet" and that *The Excursion* was "the worst poem, of any character, in the English language."[16] When another victim of the same article threatened legal action, Wilson hid in the Lake District and sent letters to William Blackwood begging him not to reveal his name for fear that he would be exposed as Wordsworth's calumniator.[17]

The attacks of 1817 and 1825 bookend a period in which the *Blackwood's* attitude to Wordsworth was nearly always one of unqualified adulation. Wilson wrote the vast majority of articles praising him, though others such as Lockhart, Patmore, and Moir also joined the chorus of approbation.[18] His genius was constantly celebrated and he was treated as a profound thinker, worthy of veneration. The following passage from 1818, with its religious overtones, is typical:

> With all the great and essential faculties of the Poet, he possesses the calm and self-commanding powers of the Philosopher. ... Hence he looks over the world of life, and man, with a sublime benignity. ... The pathos and the truth of his most felicitous Poetry are more profound than of any other, not unlike the most touching and beautiful passages in the Sacred Page.[19]

Blackwood's, of course, praised other contemporary poets at this time, but this sort of language was reserved for Wordsworth. He was marked out from "all the other first-rate writers of the age," who, Wilson argued in 1822, "have varied their moods and measures according to the fluctuations of popular feeling, sentiment, and opinion." In contrast:

> Wordsworth buries his spirit in the solitary haunts and recesses of nature, and suffers no living thing to intrude there, to disturb the dreams of his own imagination. He is to himself all in all. – He holds communings with the great spirit of human life, and feels a sanctity in all the revelations that are made to him in his solitude. ... His poetry is

to him religion; and we venture to say, that it has been felt to be so by thousands. It would be absolute profanation to speak one word against many of his finest breathings; and as the author and promulgator of such divine thoughts, Wordsworth, beyond all poets, living or dead, is felt to be the object of the soul's purest reverence, gratitude, and love.[20]

For Wilson, Wordsworth's solitary and contemplative life gives him access to "revelations" that are denied to his more worldly-minded peers. But in the final sentence of the passage, he seems less like a holy hermit and more like a sort of living God, the "author" of "divine thoughts" who should be revered above all other poets (including, presumably, Shakespeare and Milton).

What lay behind such high praise of Wordsworth? One answer is that Wilson and other *Blackwood's* writers were simply responding to his poetic gifts. This was clearly partly the case, but there were also strong commercial and ideological reasons that contributed to their representations of the poet. Jeffrey N. Cox has recently argued that the impetus behind the magazine's praise of Wordsworth was its enmity towards the "Cockney School:" "*Blackwood's* editors seem to decide that if the gathering of liberal and radical intellectuals around Hunt criticized Wordsworth and the Lakers, then *Blackwood's* would defend them: if you are my enemy's enemy, then you must be my friend."[21] But Cox, I think, accepts at face value an opposition between the two "Schools" that *Blackwood's* had actually very much exaggerated so as to pretend that it was the sole critical voice that was capable of recognizing the Lakers' genius. In fact, Hunt and Keats had also written favorably about Wordsworth in the previous year, and thus in order to protect the apparent exclusivity of *Blackwood's* cultural investment in him, Lockhart took great pains in two of the Cockney School articles to deny that the "Cockneys" could truly have the taste to appreciate such a genius.[22]

There were much more notable reasons for the *Blackwood's* interest in Wordsworth than its dislike of the Cockney School. The most important is that the journal used the poet to help create a position for itself within the increasingly competitive marketplace for periodical literature.[23] By this I do not mean that its support of Wordsworth had a direct or immediate effect on the magazine's popularity, but rather that it was a central part of *Blackwood's* claims to originality and distinction – and ultimately the strength of these claims helped the journal to sustain its early success. Before the founding of his magazine, William Blackwood had been engaged for some years in a battle with Archibald Constable for control of the Scottish literary market.[24] *Blackwood's* was started in order to mount a commercial and ideological challenge to Constable's two journals, the *Scots Magazine* and the mighty *Edinburgh Review*. In the magazine's early years, Wilson and Lockhart frequently attacked the *Edinburgh*'s editor, Francis Jeffrey. His "failure" to appreciate Wordsworth's genius was used as a prime example of his own weakness as a critic, the inadequacies of the *Edinburgh Review*, and the lamentable ignorance and partisanship of Edinburgh Whigs.[25] During the 1820s, it became customary for the magazine's writers to use their support of the poet as an example of their literary insight, and to claim that they had single-handedly rescued him from public obscurity and critical vituperation. For example, in 1826, Wilson and Maginn claimed that the magazine's inception had quickly led to "a revolution" in reviewing:

> no Zany-Zoilus in the Blue and Yellow [the cover of the *Edinburgh Review*] could any longer outcrow the reading Public. A long, prosing leading article in the Edinburgh, abusing Wordsworth, looked ineffably silly beside one splendid panegyrical paragraph in Maga on the Great Laker.[26]

It matters little whether or not this claim was accurate; the point is that *Blackwood's*' self-promotion was partly based on its professed opposition to the *Edinburgh Review*, and its support of Wordsworth was a powerful way of articulating this opposition.[27]

What other factors led *Blackwood's* to construct Wordsworth as a genius? The panegyric on him and Coleridge in the third of the "Letters from the Lakes" (March 1819) may well have been partly designed to secure the latter's approbation. In the infamous October 1817 issue of the magazine, which also contained the "The Chaldee Manuscript" and the first Cockney School article, Coleridge's *Biographia Literaria* had been savagely attacked.[28] But by 1819, William Blackwood was attempting to solicit him as a contributor and sent him the March 1819 issue.[29] In June of that year, William Davis (of Cadell and Davis, Blackwood's London agents) wrote to the publisher, stating that "[Coleridge] *must* be much influenced, I think, by what he has discovered of the altered manner in which both he himself and his friend Wordsworth have lately been mentioned in your Magazine."[30] Another reason for the journal's support of Wordsworth is simply that his Toryism, which was becoming increasingly apparent (especially after his support for Lowther in the Westmoreland election of 1818), chimed in with *Blackwood's*' own ideological stance. Finally, he was also valuable to the magazine because he could be used to strengthen its account of poetic genius as, ideally, an emanation of national culture that had to be restrained by custom and tradition, as opposed to a dangerous, transgressive force threatening social and political stability.[31] In its early years, the magazine's writers made great play of their willingness to recognize genius wherever it occurred. But when dealing with authors like Byron and Shelley this led to a tension between the journal's Tory politics and its desire to be seen, in literary terms, as meritocratic. This tension is strongly apparent in a passage Wilson wrote in 1818:

we must desire to see writers of genius and power perfectly bold and free, – submissive, indeed, where all minds should submit, – but within that circumscription, uncontrolled, impetuous, trusting to their own spirit, and by that light fearlessly exploring and fearlessly creating. A literature generous and aspiring, – yet guarded alike by wisdom and reverence from all transgression, – is alone worthy of England.[32]

Here we have, in a nutshell, the dilemma of the *Blackwood's* approach to "writers of genius." They should be "perfectly bold and free," but also "submissive" to church and state; "uncontrolled," yet "guarded;" literary republicans, but political monarchists. Wordsworth seemed to resolve this dilemma because his artistic experimentation and originality were counterbalanced by his Toryism and exemplary private life.

I now wish to consider the representation of Wordsworth in the third of John Wilson's "Letters from the Lakes," which requires a brief account of the relationship between the two men. Following a brilliant career at Oxford, Wilson had settled at the Elleray estate near Windermere in 1808. He had already written Wordsworth a fan letter in 1802, and quickly became a close friend of the poet and his family.[33] Writing in August 1808, Dorothy Wordsworth told her friend Catherine Clarkson about Wilson's reverence for her brother, and the increasing intimacy between the two households.[34] In 1810, Wilson became godfather to Wordsworth's son William, and was also, he later claimed, allowed to read the manuscript of *The Prelude*.[35] *The Isle of Palms* (1812), Wilson's first volume of poetry, bears obvious marks of Wordsworth's influence: in one poem, "The Angler's Tent," Wilson even self-deprecatingly compares his mentor's "inspired song" with his own "lowlier simple strain."[36] Shortly after its publication, however, the friendship seems to have become strained, and by 1815 a breach between the two poets had developed. In February of that year, Henry Crabb Robinson reports the following piece of gossip by De Quincey:

> Wilson, the minor poet of the Lakes, is estranged from Wordsworth. Vanity among such men produces sad effects. Wordsworth was offended that Wilson should borrow so much without acknowledgment from him and his works, and has therefore given no praise to Wilson. This pains Wilson, who has, besides, peculiarities in his manners, etc., which Wordsworth does not spare.[37]

It seems that Wilson's hero-worship of the older man became tinged with the resentment of a friend who found his merits were not acknowledged, and perhaps also with the anxiety of a poet trying to emancipate himself from the influence of a literary forebear. Thus it is hardly surprising that, when Wilson began to write for *Blackwood's Magazine* after being forced to give up his life of gentlemanly leisure due to a heavy financial loss, he was capable of attacking as well as praising Wordsworth.

The "Letters from the Lakes" purported to be translations of letters written by a young German, Philip Kempferhausen, while holidaying in the Lake District in the summer of 1818. The first letter describes his wanderings among the Lakes, the second concentrates on a trip to Ambleside and a meeting with Robert Southey, and the third recounts a visit to Wordsworth at Rydal Mount. This letter treats the poet as a celebrity and interestingly anticipates his status as a Lakeland oracle in the latter period of his life. Like most of Wilson's other articles on the poet, it seeks to defend Wordsworth's work from his critics, but in this case through a representation of his personal character and private life. He appears, in part, as a country gentleman immersed in a network of healthy, paternalistic social relations and is thus linked with *Blackwood's*' Tory ideology based on agrarian virtue, the maintenance of social distinctions, and religious orthodoxy. At the same time, despite its panegyrical tone, by breaching the boundaries between public and private in such a way the article represents a deliberate insult to Wordsworth and reveals Wilson's ambivalent feelings about his former friend.

In the third of the "Letters from the Lakes," as Peter Swaab has argued, Wilson situates Wordsworth in a pastoral context like that of *The Excursion*.[38] This is significant for, in part, the article attempts to mediate the persona that Wordsworth adopted in that poem – that of the Miltonic philosopher-poet – to the readers of *Blackwood's*. It also seeks to defend this version of genius from the criticisms of Hazlitt and Jeffrey, who had represented Wordsworth as an alienated, antisocial figure in their reviews of Wordsworth's epic.[39] Jeffrey in particular had argued that Wordsworth's artistic errors were a result of his desire to distance himself from his contemporaries both geographically and artistically. Genius, Jeffrey stated, could only succeed through "an habitual and general knowledge of the few and settled permanent maxims, which form the canon of general taste in all large and polished societies."[40] If, as Raymond Williams claims, the Romantic poets' emphasis on genius can be seen as partly a response to the alienation of the poet from his audience in an increasingly commercialized literary world, then Jeffrey's critique of genius was based on a refusal to accept that this was a real problem.[41] As far as he was concerned, Wordsworth's failure was due to his self-induced separation from the reading public, and his disdain for its feelings. *Blackwood's* attempted to show that the poet's position actually resulted from the inability of this public – misled by foolish critics like Jeffrey – to appreciate his profound philosophical poetry and that *their* readers could be taught to admire him. In sharp contrast to Jeffrey's review, the third of the "Letters from the Lakes" celebrates Wordsworth's sequestration in the Lake District, and presents it as a guarantee of the merits of his poetry.

Kempferhausen's description of his first meeting with Wordsworth is an important moment in the cultural fashioning of the poet:

> There seemed to me, in his first appearance, something grave almost to austerity, and the deep tones of his voice added strength to that impression of him. ... His mind seemed to require an effort to awaken itself thoroughly from some brooding train of thought, and his manner, as I felt at least, at first reluctantly relaxed into blandness and urbanity. There was, however, nothing of vulgar pride in all this, although perhaps it might have seemed so, in an ordinary person. It was the dignity of a mind habitually conversant with high and abstracted thoughts – and unable to divest itself wholly, even in common hours, of the stateliness inspired by the loftiest studies of humanity. ... Never saw I a countenance in which CONTEMPLATION so reigns. His brow is very lofty – and his dark brown hair seems worn away, as it were, by thought, so thinly is it spread over his temples.[42]

This early account of Wordsworth as a deep thinker is echoed in later nineteenth-century representations of him as a sort of philosopher-priest. The passage works directly against contemporary representations of Wordsworth and his work as puerile and childish: *this* man is not the writer of the widely mocked *Poems* of 1807, but the great genius who created *The Excursion*. Wilson is also careful to emphasize that Wordsworth's abstracted manner is not due to pride or egotism – epithets that were frequently hurled at the poet in the 1810s – but a sign of the "dignity" and "stateliness" of his extraordinary mind.

After describing the poet's idyllic home life and emphasizing his familial affections, Kempferhausen gives an account of a walk to Grasmere Church with Wordsworth and his family. At this point in the article the poet appears as a philanthropic country gentleman who is venerated by the local peasantry: "the old men, as they passed by, addressed him with an air of reverence, inspired no doubt by the power and wisdom of his conversation, and also by the benevolence and charities of his life" (740). And Wordsworth's virtue outshines even his poetic genius: "I less envied William Wordsworth his glory as a prevailing poet, than his happiness as a philanthropist and a Christian" (741). Whereas Hazlitt and Jeffrey had disparaged rural society, implying that it was bound to degrade a man like Wordsworth by removing him from intercourse with his equals, Wilson shows the poet as protected from the corruption of city life, and fully embedded in a network of healthy, hierarchical social relations in a devout rural community. His poetry may be revolutionary, but his politics and private life are both entirely sedate. The *Blackwood's* Wordsworth is an image of literary greatness that shows genius not as being a dangerous, transgressive force *à la* Byron and Shelley, but rather as fully reconciled with church and state.

Wilson balances his representation of Wordsworth as a sociable, family-loving gentleman with a portrayal of him as a reclusive genius. After the visit to Grasmere Church, the poet takes Kempferhausen to a "tarn of deepest solitude" in Easedale, where, the young German states:

> Wordsworth informed me, that he had meditated, and even composed, much of his poetry; and certainly there could not be a fitter study for a spirit like his, that loves to brood, with an intensity of passion, on those images of nature which his imagination brings from afar and moulds into the forms of life. It was in this naked solitude that many of the richest and loftiest passages of the "Excursion" were composed [741].

This account of Wordsworth creating his masterpiece in sublime isolation is intended to contradict utterly Jeffrey's argument in his review of *The Excursion* that the poet should restrain his imagination through a dialogic relationship with his urban readership. Wordsworth has an exemplary private life, marked by both domestic affections and social duty, but here Kempferhausen emphasizes that his poetry comes entirely from the brooding of his mind on "images of nature." This is a typically Romantic, individualistic view of composition. The explicit mention of Wordsworth's epic poem serves to emphasize the extent to which the third letter is almost a belated advertisement for the slow-selling *Excursion*. Throughout, Wilson represents Wordsworth's impressive appearance, personal happiness, sagacity, and virtue as guarantees for the merit of his philosophical poem.

A vital aspect of the Romantic account of literary production is that, for the true genius, writing is not an occasional hobby or a mere trade, but a way of life. Wordsworth speaks of poetry "like an inspired man," and his auditor declares that:

> it was evident, that poetry was the element in which he lived, and breathed, and had his being. Other poets, at least all I have ever known, are poets but on occasions – Wordsworth's profession is that of a poet; and therefore when he speaks of poetry, he speaks of the things most familiar, and, at the same time, most holy to his heart. For twenty years has he lived in this grand country, and there devoted his whole soul to his divine art [741].

Poetry is not just something that Wordsworth produces when he feels like it; it is his *essence*. In reality, of course, literature was certainly not Wordsworth's main source of income; unable to make enough money from his publications to support his family, he had taken on the post of Distributor of Stamps for Westmoreland and Penrith in 1813. Wilson is using "profession" mainly in its theological sense, meaning, in general, a declaration of faith and, more specifically, the vow made on entering a religious order. Poetry, for

Wordsworth, is like the daily work undertaken by a monk or nun: "most familiar" and "most holy." Thus although Kempferhausen emphasizes that he is generous in his praise for his contemporaries, he is marked out from them: "it was clear that his soul was with them of elder times; and who shall say, but in this he obeyed the voice of truth – the only voice to which in his solitude Wordsworth cares to listen" (742).

This account of Wordsworth's separation from the literary marketplace is emphasized further by his "unqualified contempt" for "the periodical criticism of Britain." He states that:

> The office of a periodical critic was one beneath the dignity of a great mind – that such a critic, in order to please, to startle, or astonish – without doing which he could acquire no character at all – must often sacrifice what he knew to be truth – that he must mingle truth with falsehood, or, at least, with error; and that he who wrote avowedly and professionally to the public, must respect, nay, take advantage, of its prejudices or its ignorance; and if so, surely, whatever might be the advantages or disadvantages of such writings to the public, they were not worthy [of] much notice from a poet who devoted his whole life to the study of his art, – who in his solitude sought truth, and truth alone; and who, unless he knew that it was amply deserved, and wisely bestowed, would be miserable under the world's applause [742].

Again, this is a typically Romantic account of authorship. Periodical writers, unlike poets, write "avowedly and professionally [for] the public;" they pander to their readers and thus sacrifice truth to sales. They cannot be men of "high intellect." On the other hand, the poetic genius finds truth in his solitude, caring nothing for the "world's applause," and, by implication, the concomitant financial rewards. It may seem odd that Wilson would include an attack on periodical literature in the "Letters from the Lakes." However, disquiet about the influence of the press on both authors and the reading public was a fairly common theme among magazine writers of the period. In 1818 both Wilson and Lockhart had published articles attacking the way in which literary critics sought to position themselves and their readers as judges of men of genius.[43] *Blackwood's* was often represented by its writers very differently: as a supporter of genius, and as a journal which sought to educate and improve its audience, rather than pander to its prejudices. Its readers were encouraged to believe that it should not be included as part of a pernicious magazine culture that could be so harmful to creativity. By reporting Wordsworth's comments on the press in his account of the poet, Wilson affirms the model of cultural production that pitches the disinterested genius against the debased critic, while suggesting at the same time that *Blackwood's* is the exception that proves this rule. In reality, Wordsworth would certainly not have exempted it from his remarks, and so Wilson is also having a joke at the poet's expense.

For the "Letters from the Lakes" were seen as a breach of social decorum by Wordsworth and his family. The poet had disliked *Blackwood's* from its inception, having taken umbrage at Wilson's attacks on *A Letter to a Friend of Robert Burns*, and the magazine was banned from his household.[44] Around the time of the publication of the third of the letters, he wrote to Francis Wrangham expressing his disgust at the "personal" nature of *Blackwood's* articles on him and his friends.[45] When the "Letters from the Lakes" were reprinted in the *Westmoreland Gazette*, probably with De Quincey's connivance, he was angered and tried to prevent the publication.[46] Wilson must have known that Wordsworth would be offended by *Blackwood's* account of his private life, no matter how panegyrical; in *A Letter to a Friend of Robert Burns*, the poet had attacked the contemporary culture of "personality," lamenting "the coarse intrusions into the recesses, the gross breaches upon the sanctities, of domestic life, to which we have lately been more and more accustomed."[47] Having written three articles on this text in 1817, Wilson can hardly have been unaware of Wordsworth's assertion that biography was unnecessary in the case of authors, whom he did not consider to be public figures.

Despite their eulogistic content, "The Letters from the Lakes" were criticized by an anonymous writer in the *New Monthly Magazine*, who complained of the *Blackwood's* practice

> of dragging the peculiarities, the conversation, and domestic habits of distinguished individuals into public view, to gratify a diseased curiosity at the expense of men by whom its authors have been trusted. … If the enshading sanctities of life are to be cut away – as in Peter's Letters, or in the Letters from the Lakes – its joys will speedily perish.[48]

Wilson's effusive praise of Wordsworth in the "Letters from the Lakes" is, paradoxically, a sort of revenge for Wordsworth's refusal to praise Wilson's poetry. The article is calculated both to improve Wordsworth's cultural status, and to offend the poet by revealing details of his private life to the readers of *Blackwood's*. Wordsworth's dislike of "personality" was due not simply to his sense of personal dignity, but to a desire to control the ways in which he, or different versions of him, were mediated and consumed. Throughout his career, the poet wanted public success, but was horrified by the possible development of the culture of celebrity that is a hallmark of modern capitalist society: the uncontrolled, commercialized proliferation of representations of individuals in the public eye. By publicizing the poet's private life, Wilson usurps Wordsworth's power to control representations of himself. He asserts the increasing dominance of the periodical press in the literary marketplace and also, covertly, his own power over his former friend as a writer for a powerful journal. And by including Wordsworth's disparaging remarks on the press in a magazine that is conducting a public campaign in support of the poet, he draws attention to the symbiotic relationship which commodity culture creates between artists and critics.

NOTES

I am grateful to John Barrell, Robert Morrison, and Kiera Chapman for their comments on earlier drafts of this essay.

1. Thomas De Quincey, "Sketches of Life and Manners; from the Autobiography of an English Opium Eater: Oxford," *Tait's Edinburgh Magazine* n.s. 2 (Aug. 1835), 543.
2. Ashley J. Cross, "From *Lyrical Ballads* to *Lyrical Tales*: Mary Robinson's Reputation and the Problem of Literary Debt," *Studies in Romanticism* 40 (2001), 572. As far as I am aware, Raymond Williams was the first critic to draw attention to the relationship between Romantic aesthetics and changes in the production and consumption of literature; see Williams, *Culture and Society* (London: The Hogarth Press, 1993), Ch.2.
3. For the Romantic interest in posthumous fame, see Andrew Bennett, *Romantic Poets and the Culture of Posterity* (Cambridge: Cambridge University Press, 1999). Andrew Elfenbein gives a good account of Byron and celebrity in *Byron and the Victorians* (Cambridge: Cambridge University Press, 1995), Ch.2.
4. David S. Hogsette has discussed how, in the early Victorian period, Samuel Taylor Coleridge was represented as "a secular messiah whose creative power redeems the middle classes;" see Hogsette, "Coleridge as Victorian Heirloom: Nostalgic Rhetoric in the Early Victorian Reviews of Poetical Works," *Studies in Romanticism* 37 (1998), 63–75. However, Robert Lapp has recently shown that, at least in the case of *Fraser's Magazine*, representations of the poet were much more equivocal and complex than Hogsette suggests; see Lapp, "Romanticism Repackaged: The New Faces of 'Old Man' Coleridge in *Fraser's Magazine*, 1830–35," *European Romantic Review* 11 (2000), 235–47.
5. Jon P. Klancher, *The Making of English Reading Audiences, 1790–1832* (Madison, WI: University of Wisconsin Press, 1987), 52.
6. See David E. Latané's thought-provoking article "The Birth of the Author in the Victorian Archive," *Victorian Periodicals Review* 22 (1989), 109–17. The question of how best to approach anonymous or pseudonymous periodical writing is a difficult one. I would argue that it is legitimate to consider the agency of individual authors when we study periodicals, as long as we recognize that this agency was structured and constrained by the discursive parameters of the particular periodical(s) for which they wrote; Mark Parker makes a similar point in *Literary Magazines and British Romanticism* (Cambridge: Cambridge University Press, 2000), 4–5.
7. For a stimulating discussion of these issues which focuses on the *London Magazine*, see Margaret Russett, *De Quincey's Romanticism* (Cambridge: Cambridge University Press, 1997), Ch.3.
8. Peter T. Murphy, "Impersonation and Authorship in Romantic Britain," *ELH* 59 (1992), 626.
9. Ibid., 636.
10. This is what I mean by "the construction of Wordsworth's genius." In fact, I believe that genius is *always* socially constructed. There is nothing inevitable about the process which leads a person to be described as a genius: this depends on a number of factors which are extrinsic to his or her mental abilities, and what appear as the "signs" of genius at a certain time and place may not be considered as such in other contexts. Tia DeNora and Hugh Mehan give a good account of this view in "Genius: A Social Construction, the Case of Beethoven's Initial Recognition," in *Constructing the Social*, ed. Theodore R. Sarbin and John I. Kitsuse (London: Sage Publications, 1994), 157–73.
11. For Wordsworth's reputation in the 1820s, see Stephen Gill, *Wordsworth: A Life* (Oxford: Clarendon Press, 1989), 347–52. Gill deals with the 1830s and 1840s in *Wordsworth and the Victorians* (Oxford: Clarendon Press, 1998), Ch.1.

12. For example, see [John Scott], "Living Authors No.II: Wordsworth," *London Magazine* 1 (March 1820), 275–85; "G.M.," "On the Genius and Writings of Wordsworth," *Imperial Magazine* 3 (July 1821), 598–602; and [Thomas Noon Talfourd], "On the Genius and Writings of Wordsworth," *New Monthly Magazine* 14 (Nov. and Dec. 1820), 483–508 and 648–55.

13. Alan Lang Strout, "John Wilson, 'Champion' of Wordsworth," *Modern Philology* 31 (1934), 383–94.

14. Ibid., 392–3.

15. J.H. Alexander, *"Blackwood's*: Magazine as Romantic Form," *Wordsworth Circle* 15 (1984), 61.

16. [John Wilson], "Noctes Ambrosianae. No.XXI," *Blackwood's Edinburgh Magazine* 18 (Sept. 1825), 380–81.

17. Margaret Oliphant, *Annals of a Publishing House: William Blackwood and His Sons*, 3 Vols. (Edinburgh: William Blackwood, 1899), I:277–87. Three years later, Wilson published a lengthy attack on *The Excursion* for its lack of Christian doctrine: John Wilson, "Sacred Poetry," *Blackwood's Edinburgh Magazine* 24 (Dec. 1828), 917–38.

18. For example, see "Essays on the Lake School of Poetry No.I: Wordsworth's *White Doe of Rhylstone*," *Blackwood's* 3 (July 1818), 255–63; "Essays on the Lake School of Poetry No.II: On the Habits of Thought, Inculcated by Wordsworth," *Blackwood's* 4 (Dec. 1818), 369–80; "Letters from the Lakes," *Blackwood's* 4 (Jan. and March 1819), 396–404 and 735–44 – all by John Wilson. Wilson also wrote a number of reviews of Wordsworth: *"Peter Bell*," *Blackwood's* 5 (May 1819), 130–36; *"The Waggoner*," *Blackwood's* 5 (June 1819), 332–4; *"The River Duddon*," *Blackwood's* 7 (May 1820), 206–13; *"Ecclesiastical Sketches* and *Memorials of a Tour on the Continent*," *Blackwood's* 12 (Aug. 1822), 175–91. He praised Wordsworth strongly in a review of Crabbe's *Tales of the Hall*, *Blackwood's* 5 (July 1819), 469–83. Patmore's two "Sonnets to Mr Wordsworth" appeared in *Blackwood's* 2 (Feb. 1818), 512–13. Moir published a sonnet on the poet in *Blackwood's* 8 (Feb. 1821), 542. John Gibson Lockhart praised Wordsworth in several passages in *Peter's Letters to His Kinfolk*, 2nd Edn., 3 Vols. (Edinburgh: William Blackwood, 1819): for example, I:121–3 and 179; II:143–4; III:130.

19. [John Wilson], "Essays on the Lake School of Poetry No.I: Wordsworth's *White Doe of Rhylstone*," *Blackwood's Edinburgh Magazine* 3 (July 1818), 371.

20. [John Wilson], "Wordsworth's Sonnets and Memorials," *Blackwood's Edinburgh Magazine* 12 (Aug. 1822), 175.

21. Jeffrey N. Cox, "Leigh Hunt's Cockney School: The Lakers' 'Other,'" *Romanticism on the Net* 14 (1999), para.4, 8 Jan. 2002: http://users.ox.ac.uk/~scat0385/huntlakers.html.

22. See "Z." [John Gibson Lockhart], "On the Cockney School of Poetry No.I," *Blackwood's Edinburgh Magazine* 2 (Oct. 1817), 41, and "On the Cockney School of Poetry No.IV," *Blackwood's Edinburgh Magazine* 3 (Aug. 1818), 520.

23. Its championing of Shelley was also used for this purpose; see Robert Morrison, "'Abuse Wickedness, but Acknowledge Wit:' *Blackwood's* and the Shelley Circle," *Victorian Periodicals Review* 34 (2001), 160.

24. See Oliphant, *Annals of a Publishing House*, I, Ch.2 and 3.

25. For example, [John Wilson], "An Hour's Tête-à-Tête with the Public," *Blackwood's Edinburgh Magazine* 8 (Oct. 1820), 93.

26. [John Wilson and William Maginn], "Preface," *Blackwood's Edinburgh Magazine* 19 (1826), xxii.

27. I do not mean to suggest that *Blackwood's*' literary criticism was straightforwardly "Romantic," or that the *Edinburgh's* was consistently "Augustan." It is simply that *Blackwood's* represented its criticism as revolutionary and the *Edinburgh's* as reactionary.

28. [John Wilson], "Observations on Coleridge's *Biographia Literaria*," *Blackwood's Edinburgh Magazine* 2 (Oct. 1817), 3–18.

29. See Nicholas Roe, *John Keats and the Culture of Dissent* (Oxford: Clarendon Press, 1997), 272–3, and Alan Lang Strout, "Samuel Taylor Coleridge and John Wilson of *Blackwood's Magazine*," *PMLA* 48 (1933), 108–10. Robert Morrison gives an account of Coleridge's association with *Blackwood's* in his article "Opium-Eaters and Magazine Wars: De Quincey and Coleridge in 1821," *Victorian Periodicals Review* 30 (1997), 27–40.

30. Quoted in Roe, *John Keats*, 273.
31. See, for example, two anonymous articles by John Wilson: "On Literary Censorship," *Blackwood's Edinburgh Magazine* 4 (Nov. 1818), 176–8, and "On the Analogy between the Growth of Individual and National Genius," *Blackwood's Edinburgh Magazine* 6 (Jan. 1820), 375–81.
32. [Wilson], "On Literary Censorship," 177.
33. For a detailed account of the relationship between Wilson and Wordsworth up to 1817, see Alan Lang Strout, "William Wordsworth and John Wilson: A Review of their Relations between 1802 and 1817," *PMLA* 49 (1934), 143–83. See also Mary Gordon, *Christopher North: A Memoir of John Wilson*, 2nd Edn. (Edinburgh: Thomas C. Jack, 1879), Ch.5, and Elsie Swann, *Christopher North* (Edinburgh: Oliver and Boyd, 1934), Ch.3.
34. Ernest de Selincourt (ed.), *The Letters of William and Dorothy Wordsworth*, 2nd Edn., revised by Mary Moorman and Alan G. Hill, 8 Vols. (Oxford: Clarendon Press, 1967–93), II:260.
35. Robert Morrison, "*Blackwood's* Berserker: John Wilson and the Language of Extremity," *Romanticism on the Net* 20 (2000), para.4, 20 May 2002: http://users.ox.ac.uk/~scat0385/20morrison.html.
36. John Wilson, *The Isle of Palms and Other Poems* (Edinburgh: Ballantyne, 1812), 186.
37. Edith Morley (ed.), *Henry Crabb Robinson on Books and their Writers*, 3 Vols. (London: J.M. Dent & Sons, 1938), I:160.
38. John Mullan, Chris Hart, and Peter Swaab (ed.), *Lives of the Great Romantics*, 3 Vols. (London: William Pickering, 1996), III (ed. Peter Swaab):7.
39. [William Hazlitt], "Character of Mr Wordsworth's New Poem, The Excursion," *The Examiner* (21 Aug., 28 Aug., and 2 Oct. 1814), 541–42, 555–8, and 636–8; rpt. in *The Complete Works of William Hazlitt*, ed. P.P. Howe, 21 Vols. (London: J.M. Dent & Sons, 1930–33), XIX:9–25.
40. [Francis Jeffrey], "Wordsworth's *Excursion*," *Edinburgh Review* 24 (Nov. 1814), 3.
41. Williams, *Culture and Society*, Ch.2.
42. Philip Kempferhausen [John Wilson], "Letters from the Lakes: Written during the Summer of 1818. Letter III," *Blackwood's Edinburgh Magazine* 4 (March 1819), 739–40. All further references to this article are within the text.
43. Baron von Lauerwinkel [John Gibson Lockhart], "Remarks on the Periodical Criticism of England," *Blackwood's Edinburgh Magazine* 2 (March 1818), 670–79. Also [Wilson], "On Literary Censorship," 176–8.
44. Mary Moorman, *William Wordsworth: A Biography*, 2 Vols. (Oxford: Clarendon Press, 1957–65), II:409; Swaab, *Lives of the Great Romantics*, III:6; Grevel Lindop, *The Opium Eater; A Life of Thomas De Quincey* (Oxford: Oxford University Press, 1985), 228.
45. Selincourt (ed.), *Letters of William and Dorothy Wordsworth*, III:522–4.
46. Moorman, *William Wordsworth*, II:409.
47. William Wordsworth, *Prose Works*, ed. W.J.B. Owen and Jane Worthington Smyser, 3 Vols. (Oxford: Clarendon Press, 1974), III:122. Significantly, during the period in which Wordsworth composed the *Letter* (Dec. 1815 to Feb. 1816), Byron's separation from his wife was prompting intense speculation and savage attacks in the press. This partly explains the strength of Wordsworth's dislike of literary biography, for the Byron scandal revealed all too clearly the unpredictable, double-edged nature of celebrity – the way in which public adulation could quickly turn to public revulsion.
48. [Anon.], "Modern Periodical Literature," *New Monthly Magazine* 14 (Sept. 1820), 309–10.

Detaching Lamb's Thoughts

PETER J. MANNING

"Mr Lamb, from the peculiarity of his exterior and address as an author, would probably never have made his way by detached and independent efforts," wrote Hazlitt in *The Spirit of the Age*, continuing:

> but fortunately for himself and others, he has taken advantage of the Periodical Press, where he has been stuck into notice, and the texture of his compositions is assuredly fine enough to bear the broadest glare of popularity that has hitherto shone upon them.[1]

For Hazlitt here the periodical press functions as a welcome supplement: the regular repetition that is the essence of the journal consolidates the fragments of a peculiar and recessive author into a substantial identity, and its already existent audience delivers his compositions the attention they deserve but would not otherwise receive.

In studying Lamb's essays in the context of their first magazine publication recent scholarship may be said to follow Hazlitt's lead. Mark Parker has argued that "attention to [John] Scott's use and placement of the essays in the *London Magazine* becomes crucial in redressing the formal and autobiographical orientation of the criticism of Lamb."[2] Through a subtle examination of the ways Lamb's "The Old and the New Schoolmaster" is "pressured" by Hazlitt's "On Antiquity" in a single issue of the *London Magazine* Mark Schoenfield has demonstrated the play of competing voices in which Lamb's writings participate.[3] The gain in historical specificity and vitality from such maneuvers has been immense, nor would this essay be possible without their example. Yet thus resituating Lamb within the pages of the *London Magazine* risks circumscribing his effects in the exact proportion that one recovers their original richness. James Treadwell has shown, in a detailed contextual reading of Lamb's two Christ's Hospital essays, that circumstantiality need not lead to reduction; as he concludes, this case reveals that "autobiography is an ambiguous, contestable, self-interrogating proposition which calls into play the historical moment of the two texts."[4] The question of Lamb's relation to the *London Magazine* is the question of any author's relation to the medium in which he appears. To what degree is Lamb contained by the institutional matrix of the *London Magazine*, the voice of Elia incorporated into the Toryism of the editor, John Scott, and spoken for by the audience whose urban, bourgeois cast can be traced in the departments of the journal: Abstracts of Foreign and Domestic Occurrences, the monthly register of agriculture and commerce, the list of ecclesiastical and other preferments? This essay might be considered as a meditation on Hazlitt's word "detached," a speculation on the ways in which Lamb's texts seek to detach themselves from, or at any rate to resist absorption by, the particular circumstances of the *London Magazine* to which they nonetheless remain tied. Its argument is that Lamb draws out of periodical publishing an identity that disguises the commercial nature of that enterprise, and that he then seeks to elude the concretion, the historical embedding, of that identity. The name of this double process is Elia, and it is the workings of this persona that mark the unsettled situation of the text.

"Detached" is Lamb's word too, in the title of "Detached Thoughts on Books and Reading," published in the *London Magazine* of July 1822, on which I shall focus. Its ends are thrown into relief by another essay earlier in the same issue, "On Magazine Writers." The author of that piece, signed merely "P.," looks back on his experience "some five and twenty years ago ... when magazines were quite another sort of thing" (21).[5] The contrast is immediately undone by the portrait of the author, who despite lacking a subject determines to produce:

> The writer sits down to compose – not because his brain labours in the parturition of some long meditated matter – not because he has reflected deeply, and acquired much – but he is feverish with some vague longing after literary notoriety. He resolves to write before he has learned to think [21].

As the essay proceeds it becomes clear that this state of affairs owes less to the ambition, however misguided, of aspiring authors than to the conditions that have called them forth. Magazines, the essay observes, "have in some respects followed, in others formed, that part of the public taste which depends upon the public manners. They have changed their place in the system of literature" (22). The putative distinction between mere following and creative forming is neutralized by the alliteration that joins them, and then swallowed up entirely by the dependence of both positions on the public taste. In these circumstances the contributors to magazines are ruled by their market: "the deep thinkers and laborious writers of the last century are obliged to yield to the light, smart, and sketchy writers of the present" (23). The requirements of the magazine format are so dominant as to efface the individual subjectivities of the suppliers of copy. "The general run of contributors," the essay continues, "seems ... to be in the least danger of suffering from any modifications in the character of magazines; inasmuch, as having no fixed and certain colours of their own, they imbibe, like the cameleon, the hues of their domiciles" (23). This natural image of complete adaptability soon transforms into a vision of entirely mechanical production:

> I have heard, that a patent has been, or is about to be, taken out for an automaton writer, the principle of which is, that after being wound up it is only necessary to fling in it a certain number of pages of Johnson, or any other vocabulary, and they come out completely formed into the shape of an article [25].

The essay concludes with a grand fantasy based on the interchangeability and reproducibility of print: "sets of magazine articles might be manufactured for every month of the year, with blank titles" (26).

Like much nineteenth-century humor, "On Magazine Writers" is a good example of the very "light, smart, and sketchy" style it satirizes. The evident continuity of its concerns with Lamb's "Detached Thoughts on Books and Reading" declares the inability of Lamb's essay to detach itself from its surroundings; "Detached Thoughts," the informal, unsequential reflections that make up Lamb's essay, epitomize the sketch as the first essay defines it. To juxtapose the two essays – only six pages apart – is to see what appears most personal and spontaneous in Lamb as most typical and predetermined, an exercise in the form most favored by the conditions of publication. Moreover, the insight of the first essay, that article-making advances by recycling the words of the past – "a magazinist looks upon a library as his domain, and the works of all who have preceded him as his fair property" (26) – applies with especial force to Lamb, whose piece is made up of reminiscences of Shaftesbury, Fielding, Smollett, Sterne, Burton, Milton, Fuller, and so on: more than 40 names in a bare six-page essay.

Lamb's recognition of his inseparability from his precursors is signaled by his epigraph, a quotation from Lord Foppington in Vanbrugh's *The Relapse*: "To mind the inside of a book is to entertain oneself with the forced product of another man's brain. Now I think a man of quality may be much amused with the natural sprouts of his own."[6] To open with a gambit that places the question of originality in the mouth of a fool from Restoration comedy and that renders it already a matter of quotation sidesteps the desire to be a genius that paralyzes the neophyte author of "On Magazine Writers." Lamb develops his immersion in the world of letters in his first paragraph:

> An ingenious acquaintance of my own was so much struck with this bright sally of his Lordship, that he has left off reading altogether, to the great improvement of his originality. At the hazard of losing some credit on this head, I must confess that I dedicate no inconsiderable portion of my time to other people's thoughts. I dream away my life in others' speculations. I love to lose myself in other men's minds. ... Books think for me [33; 172].

By embracing the secondary in "Detached Thoughts on Books and Reading," Lamb circumvents the dilemma of the hacks in "On Magazine Writers:" books are more honorific than magazines, a more potent image of authorial identity than writing for a journal can produce; reading, though dependent on prior writing, is free of the taint of commodity production, and suggests an act performed by a subject.

The task of the essay is to generate that distinctive subjectivity from the library echoes stigmatized by "On Magazine Writers." The speaker who announces "I have no repugnances" turns out to have several: *"books which are no books – biblia a-biblia,"* such as court calendars and statutes, serious historians, modern philosophy, treatises on population, encyclopedias. "I confess that it moves my spleen to see these *things in book's clothing* perched upon shelves" (33; 172–3). Gradually the subject shifts from the contents of books to their covers, their clothing, but this shift to the external paradoxically founds inwardness. The choice of how to bind a book is what binds it to us, the sign of appropriation, the impress that converts the impersonal repertory into personal possession. The magazine, the medium of the essay, is only partly susceptible to this recuperation: "I would not dress a set of Magazines, for instance, in full suit. The dishabille, or half-binding (with Russia backs ever) is *our* costume" (34; 173). Lamb here both concedes his complicity with the ephemera of the journals and insinuates a world beyond, the world of "my shivering folios ... my ragged veterans" (33; 173), a world in which higher status goes hand-in-hand with fragility and indifference to conventional standards. Idiosyncratic affections supersede canonical judgments; when "[m]uch depends upon *when* and *where* you read a book," then "Kit Marlowe" (it would be the intimate diminutive) and Drayton can outrank Shakespeare and Milton (35; 175/174). Like Walter Benjamin unpacking his library, Lamb joins the book to his personal history or, more accurately, enacts the simulacrum of a personal history upon his "tickling sense of property" (34; 173), his disposition of citations.[7] Lamb, to use Susan Stewart's lexicon, *collects*.[8]

The opinion that some books are better not rebound by their owners is Lamb's mode of establishing the subjectivity of all readers, and not only his own:

> How beautiful to a genuine lover of reading are the sullied leaves, and worn out appearance, nay the very odour (beyond Russia), if we would not forget kind feelings in fastidiousness, of an old "Circulating Library" Tom Jones, or Vicar of Wakefield! How they speak of the thousand thumbs, that have turned over their pages with delight! of the lone sempstress, whom they may have cheered (milliner, or harder-working mantua-maker) after her long day's needle-toil, running far into midnight, when she has snatched an hour, ill spared

> from sleep, to steep her cares, as in some Lethean cup, in spelling out
> their enchanting contents! Who would have them a whit less soiled?
> What better condition could we desire to see them in? [34; 173]

In this fantasy, in which books are imagined as speaking of their previous
readers, subjectivity circulates and forms a community that answers to our
wishes: what better condition could *we* desire? If the image of those readers
is sentimentalized and feminized, their cherished privacy, their frail
intentionality, is the opposite of the patent mechanical reproduction
envisioned in "On Magazine Writers."

Lamb concludes "Detached Thoughts" with the verses of a "quaint
poetess of our day," an appropriate ending for this dance of derived and
feminized subjectivities.[9] The first stanza tells of a boy who reads at a
bookstall until interrupted by the shopman:

> "You, Sir, you never buy a book,
> Therefore in one you shall not look."
> The boy pass'd slowly on, and with a sigh
> He wish'd he never had been taught to read,
> Then of the old churl's books he should have had no need.

The second stanza tells of another boy:

> Who look'd as if he'd had not any
> Food, for that day at least – enjoy
> The sight of cold meat in a tavern larder.
> This boy's case, then thought I, is surely harder,
> Thus hungry, longing, thus without a penny,
> Beholding choice of dainty-dressed meat:
> No wonder if he wish he ne'er had learn'd to eat [36; 177].

In one sense the two boys make up the author's situation: the insistence on
buying in the first stanza holds for the magazine too: if readers don't
purchase, authors don't eat. Reading is thus a commodity to be consumed at
a price, like items in a tavern larder. At the same time, by maintaining that
the second boy's case is harder, the verses block the complete equation of
the two situations, and thus remove reading from the circuit of need and
consumption. Through its very marginality reading acquires a sublime
spiritual power attested by an echo of Gray's "Ode on a Distant Prospect of
Eton College;" in "filch[ing] a little learning," the boy manages to "snatch
a fearful joy" (36; 176).

This illegitimate pleasure, escaping the regulatory eye of the merchant,
grounds the subjectivity the essay offers. As with the sempstress, milliner,

or mantua-maker, who have likewise "snatched an hour" after a day of oppressed labor, the pleasures of reading challenge the all-sufficiency of the norms of commercial society. The rhetorical questions of the sempstress passage – who would have the common books less soiled? what better condition could we desire to see them in? – draw the reader into this transgressive economy of desire.

The model for these questions had already been posed in the second of the Elia essays: "methinks I hear you exclaim, Reader, *Who is Elia?*"[10] Indeed the subjectivity created by these essays is not Lamb's, but Elia's. The name, Lamb told his publisher, belonged to an Italian clerk now "no more than a name, for he died of consumption:"[11] the signature on the essays is beyond consumption. Or, as Lamb himself remarked, "Elia" is anagrammatically a lie. As he put it in "A Character of the Late Elia, by a Friend," in the January 1823 issue of the *London Magazine*, the "*first person*" was "his favourite figure."[12] Lamb's achievement was to make the "person" emerge from the rhetorical figure; the rhetorical questions make clear that he did so by eliciting the curiosity of his readers. As Hazlitt saw, the response to the accumulating essays in the periodical conferred an identity on their peculiarly absent(minded) author. "Losing some credit" on the head of originality, as he mused at the beginning of "Detached Thoughts," Lamb more than compensates by becoming the most highly paid contributor to the *London Magazine*.[13] Elia is the human face of the article-manufacturing machine of "On Magazine Writers."

A brief glance at two of Lamb's theatrical essays will clarify this process. In "On Some of the Old Actors," Lamb remarks of an actor that he:

> had two voices, – both plausible, hypocritical, and insinuating; but his secondary or supplemental voice still more decisively histrionic than his common one. It was reserved for the spectator; and the dramatis personae were supposed to know nothing at all about it. The *lies* of young Wilding, and the *sentiments* in Joseph Surface, were thus marked out in a sort of italics to the audience. This secret correspondence with the company before the curtain (which is the bane and death of tragedy) has an extremely happy effect in some kinds of comedy.[14]

Exciting our desire to penetrate the mystery of Elia – a mystery which in literary London was no mystery at all – Lamb entices his readers into a conspiracy, a secret correspondence, the shared pleasure in the play of sentiments and lies. For this collaboration to work, however, the text must be granted the immunity of a play space. In "On the Artificial Comedy of the Last Century" Lamb laments the disappearance, and so postulates the existence, of a detached aesthetic realm:

that happy breathing-place from the burthen of a perpetual moral questioning – the sanctuary and quiet Alsatia of hunted casuistry – is broken up and disfranchised, as injurious to the interests of society. The privileges of the place are taken away by law. We dare not dally with images or names of wrong.[15]

Alsatia, where debtors may escape their creditors, like the text (where casuistry and names of wrong, or wrong names, thrive), both transgresses norms and is licensed by them. "I wear my shackles more contentedly for having respired the breath of an imaginary freedom" (306; 287). But this is Elia speaking. Lamb, so far from being the progenitor of Elia, functions rather as Elia's reserve, the belief fantasized by reader and author alike of an identity beyond the words on the page, beyond exhaustion in the gestures of daily business, or, for our purposes, in the accounts of materialist explanation, a freedom that is no more – but no less – than the imagined difference between Elia and Lamb.

The supplementary space between Lamb and Elia is most visible in the announcements of Elia's death, begun in the January 1823 *London Magazine*. Proclaimed by Lamb in the "Character of the Late Elia, by a Friend" already cited, it was introduced at the front of the issue in The Lion's Head, the editor's column begun by John Scott and carried on after Scott's death by Thomas Hood:

> Elia is dead – at least so a *Friend* says; but if he be dead, we have seen him in one of those hours "when he is wont to walk;" and his *ghostship* has promised us very *material* assistance in our future Numbers [3].

Elia's ghost, Hood continues, "must still write for its peace of mind," and "the first paper in our present Number is one of its *grave* consolations" (4). That essay duly appeared over the signature "Elia's ghost;" figuring himself as Elia's ghost, Lamb located his text yet further from historical actuality.

The next issue of the *London Magazine*, February 1823, extended the joke and Lamb's deliberately indeterminate "posthumous" existence. The Lion's Head advised that:

> the Author of the Essays of Elia has promised A SERIES OF CRITICAL AND MISCELLANEOUS PAPERS, the first of which will appear in our next number. This intelligence will raise the spirits of Leila, who, since the death of Elia, has written a most feeling letter to his "Shade," from the shades below [123].

In January "Janus Weathercock" had pronounced a eulogy upon Elia (51–2); now Bernard Barton witnessed Elia's passing with a valedictory sonnet (194).[16] Another sketch reveals the serious grounds of this equivocation. "The Literary Police Office, Bow Street" stages a scene, modeled upon the Police Reports found in other publications, in which various writers are hailed before the magistrates and charged as public offenders.[17] Wordsworth, the first, is accused of stealing a pony from Betty Foy, but dismissed on the excuse that "he was *beside himself*" (158); Coleridge is accused of idling, and committed to two months' hard labor at the Muses' Treadmill; Tom Moore undergoes "a long examination for picking the pocket of the public of nine shillings, in Paternoster Row, under the pretence of selling a book." "But as it was proved that there were five partners concerned in this transaction [the firm of Longman, which had recently published Moore's *Loves of the Angels*], and that he was a mere instrument in their hands," he is acquitted (158).

This mixture of legally supported commerce and criminal responsibility perfectly defines the world in which the magazines operated. Lamb stands at the dock under suspicion of homicide:

> Charles Lamb was brought up, charged with the barbarous murder of the late Mr Elia. He was taken late in the evening, at a house of resort for characters of his description, in Fleet Street – and he had with him at the time of his caption a crape mask – a phosphorus (or hock) bottle – a dark lanthorn – a *skeleton* key – a centre bit (out of the haunch) – and a large clasp knife (and fork). The evidence was indisputable – and Mr Lamb was committed. There appears to have been no apparent motive for this horrible murder, unless the prisoner had an eye to poor Mr Elia's situation in the LONDON MAGAZINE. The prisoner is a large gaunt-looking fellow, with a queer eye, and a broad overhanging brow. If no witnesses had come forward – his looks would *have appeared against him*! [160]

Here the signs of the gustatory pleasures for which Lamb was long appreciated in the belletristic tradition – the hock bottle, the bit of the haunch, the clasp knife – are revealed as the tokens that impute a bodily reality to a figment; more precisely, the repeated pattern of a delayed increment (a large clasp knife … and fork) which converts a potentially incriminating meaning into the mark of an innocent appetite reveals that it is the sense of a real body that shields Lamb from the crimes of fraud and impersonation, the improprieties of unanchored writing.[18]

At the same time, the crime of murdering Elia is the mirror image of the dilemma the invention of him was designed to forestall. For if Lamb eludes the specter of mechanical article-production that troubles the author of "On Magazine Writers" by centering his work in a unique personality, a real person as authoring subject (as differentiated from an intriguing subjectivity) could not escape the disciplinary mechanisms the trial scene represents. As Lamb discovered to his cost when his "Confessions of a Drunkard" was taken as literal autobiography, an author of peculiar exterior and address, in Hazlitt's terms, would always find his looks appearing against him, in the terms of the sketch. The "glare of popularity" generated by the verisimilitude of his character solicited that regulation of art by the standards of ordinary life that Lamb protested in "On the Artificial Comedy of the Last Century," the situation in which "the measure of *poetical justice*," like that of political justice, is "the standard of *police*" (306; 287). By 1823 the Londoners had a frightful example, in the death of John Scott in a duel over a quarrel with *Blackwood's*, of the degree to which bodies could become the victims of the words of the magazine. If in "On Some of the Old Actors" Lamb praised a mode "which is the bane and death of tragedy," it was in part to stave off such consequences: to kill tragedy through Elia was to prevent becoming a ghost-writer in an all too literal sense. The rhetorical, deceptive figure of Elia is the sign of Lamb's efforts to resist this incorporation; if Lamb remained in the marketplace the journals fed, and subject to its tastes and rules, Elia was his recourse: "if I tread out of the way of thy sympathy, and am singularly-conceited only, I retire, impenetrable to ridicule, under the phantom-cloud of Elia" (6; 29).[19] The logic of the persona may be mapped in the historical circumstances of magazine writing in the 1820s, but the fraught but unspecifiable difference between Lamb and Elia is the productive element that prevents the reduction of the essays to their context. Elia escapes the critical police, or, as Hazlitt put it of Lamb: "He evades the present, he mocks the future" (346).[20]

NOTES

1. William Hazlitt, *The Spirit of the Age*, ed. Catherine Macdonald Maclean (London: Dent, 1967), 348. Hereafter cited parenthetically in the text.
2. Mark Parker, "Ideology and Editing: The Political Context of the Elia Essays," *Studies in Romanticism* 30 (1991), 473–94; revised as Ch.1 of Parker's *Literary Magazines and British Romanticism* (Cambridge: Cambridge University Press, 2000).
3. Mark Schoenfield, "Voices Together: Lamb, Hazlitt, and the *London*," *Studies in Romanticism* 29 (1990), 257–72.
4. James Treadwell, "Impersonation and Autobiography in Lamb's Christ's Hospital Essays," *Studies in Romanticism* 37 (1998), 499–521.
5. "P.", "On Magazine Writers," *London Magazine* 6/31 (July 1822), 21–7. "P." is identified as Peter G. Patmore by Frank P. Riga and Claude A. Prance, *Index to the London Magazine* (New York: Garland, 1978).
6. Charles Lamb, "Detached Thoughts on Books and Reading," *London Magazine* 6/31 (July 1822), 33–6. In the parenthetical references hereafter in the text I give first the page number of the magazine publication of Lamb's essays, from which I quote, and then, for the sake of convenience, a reference to *Elia and The Last Essays of Elia*, Vol.2 of *The Works of Charles and Mary Lamb*, ed. E.V. Lucas, 6 Vols. (1903; rpt. New York: AMS, 1968). "Detached Thoughts" runs from p.172 to p.177 in the Lucas edition. The epigraph is on p.33; p.172.
7. See Walter Benjamin, "Unpacking My Library," in *Illuminations*, ed. Hannah Arendt and trans. Harry Zohn (New York: Schocken, 1969), 59–67.
8. See Susan Stewart, *On Longing: Narratives of the Miniature, the Gigantic, the Souvenir, the Collection* (Baltimore, MD: Johns Hopkins University Press, 1984).

9. The unnamed "quaint poetess" was Mary Lamb, and the poem had been published in *Poetry for Children* (1809). Charles becomes Elia, but Mary here is not permitted even her usual pseudonym of Cousin Bridget. The preceding anecdote in which Elia recounts the mutual embarrassment of "having been once detected – by a familiar damsel – reclined at my ease upon the grass, on Primrose Hill (her Cythera), reading – *Pamela*" marks the limiting of the sexuality that hovers throughout the essay. On the "atypical merging of gender roles" (6) in the work of the Lambs, see Jane Aaron, *A Double Singleness* (Oxford: Clarendon Press, 1991).

10. [Charles Lamb], "Oxford in the Vacation," *London Magazine* 2/10 (Oct. 1820), 365–9; p.365; p.7.

11. Charles Lamb, letter to John Taylor, 30 June 1821, in *The Letters of Charles and Mary Lamb*, ed. E.V. Lucas, 3 Vols. (London: Dent, 1935), 2:302.

12. Charles Lamb, "A Character of the Late Elia, by a Friend," *London Magazine* 7 (Jan. 1823), 19–21. The piece reappears as the "Preface By a Friend of the Late Elia" to *The Last Essays of Elia* (Lucas, 151–3); p.20; p.151.

13. The going rate would appear to have been ten guineas a sheet; Lamb received 20. See Josephine Bauer, *The London Magazine* (Copenhagen: Rosenkilde and Bagger, 1953), *Anglistica* 1:68.

14. [Charles Lamb], "On Some of the Old Actors," *London Magazine* 5/26 (Feb. 1822), 174–9; Lucas, *The Last Essays of Elia*, 279–85; p.178; p.284.

15. [Charles Lamb], "On the Artificial Comedy of the Last Century," [I give the essay its familiar title], first published as "The Old Actors," *London Magazine* 5/28 (April 1822), 305–11; Lucas, *The Last Essays of Elia*, 285–94; p.305; p.286.

16. "Janus Weathercock" was the pseudonym of Thomas Griffiths Wainewright, another regular contributor; subsequently convicted of forgery while under suspicion of insurance fraud and poisoning, he was transported to Tasmania, where he died. De Quincey's essay "On Murder Considered as One of the Fine Arts" (*Blackwood's Magazine* [1827]) offers a further instance of the "crimes of writing," in Susan Stewart's phrase. See Susan Stewart, *Crimes of Writing: Problems in the Containment of Representation* (New York: Oxford University Press, 1991).

17. "The Literary Police Office, Bow Street," *London Magazine* 7 (Feb. 1823), 157–61. The skit was signed "Edward Herbert," the pseudonym of John Hamilton Reynolds.

18. Fred V. Randel studies the appetitive tropes in *The World of Elia* (Port Washington, NY: Kennikat Press, 1975).

19. [Charles Lamb], "New Year's Eve," *London Magazine* 3/13 (Jan. 1821), 5–8; Lucas, *The Last Essays of Elia*, 27–32; p.6; p.29.

20. In its publication in the *London Magazine* "Detached Thoughts" concludes with the words "To be continued" (p.36), which it wasn't: a final sly indication of Lamb's evasion of consequence and determination?

The New Monthly Magazine *and the Liberalism of the 1820s*

NANORA SWEET

> The great merit of the publication is that it does not meddle in politics; but – it is too decidedly a Tory work, the editor is a reputed Whig, and half the contributors downright Radicals.[1]

Thus an 1823 "Letter to the Editor," probably an "in-house" plant, "outed" the politics of the purportedly apolitical *New Monthly Magazine*. In 1821 its editor Thomas Campbell had introduced his first issues by saying that the journal would be "literary, not political," "a calm spot in the world of periodical literature ... without the asperities of party feeling."[2] Yet in the years leading up to 1821, to edit a "literary" periodical was to risk partisan "asperity," with *Blackwood's Edinburgh Magazine* serving as Tory attack dog against the upstart "Cockney School" and the *Quarterly Review* taking on the blasphemous "Satanic School." A "new era of magazines" began in the late 1810s with the growth of middle-class readership, but a monthly came to the fore very much at its peril.[3] John Scott, editor of the *London Magazine*, the most literary of the monthlies, died in a duel with a *Blackwood's* supporter just weeks after Campbell assumed the editorship of the *New Monthly*.[4] Scott's death would mean literary and commercial losses for the *London*, whose most talented and popular writers (Hazlitt, Lamb, Horace Smith, Barry Cornwall) left one by one for the *New Monthly*. By the mid-1820s the *New Monthly Magazine* reached a circulation of 5,000, easily surpassing the *London*'s 1,700 and competing well with *Blackwood's'* 3,000–8,000: it had become "the leading magazine published in London."[5]

The *New Monthly Magazine* found success, not by avoiding politics, but by adapting its politics to the liberal coalition-building that replaced strict partisanship in the 1820s. Overt partisanship could not further political goals in a decade at odds over corn laws, Catholic emancipation, and electoral reform. Solutions lay in accommodation, and by the mid-1820s a coalition of Whigs and moderate Tories under George Canning had begun to meet demands for freer trade and constitutional reform.[6] Literary success too lay beyond the oppositions of the late 1810s, when the now perishing generations of "Cockney" and "Satanic" poets gave journalists their punching bags. In the 1820s, literary success lay in the new poetry of Felicia

Hemans, Letitia Landon, and Elizabeth Barrett; the prose of Lady Morgan, Mary Russell Mitford, Mary Shelley, the Countess of Blessington, and Edward Lytton Bulwer – all appearing in Henry Colburn's *New Monthly*; the books of Anna Jameson and Benjamin Disraeli published by Colburn's press. Essayists like Hunt, Hazlitt, and Lamb whose names elsewhere spelled affiliation with Cockney, Satanic, or Lake Schools also continued their careers profitably under the magazine's auspices. The *New Monthly* succeeded because it was a seat of literary culture suited to the 1820s: universalized in style, free of personalized controversy, and supportive of constitutional and institutional reform at home and abroad.

II

Owned by Henry Colburn from 1814 until 1845, the *New Monthly* strove to meet a changing political scene by being saleable enough to meet costs while advertising the popular books that were its publisher's main business.[7] The magazine's first series from 1814 to 1820 was a "King," "Country," and "God" effort intended to answer the liberal *Monthly Review* and coincide with postwar reaction.[8] A sober, double-columned product, this *New Monthly* was soon outgunned by *Blackwood's*. Despite late efforts like the publication of Polidori's "The Vampyre; a Tale by Lord Byron," circulation lagged, and Colburn sought a change.[9] To edit the *New Monthly*'s New Series from 1821, Colburn chose Thomas Campbell, a well-connected Whig poet known for his reluctance to be controversial. By 1831, with *Fraser's Magazine* offering fresh competition from the Tory side, Edward Lytton Bulwer was made editor of the *New Monthly* and permitted to promote electoral reform overtly in all sections of the magazine. When circulation dropped, Bulwer was let go, and a magazine emphasizing humor followed under Theodore Hook and Thomas Hood until Colburn sold out in 1845. The first ten years of the magazine's New Series, 1821 to 1831 under Campbell, have attracted the lion's share of critical attention given the *New Monthly*, and they will do so here.[10]

In an era when Whigs were on the defensive and the wise editor remained anonymous, Colburn publicized Campbell's appointment and high salary of £500. Colburn's stroke was less counterintuitive than it seemed, for Campbell's identity as author of the innocuous-sounding *The Pleasures of Hope* gave gallant coverture to contributors and readers alike. Colburn also hired the energetic Cyrus Redding, previously editor of *Galignani's Messenger*, as sub-editor and compiler of the magazine's Register sections. Politically restive, Redding regretted that Colburn's caution and Campbell's timidity prevented the magazine from making an explicit "promulgation of those great public truths which time has successively developed," presumably as the fruits of reform.[11] While Colburn would be a constant in the magazine's life from 1814 to 1845, this study highlights what was distinctive about the *New Monthly* of the 1820s, namely, its conduct by the gun-shy liberal Campbell and the would-be reformer Redding.[12] First examining the New Series's format, content, and political context, this essay also considers the *New Monthly* of the 1820s as an institution in a time of institutional change, finally arguing that beneath its self-description as a "calm spot," it was the dialectical product (Tory, Whig, Radical) of its three individual coadjutors and their collective projects and paradoxes.

The magazine's format changed in 1821 in ways that seemed to divide literary from political content. It reached out to readers with single-columned pages for "Original Papers" – columns, essays, reviews, poems – and devoted a separate "Historical Register" section to reports on politics, commerce, and the arts. The Register section remained double-columned and formed a separate third volume in the yearly reissue. The resulting division between the magazine's literary and topical contents was more apparent than real, however, for the political and controversial topics of the Register also informed the Original Papers (as examples, the career of Canning, the progress of republicanism in South America and southern Europe, and Catholic emancipation).[13]

Redding and his liberal politics forged a further link between politics and literature in the *New Monthly*. Besides compiling the Register and writing several of its sections – starting with the crucial "Political Events" that headed the Register – Redding was a major contributor to the Original Papers, claiming 160 articles and in addition numerous poems.[14] The mostly anonymous Original Papers were not sorted into sub-categories; its lectures, ongoing series, various articles serious and light, reviews, and poems formed a stream of variable contents. In this context the literary controversies of the late 1810s lost their sting, and ongoing political controversy took place in the context, and often in the guise of, humor and fiction. Notable examples of the latter were "Sketches of the Irish Bar" that promoted Catholic emancipation and Irish home rule, and "Jonathan Kentucky's Journal," a critique of English life from an American viewpoint offering liberal commentary on matters from flogging to George IV's coronation.

At its height in the 1820s, the *New Monthly* was as multifaceted as the term *magazine* implies. Its stable of writers included male essayists; popular women writers; continental correspondents and émigrés; and Irish, American, and other topical correspondents, including abolitionists. Its editors and in-house factotums contributed often. Among London-based writers, the essayists William Hazlitt, Charles Lamb, and Leigh Hunt made 91 contributions altogether, and producers of lighter fare (Horace Smith, James Smith, John Poole) were even more prolific. Most of these London essayists and humorists had been pirated from the *London Magazine*. Never

named in the *New Monthly*'s tables of contents, they offer fewer clues to its
distinctiveness in the 1820s than the female and foreign writers recruited by
Campbell and Redding. Among students of the *New Monthly* of 1821–30,
Linda Jones has analyzed the topic in the most depth and detail: when she
selects the writers whose names drew the most readers, she lists an offshore
writer, Lady Morgan; a London writer, Charles Lamb; and a woman from
the western provinces, Felicia Hemans.[15] Contributions to the *New Monthly*
were rarely attributed in its table of contents (exceptions are authors in
translation and established figures appearing the odd time: Joanna Baillie,
Ann Radcliffe, Lord Byron, John Clare, William Wordsworth). In some
years, Campbell was the only author named. In the later 1820s, the only
writers named alongside Campbell were women.

Women writers from throughout the British Isles made significant
contributions to the *New Monthly*, especially Morgan, Hemans, Elizabeth
Barrett, Mary Russell Mitford, and Letitia Landon, with Eliza Walker a
humor contributor.[16] Campbell readily drew women contributors and
particularly admired Hemans' work: 107 poems attributed to her appear in
the *New Monthly* between 1823 and 1830, including "Greek Songs," "Songs
of the Cid," and most of the "Records of Woman" series.[17] Hemans
frequently depicted scenes of unrest in lands where resistance movements
were a contemporary reality, and Morgan's presence ensured that Ireland's
volatile politics would be a presence in the *New Monthly*. According to John
Sutherland, Lady Morgan was given *carte blanche* at the magazine, for her
1817 book *France* had "made" Colburn as a book publisher.[18]

Morgan's "The Last Night of the Last Year: Ireland As It Is" combines
novelistic devices and editorial warnings to convey Ireland's response to
Catholic emancipation.[19] Its 1829 New Year's Eve in Ireland is a ringing out
of religious disabilities by all who, whatever their religion, join in Ireland's
noted sociability because their "happiness is dependent upon the general
happiness of the community." She paints a scene at Dublin Castle where
"leading families, of all sects and all parties" celebrate 1829 as "the happiest
year which Ireland had yet to record" and contrasts this ball with the one just
preceding, when the ruling class bade a fearful farewell to a governor known
for moderation toward Catholics. Noting that discontent and apprehension
were still at work in the land, she lays bare their causes with the sympathetic
attention of a novelist imagining the motives of her characters.

Émigrés, foreign correspondents, and offshore dissidents like Lady
Morgan formed an influential group of contributors in their own right
through the 1820s, with Campbell and Redding directly recruiting those from
the Continent.[20] Stendhal contributed regularly from 1824 to 1829 ("Letters
from Rome," "Sketches from Paris"). Continental contributors describable as
dissidents or émigrés include Ugo Foscolo, Giuseppe Peccio, Manuel

Eduardo de Gorostiza, Joseph Blanco White, and J.-C.-L. Sismondi, while liberal-minded correspondents wrote from and about Central and South America, the Near East, and Africa.[21] Writers on North America such as John Galt and Henry Matthews form a small group buttressed by American controversies elsewhere in the magazine.[22] Irish spokespeople besides the Morgans were John Baynim, and Richard Lalor Sheil and William Henry Curran whose "Sketches from the Irish Bar" ran from 1822 to 1829. The controversial politics of these "Sketches" cannot be overestimated, with Sheil "a popular orator" (who appeared with Cobbett and Henry "Orator" Hunt) and "a leader of the Catholic Association," the "State within the State" at the center of Irish and Catholic emancipation controversy in the mid-1820s.[23] Thomas Pringle sustained a series of "Letters from South Africa" expressing his anti-slavery views. With its polemics cast in poetry and fictive prose from beyond Great Britain, the *New Monthly* was inextricably "literary" *and* "political," a testing ground for liberal interests like constitutionalism, Catholic emancipation, and abolitionism.

The *New Monthly*'s politics mirror those of the reform era itself, and these cut across party lines in pursuit of a new liberalism: when Redding said that he kept his "Political Events" section of the Register free from "all party spirit," strictly speaking he was quite correct.[24] The liberalism of the 1820s was not Tory, though it was furthered by the Tory minister Canning; it was not Whig in the traditional "great families" sense, though it was supported by Foxites like Lord Holland. It was not doctrinaire, not quite republican, not especially French; it was foreign-born yet natively British.[25] Its rallying point was Spain's Constitution of 1812, whose weak monarchy and responsible legislature are traceable to the enlightened constitutionalism that Britain's Whig Holland House brought to Spain in 1808.[26] Invoked by Spain's *liberales* between 1820 and 1823, the Constitution informed Italy's revolts during 1820 and coincided with the Greek War of Independence.[27] The new liberalism provided a rationale for a British government seeking to distance itself from the Holy Alliance while sponsoring constitutional governments in new spheres of influence. It also stiffened the resolve of George IV's ministers against his exercise of royal prerogative.[28] With interests in trade and constitutionalism, the new liberalism resembled the radicalism of Ricardo and Bentham without its high rationalism. The reform movement of the 1820s was more than a prelude to the Great Bill of 1832. Guided by the new liberalism, reform was a process that included steps toward free trade, the repeal of the Combination Laws in 1824, the repeal of the Test and Corporation Acts in 1828, Catholic emancipation in 1829, electoral reform in 1832, the abolition of slavery in 1833, and the Municipal Reform Act of 1835.

The *New Monthly* engaged nearly all of these topics and the political and intellectual factions behind them. Poet Campbell labored over political economy for the magazine (Redding reports him pondering Godwin and Malthus and procuring an article by Francis Place for the New Series's second issue).[29] Whig Holland House was Campbell's conduit for émigré writers, but Tory leader Canning courted the *New Monthly* as an important organ for the "public opinion" that he would use to govern over the heads of "ultra-Tory" obstructionists.[30] Canning failed the liberal litmus test in 1823 – his government did not intervene when Bourbon France entered Spain to topple the *liberales* – but by way of redress he recognized the independence of Spain's former American colonies, declaring them off-limits to continental powers.[31] Under the cloak of the *New Monthly*'s anonymity and in the semi-privacy of their table-talk, Redding and Campbell welcomed Canning's (and soon Peel's) apostasies from Toryism by which new republics were recognized and Catholic emancipation achieved.[32]

Students of the early nineteenth-century periodical press in Britain have tended to regard the *New Monthly* as a merely commercial, "fashionable" product.[33] They have looked elsewhere for politics and literature – in the obviously polemical *Blackwood's*, or the proto-canonical *London* which introduced Lamb's "Elia" and De Quincey's "Confessions" to the world.[34] For these students, the foreign interests that fill the *New Monthly* must seem fashionable travel writing, but clearly the magazine's poetry and prose from the Mediterranean and the New World is topical and programmatic. Poems like the anonymous "The Genius of Spain" and Hemans' "Greek Song: The Bowl of Liberty" are typical of the *New Monthly* in this vein.

In "The Genius of Spain" (1823), a "recreant France" in (un)holy alliance with "Croats and Muscovites" is invading Spain. Unless England stands firm, Bourbon rule and the Inquisition will be reimposed (and they were). Hemans' "The Bowl of Liberty" (1823) alludes to the ongoing Greek War of Independence. It invokes the pledge of freedom by the ancient Plataeans, perennial subjects of Thebes, and ends with the question, "When shall *we* crown the Bowl of Liberty?" (emphasis original). Read among the magazine's numerous pieces by Italian, Spanish, Greek, and Latin American revolutionaries, Hemans' poem must apply to modern as well as ancient Greece; and its "*we*" could well intimate a Britain still hesitant to reform its own constitution. More confidently, "To Greece" (by "A.S.") favorably compares modern Greek patriots with ancient Greek warriors. Again, in 1825 "To Spain" (by "J.") compares "suffering Spain" to the free nations of South America and urges Spain to regain its former strength and independence.[35]

The *New Monthly*'s prose contributors also use other times and places to address current issues. The series' first issue printed Ugo Foscolo's "An Account of the Revolution of Naples during the years 1798, 1799," a depiction critical of Nelson's command and relevant to Naples's short-lived republic of 1820–21: "The present state of commotion at Naples invites us to extract from a manuscript historical work the following narrative ..." reads the headnote.[36] In January 1823, an anonymous "Sketch of the Political Career of Simon Bolivar" ends with the recommendation "that England recognize the free states of South America," the very step taken by Canning in October of that year.[37] John Carne's "Letters from the East" (No.II, June 1824) laments the wretched conditions of the Greeks in Constantinople, a commentary clearly related to debate over whether the Greek independence movement should set its sights on the Turkish capital. Also in June 1824, the anonymous "Secrets of the Modern Spanish Inquisition" compares the state of modern Spain under Ferdinand VII to the sixteenth-century Inquisition. Further examples abound.

The *New Monthly*'s most striking use of distant time or place to address current European politics may be the anonymous "Appeal from the Old World to the New World" (August 1825), which uses evidence of enlightened civilization in Van Diemen's Land and Tahiti as a beacon for a Europe laboring under the Holy Alliance:

> if we take a more enlarged view of the globe, and reflect that nearly the whole South American continent is starting upon a new career of improvement, under the powerful stimulus of free institutions, that the extensive regions of New South Wales, the island of Madagascar, and all those with which the Southern Ocean is studded, are following the progress of knowledge and civilization, we may be well assured that the Holy Alliance, though they may have darkened their own domains, have not prevented the sun from shining upon others; and when we feel any desponding apprehensions for the cause of human nature, on account of certain benighted portions of Europe, we may pleasantly dispel them by looking out beyond our own immediate horizon, and console ourselves for the fate of the Old World by appealing to the New.[38]

This passage takes its ironic point that Europe's (and Britain's) acquiescence to the Holy Alliance enforces an "enlarged view" of the world in response. In that view, it is the new nations and regions of the "Southern Ocean" – from Venezuela to Madagascar to Tasmania (Van Diemen's Land) – that exemplify "the progress of knowledge and civilization" for the rest of the world, most especially a Europe "benighted" by old regimes. The "Appeal" ends with an echo of Canning's noted speech of 12 December 1826, "I called the New World into existence to redress the balance of the Old." The obituary for Canning that Redding authored for the *New Monthly* in 1827 also echoes Canning's appeal, suggesting that Redding may have authored "An Appeal," which also bears his table-turning, anti-authoritarian stamp.[39]

The *New Monthly* was both literary and political – insistently so; it simply avoided an overt partisanship in either domain that would in any case be self-defeating in an era of accommodation between parties (or, as some thought, apostasy from them). Commercial success lay elsewhere, among middle-class and women readers who bought the periodical and the books advertised there or otherwise paid to read both in circulating libraries. Literary success lay elsewhere, in a broader, suppler, but still political program already at work in salons, extramural lectures, provincial and female poetries, and émigré literatures.

III

> All topics became blended, known, and discussed. The domain of knowledge was unenclosed, – thrown into a common, and now the tripping step of the fair may as well stray over it as the dull plod of the university professor.[40]

While transacting the changing politics of the 1820s, the *New Monthly Magazine* also modeled its changing cultural institutions. In an anonymous article of 1821 entitled "Blues and Anti-Blues," the contributor, probably the magazine's sub-editor Redding, describes a setting very like the *New Monthly*: "unenclosed" from the landed establishment with its church and universities, catering to women and middle-class readers, a "common" where "all topics become blended, known, and discussed."[41] In a sly allusion to the culture wars of the 1810s, Redding calls himself "Y." as against the "Z." (John Gibson Lockhart) of *Blackwood's* who tried to preserve literature from the "Cockney" poets. Redding's bluestocking "domain of knowledge" is the site of adult education, which in the *New Monthly* begins with an introduction to ancient and foreign literatures. Nine of the magazine's first 17 issues under Campbell open with his "Lectures" on Greek and Hebrew literature, originally delivered to mixed-gender audiences at London's Royal Institution and then similar audiences in the provinces. Italian, Spanish, and German literature and history are soon introduced to *New Monthly* readers by Foscolo and others. Among Campbell's further contributions to the magazine are his "Suggestions" for a new institution of higher learning, a secular University of London. As Redding reports, the first organizational meeting for this successful middle-class project was attended by women as well as men.[42]

The *New Monthly*'s commercial "domain" was as unbounded as its educational one, both illustrating the uncharted waters of middle-class enterprise. As John Sutherland observes, Colburn's seamless or "blended" combination of circulating library, trade publishing, and magazine ownership resembles today's "synergistic patterns of publishing."[43] Jon Klancher extends this point, saying that the magazine "represented itself as an institution blending writer, editor, and publisher in what could only appear to be an essentially authorless text."[44] As the reform era's hard-won coalition politics suggest, however, that smooth exterior – Campbell's "calm spot in the world of periodical literature" – was something of an illusion. All apparent efforts at disinterest and anonymity notwithstanding, the *New Monthly* was no more "authorless" than it was apolitical. Its great success in the 1820s was managed precisely "by a name," as Redding explains of Campbell's appointment.[45] This is not to say that it was managed with a "personality" but rather with the "name" of a real figure with a known curriculum vitae.

It is instructive to compare the *New Monthly*'s use of anonymity behind Campbell's "name" with the anonymity or "chameleonic" pseudonymity that Margaret Russett has theorized for *Blackwood's* and the *London*.[46] In Russett's analysis, the pseudonyms of *Blackwood's* produced "personality," which the magazine then used to discipline certain of its readers and even contributors as upstart Cockneys and bumpkins out of their depth; and the *London* used pseudonymity to produce reflections on authorship sufficient to an aura if not a reality of gentlemanly authorship. In each case, anonymity or pseudonymity expressed, or better *managed*, a collective anxiety about downward literary mobility. In contrast, *New Monthly* writers seldom cast themselves as gentlefolk lowering themselves to contribute or even as upwardly-mobile individuals jockeying for a space made narrow by ideas of gentility. The *New Monthly* proposed instead to open "knowledge" to the many and to broaden knowledge itself.[47] The *New Monthly* used Campbell's "name" and otherwise a general anonymity to cover the emergence of the middle-class writer and the more profoundly unenfranchised female and émigré writer: this anonymity was punctuated with Campbell's gallant presentation of literary relics like Ann Radcliffe or plucky women writers like Morgan and Hemans. With Redding's help, this cover was quickly converted to an open invitation to "stray" over "commons" that were in truth neither Campbell's nor his coadjutor's to unenclose.[48]

Redding's anonymity is interesting in its own ways. It presents the insertions of an editor as those of a contributor; it distances what are often political contributions from the magazine's supposedly apolitical editorship; it maintains the fiction that the Historical Register's political reporting is separate from the more literary Original Papers. In these ways and more, the cross-purposes of a Tory-associated publisher, a liberal editor, and a yet more liberal sub-editor were, like the magazine's public, "managed by a name." Under this cover the *New Monthly Magazine* 1821–30 was not a seamless institution but the work of three particular men with three particular curricula vitae. It bears the marks of their individual projects and the politics informing them, and those particularities form the subject of the balance of this essay.

IV

Each of the magazine's coadjutors, Colburn, Campbell, and Redding, brought paradoxes ample to disturb a "calm" surface: the publisher of "silver fork" novels known for his crudity, the non-controversial poet with incendiary ways, the anonymous sub-editor whose memoirs promoted self through a barrage of other people's names. Henry Colburn's politics and even his paternity have eluded biographers. According to Gregg Johnson, Colburn displayed "extreme Tory sympathies;" according to John Sutherland, "his politics were generally Liberal;" in any case, he answered to conservative associates.[49] Sutherland further reports that Colburn was rumored to be illegitimate, perhaps a royal's natural son; he was also childless; for him there was no dynasty building *à la* John Murray. Colburn stood apart from establishment culture, living for business in the moment. Certainly his "puffing" and other publicizing raised eyebrows and angered his editors (he owned part or all of three other magazines as well). His terms with authors were generous – *New Monthly* contributors often got 20 guineas a sheet, occasionally much more. Luring authors, he cheated them too and was labeled, as John Sutherland reports, "a publishing bawd." Furthering the slide of Colburn's reputation from the illegitimate to the prostituted to the feminized, Sutherland also describes him as once bringing a "negative dowry" into a partnership.[50]

Colburn operated, then, as though under a feminized bar-sinister, prostituting himself and his editors. He needed Campbell's coverture more than any other party to the project. Among the most interesting commentators on Colburn is Janet Courtney, who calls the 1830s an "adventurous ... chapter in the women's movement" and gives Colburn a major role in that chapter, along with *salonnières* like Lady Holland and the Countess of Blessington (who gained their pre-Victorian salons by adultery or courtesanship).[51] How successful was Colburn with the *New Monthly*? At the good price of three shillings sixpence and strong circulation, he earned well: Jones gives £1,800 as his profit in 1826. Yet printing debts, that "negative dowry," drove him into forced partnership in 1829 – from which he emerged the gainer. The *New Monthly* was a necessary business expense for Colburn, to be recouped by a profitable business marriage and divorce.[52]

What were Thomas Campbell's motives at the *New Monthly* and what did he bring worth £500 a year? His motives seem to have been to earn handsomely while remaining in a wide circle of Whig associates and pursuing projects like the University of London and a Polish Association. Campbell's qualifications to edit and his achievements on the *New Monthly* have been as elusive as Colburn's origins and politics. His dilatoriness and abstraction, desultory studies and unfulfilled promise, make him seem a Whig Coleridge – as do his mildly erotic romances, lectures at the Royal Institution, Germanism, and reputation for plagiarism. Like Coleridge, he also accomplished rather more in the way of prose works (history, biography, criticism) and oft-repeated poetry than his critics care to remember. At times, Campbell seemed to contribute to the magazine only his reluctance to contribute – but, after all, he was there to "manage the public" with his "name."

How did this work? The answer lies in Campbell's contacts, his poetry, and his ability to rouse and then evade controversy. Campbell brought contacts in virtually every Whig circle and several Tory ones.[53] He remained in close correspondence with Scottish Enlightenment circles at Edinburgh, specifically the Archibald Alisons and the Dugald Stewarts. He collaborated with Walter Scott over war poetry and a projected anthology of English poetry. He met the Joseph Johnson circle in London and lived to attend the celebrated anti-slavery convention there in 1840. He associated with the Currie-Roscoe group in Liverpool, retaining young Henry Roscoe as a staff writer. He was welcome at Holland House, where he met Byron, discussed Virgil with Charles James Fox, and enlisted Foscolo and Blanco White for the magazine. He became a friend of Princess Charlotte after her lady-in-waiting attended his 1812 Royal Institution lectures; he befriended Lady Byron. On Germaine de Staël's visit to London in 1813–14, he received her enraptured recitation from his *The Pleasures of Hope* and gave her a private performance from his lectures: among her close associates A.W. Schlegel became an intellectual sparring partner and Sismondi a contributor to his magazine. Campbell was sponsored by such leading Whigs as James Macintosh, Sydney Smith, and Henry Brougham; in 1806 he was put on the civil list for a pension of £200, lucrative over a long lifetime.

Part of Campbell's "name" was his poetry, his lifelong fame as author of *The Pleasures of Hope*, a catalog of Whiggish hopes in 1799 and veritable *magazine* of "the reigning topics of the day" from the French Revolution and African slavery to the partition of Poland.[54] This poem's long fame and equally long-deferred Whig hopes reinforced each other, ensuring that his "name" as poet and editor spelled Whig "hope." Reportedly, Campbell was often quoted by legislators, at least in the US House.[55] In the 27 poems he placed in the *New Monthly*, Campbell's "hope" can be iconographic as in "To a Rainbow," or metaphysical as in "The Last Man." It appears with greatest power, however, in his most topical poems, such as "Stanzas to the Memory of the Spanish Patriots." There, although "brave men" have fallen "Cursing the Bigot's and the Bourbon's chain," "Hope is not wither'd;" and "Long trains of ill may pass unheeded, dumb, / But vengeance is behind and justice is to come."[56]

Standing for Whig "hope," Campbell's "name" also stood for a reluctance to make political hope partisan and thus self-defeating. Campbell claimed, somewhat incredibly, that his £200 pension from the days of Fox made him politically "disinterested," but his fastidiousness accompanied a lifelong flirtation with high-stakes controversy.[57] He traveled to Edinburgh during its treason trials and to Germany during the French war. He returned home to be arrested, mistakenly, for high treason (collaboration with a United Irishman in Hamburg). He considered a professorship in Lithuania while consorting with Polish patriots. Finally, he ignited the most celebrated literary pamphlet war of the early nineteenth century, the Pope-Bowles controversy. Campbell's 1819 *Specimens of the British Poets* swiped at Bowles's long-dormant critique of Pope as a poet of art, not nature, and the war was on. Twenty-six books, pamphlets, and articles later, and Byron, Hazlitt, Roscoe, and lesser lights had had their say, with Campbell answering once and anonymously in the Register section of the *New Monthly*.[58] Campbell was only defending the removed, universalized style that allowed him to forward Whig visions while keeping out of harm's way. It is worth remembering that it was at the height of the Bowles controversy that Colburn recruited Campbell as purportedly a non-controversial name.

The anonymous sub-editor Cyrus Redding knew the value of "a name," a commodity sprinkled liberally through his memoirs of life in and around the *New Monthly Magazine*. Redding might have met Campbell in the occupied Paris of 1814, the poet gazing at the Apollo Belvedere in the Louvre by the side of Sarah Siddons, the journalist seeking relics of the Revolutionary and Napoleonic eras.[59] Redding edited *Galignani's Messenger* from 1815 to 1818 and corresponded for the *Examiner*. With poems, translations, contacts, and a new cosmopolitanism in hand, this son of Devon returned to a "joy-killing" London and work on the *New Monthly Magazine* late in its first series.[60] Once Campbell was on board, Redding began his ten years of continuous work as sub-editor. His position under the inattentive Campbell and the magazine's policy of anonymity allowed him to contribute much prose and poetry that intimated his "Liberal" views, except when checked by the savvy Colburn or the squeamish Campbell.[61]

Redding and Campbell agreed on literary and liberal politics and the value of "classicism" as a bulwark against provincial, politically regressive writing. Just as Campbell stood against the Lake School in the Bowles controversy, Redding faulted the Cockney School for its "habit of dwelling on trifles and holding circumscribed views of things."[62] Redding's "Spes Rediviva, or Lines on the Death of Alexander" barely cloaks its liberalism in a Latin title and Shakespearean stanza. This February 1826 poem registers the death of the Czar and ideological architect of the Holy Alliance, and it challenges England:

> […] though your state
> And law may loaded be,
> With evils that deteriorate
> Your chart of liberty, […]
> Go, place the freedom that is yours

> By the 'slaved Russian's side,
> The Austrian serf's, the German boor's,
> Or Spain's, that suicide![63]

Redding's "spes rediviva" or "second-hand hope" affirms that Whig hope must now be reclaimed from abroad. His allusions play to the keenest ears on the government's bench, those of George Canning, who in the spring of 1826 was engineering an alliance with France and Russia and sending an allied fleet to counter Turkey's taking of Athens from Greek insurgents. The Battle of Navarino was the result, celebrated by Campbell himself in the January 1828 issue.

Nothing illustrates the unvarnished politics of the *New Monthly* better than the signals passing between it and Canning, the decade's most spectacular politician, whose youthful fame rested in Tory literary exercises for the *Anti-Jacobin Review*. According to Redding, Campbell's "name" drew Canning to grant the magazine two exclusives in 1821, one an epitaph on his young son, the other a letter conveying his resignation from Lord Liverpool's government in protest over the treatment of Queen Caroline. Redding bitterly regretted his boss's unthinking instruction to publish the letter verbatim, which lost the government leader as a contributor.[64] When Redding authored the *New Monthly*'s obituary on this Tory premier beloved of liberals, he used the occasion to do what Colburn and Campbell ordinarily would not allow: use the *New Monthly* as a "great engine ... for guiding opinion or enforcing great truths."[65] Here the liberal platform spills out in epic terms:

> He had disconcerted the Holy Alliance; called a new world into existence; negotiated for the independence of Greece; maintained the honour of England with Portugal; heard his name re-echoed from remote shores; ... begun to apply the principles of philosophy to politics; ... and maturing plans for universal good ... died in the field, harnessed, and at the post of honour.[66]

That Canning, who ruled by way of "public opinion upon the ruins of the old parties," saw the *New Monthly Magazine* as a choice site for such rule speaks volumes to its role in the literature, politics, and commerce of the 1820s.[67]

NOTES

Thanks to Susan Todd for research assistance on the *New Monthly*.

1. "Letter to the Editor," *New Monthly Magazine* 7 n.s. (Jan. 1823), 4. *The Wellesley Index to Victorian Periodicals 1824–1900*, Vol.3, ed. Walter E. Houghton and Esther Rhoads Houghton (Toronto: University of Toronto Press, 1979) gives T.C. Morgan as probable author (182). Below, the magazine's name will be abbreviated *NMM*, with all citations being to its second series unless otherwise noted.
2. "T.C.," "Preface," *NMM* 1 (1821), v–vi. (Preface composed in December.)

3. Charles Payne Knight, *Passages of a Working Life During Half a Century* (London, 1864), 1:265, quoted in Linda Bunnell Jones, "The *New Monthly Magazine*, 1821 to 1830" (Ph.D. dissertation, University of Colorado, 1970), 13.

4. Campbell suspected that William Hazlitt urged Scott on to the duel: for sources of tension between Campbell and Hazlitt, see Cyrus Redding, *Fifty Years' Recollections, Literary and Personal*, 2nd Edn. (London: Skeet, 1858), 2:218, 269; and Redding, "Life and Reminiscences of Thomas Campbell," *NMM* 78 (1846), 427; and *NMM* 82 (1848), 173. Redding's "Reminiscences" appear in the *NMM* over three years, first as "Literary Reminiscences of Thomas Campbell" (months not cited in annual volumes); for detail see Jones, "The *New Monthly Magazine*," 172.

5. Quoting from Jones, "The *New Monthly Magazine*," 17–18: circulation was augmented by periodic second editions and pirated copies in America.

6. A detailed account of these dilemmas and progress through them appears in Elie Halévy's *The Liberal Awakening (1815–1830)*, Vol.2 of *A History of the English People in the Nineteenth Century*, trans. E.J. Watkin ([1923] New York: Barnes, 1961), 80–259.

7. Standard sources on the *New Monthly* are Alvin Sullivan, *British Literary Magazines: The Romantic Age, 1789–1836* (Westport, CT: Greenwood Press, 1983), 331–9; and Houghton and Houghton, *Wellesley Index*, 3:161–302, and see xiv–xv. Jones's dissertation on the *NMM* 1822–30 is indispensable ("The *New Monthly Magazine*").

8. Preface to Vol.4, *New Monthly Magazine and Universal Register* 4 (1815), iii.

9. *NMM* 11 (April 1819), 195–206.

10. See Jon P. Klancher, *The Making of English Reading Audiences, 1790–1832* (Madison, WI: University of Wisconsin Press, 1987), 62–8; Marilyn Butler, "Culture's Medium: The Role of the Review," in *The Cambridge Companion to British Romanticism*, ed. Stuart Curran (Cambridge: Cambridge University Press, 1993), 131, 143–5; Mark Parker, *Literary Magazines and British Romanticism* (Cambridge: Cambridge University Press, 2000), Ch.4 (135–56); and Diego Saglia, "Hispanism in *The New Monthly Magazine*, 1821–1825," *Notes and Queries* 49 n.s. (March 2002), 49–56.

11. Cyrus Redding, "Life and Reminiscences of Thomas Campbell," *NMM* 79 (1847), 52.

12. Other students of the 1821–30 run have emphasized the magazine's business side and Colburn's impact there, muting the roles of Campbell and Redding as editors see Butler ("Culture's Medium," 143), Klancher (*The Making of English Reading Audiences*, 62), and Parker (*Literary Magazines*, 139).

13. As one example, Redding reports on Catholic emancipation in the June 1822 Register, and the August 1822 Original Papers begin the "Sketches of the Irish Bar" (5, 97–106).

14. See Jones, "The *New Monthly Magazine*," 90–93. In contrast to these findings, Parker takes the 1821–30 series' apparent division of literature and politics as an accomplished fact and a sort of aestheticized subjectivity as its reigning ethos (*Literary Magazines*, 137–40).

15. Jones, "The *New Monthly Magazine*," 98. In contrast, critics interested in large units of dominant discourse are inclined to see London writers as most typical of the *New Monthly*. In keeping with their interest in Bourdieuan social semiotics of fashion, Klancher (*The Making of English Reading Audiences*) and Butler ("Culture's Medium") associate the *New Monthly* principally with these writers, and Parker's interest in a popularized "Romanticism" (theorized by Carl Schmitt as "subjective occasionalism") coincides with his interest in the bemused Horace Smith (Parker, *Literary Magazines*, 138–9).

16. Two items have been attributed to Mary Shelley (see Houghton and Houghton, *Wellesley Index*, 3:187, 213). Maria Jane Jewsbury contributed "Regulus before the Senate," *NMM* 14 (Oct. 1825), 342.

17. On Hemans and Campbell, see William Beattie, *Life and Letters of Thomas Campbell*, 3 Vols. (London: Moxon, 1847), 2:418 and 3:60; Cyrus Redding, "Life and Reminiscences of Thomas Campbell," *NMM* 79 (1847), 246. In "Felicia Dorothea Hemans, née Browne," I supplement Jones' attributions to Hemans: Nanora Sweet, "Felicia Dorothea Hemans, née Browne," in *Cambridge Bibliography of English Literature*, ed. Joanne Shattock, 3rd Edn., Vol.4 (Cambridge: Cambridge University Press, 2000), 356–7.

18. On Colburn (principally as a book publisher), see John Sutherland, "Henry Colburn, Publisher," *Publishing History* 19 (1986), 59–84.

19. Lady Morgan's Ireland articles appeared in the *New Monthly* as follows: "Absenteeism," *NMM* 10 (June 1824), 481–95, and *NMM* 11 (Aug. 1824), 162–76; "Old Dublin," *NMM* 14 (July 1825), 57–67; "Irish Lords Lieutenant," *NMM* 25 (Feb. 1829), 105–17; "The Last Night of the Last Year: Ireland As It Is," *NMM* 28 (March 1830), 105–13. Quotations below are from p.106 of "Last Night."

20. Memoirs about Campbell and by Redding abound in references to these contacts; a focused note is Mary Ruth Miller's "Thomas Campbell and General Pepé," *Notes and Queries* 45 n.s. (June 1998), 211–14.

21. Saglia's study of "hispanism" in the *New Monthly* yields 53 items between 1821 and 1825 ("Hispanism in *The New Monthly Magazine*").

22. See Thomas Campbell's "Preface," *NMM* 1 (Jan. 1821), vi–xii; and his "Letter to the Mohawk Chief Ahyonwaeghs," *NMM* 4 (Feb. 1822), 97–101.

23. Jones, "The *New Monthly Magazine*," 145; Halévy, *Liberal Awakening*, 222.

24. Cyrus Redding, "Life and Reminiscences of Thomas Campbell," *NMM* 78 (1846), 431.

25. Study of this liberalism begins with Halévy (see his tracing of the term to the *liberales* of Spain: *Liberal Awakening*, 81–2, n.8). See Marilyn Butler, *Romantics, Rebels, and Reactionaries, 1815–1845* (Oxford: Oxford University Press, 1981), 113–37, and Peter L. Thorslev, Jr., "Post-Waterloo Liberalism: The Second Generation," *Studies in Romanticism* 28 (1989), 437–61.

26. See Martin Murphy, *Blanco White: Self-Banished Spaniard* (New Haven, CT: Yale University Press, 1989), 52, 72–4.

27. Halévy, *Liberal Awakening*, 81. According to Peter Thorslev, this constitution inspired the Hunt-Byron journal of those years, the *Liberal* ("Post-Waterloo Liberalism," 444).

28. See Halévy on George's challenges to parliamentary order and responsibility (*Liberal Awakening*, 84–100, 182–4).

29. Francis Place, "On the Theories of Malthus and Godwin," *NMM* 1 (Feb. 1821), 195–205. See Redding, "Literary Reminiscences of Thomas Campbell," *NMM* 78 (1846), 428.

30. On Canning's governing by "public opinion," see Halévy (*Liberal Awakening*, 182, 188) and Arthur Aspinall, *Politics and the Press, c.1780–1850* (London: Hom and Van Thal, 1949), 326.

31. See Halévy on this episode, *Liberal Awakening*, 163–91. For trade and politics triangulated among Britain, Spain, and Spanish America and its literary analogues in Blanco White and Hemans, see my "'Hitherto closed to British enterprise':" Trading and Writing the Hispanic World circa 1815," *European Romantic Review* 8/2 (Spring 1997), 139–47.

32. Redding, "Life and Reminiscences of Thomas Campbell," *NMM* 83 (1848), 41.

33. See Klancher, *The Making of English Reading Audiences*, 62–8, and, following him, Butler, who terms the magazine from 1814 "middlebrow" (131) and "resolutely middle-class," a periodical that "seemed to exist to catch 'fashion as it flies'," "Culture's Medium," (143).

34. On the *London Magazine*'s incipient yet complicated relationship with "the essentialist canon," see Margaret Russett, *De Quincey's Romanticism: Canonical Minority and the Forms of Transmission* (Cambridge: Cambridge University Press, 1997), 134.

35. [Anon.], "The Genius of Spain," *NMM* 5 (Jan. 1823), 78; Felicia Hemans, "Greek Song: The Bowl of Liberty," *NMM* 5 (April 1823), 337. Further examples of the *NMM*'s topical, liberationist verse are Thomas Campbell's "Spanish Patriots' Song," *NMM* 7 (June 1823), 491, and "Stanzas to the Memory of the Spanish Patriots," *NMM* 8 (Dec. 1823), 480; and Elizabeth Barrett's "Stanzas, Excited by some Reflections on the Present State of Greece," *NMM* 1 (May 1821), 523; examples are legion.

36. Ugo Foscolo, "An Account of the Revolution of Naples during the years 1798, 1799," *NMM* 1 (Jan. 1821), 33.

37. Foscolo, "An Account," *NMM* 1 (Jan. 1821), 33–64; [Anon.], "Sketch of the Political Career of Simon Bolivar," *NMM* 7 (Jan. 1823), 4–17. Further pieces appeared on Latin American countries, Guatemala 1825–26, Mexico 1827, 1829, Brazil 1829.

38. John Carne, "Letters from the East," *NMM* 10 (June 1824), 275–82; [Anon.], "Secrets of the Modern Spanish Inquisition," *NMM* 10 (June 1824), 522–6; [Anon.], "An Appeal from the Old World to the New World," *NMM* 14 (Aug. 1825), 163.

39. For more on Canning's speech, see Halévy, *Liberal Awakening*, 247. For its echo in Redding's obituary, see *NMM* 20 (Sept. 1827), 276.

40. "Y.," "Blues and Anti-Blues," *NMM* 2 (Aug. 1821), 223. Redding always contributed anonymously, often as "Y."

41. Redding's welcome might have countered Ugo Foscolo's article "Learned Ladies" (*NMM* 1 [Feb. 1821], 223–30) which rowed in another direction, critiquing the poor Italian of drawing-room lessons for women.

42. *NMM* 13 (Apr. 1825), 404–19; *NMM* 14 (July 1825), 1–11; Redding, *Fifty Years*, 2:322.

43. Sutherland, "Henry Colburn," 80.

44. Klancher, *The Making of English Reading Audiences*, 51.

45. Colburn "knew how the public were managed by a name." Redding, *Fifty Years*, 2:162.

46. Russett, *De Quincey's Romanticism*, 92–134.

47. Gregory Dart has written interestingly on Hazlitt's particular (and productive) struggles in this narrow space: "Romantic Cockneyism: Hazlitt and the Periodical Press," *Romanticism* 6/2 (2000), 143–62.

48. Yet Campbell's actions as Rector of Glasgow University showed his penchant for liberalizing academia: his student-friendliness made for a third term over the expected Tory victor, Sir Walter Scott, and he inserted his letters to the students in the *New Monthly*.

49. Gregg Johnson, "Henry Colburn (?–1855)," in *Encyclopedia of Romanticism: Culture in Britain, 1780s–1830s*, ed. Laura Dabundo *et al.* (New York: Garland, 1922), 100; Sutherland, "Henry Colburn," 65; Redding, *Fifty Years*, 2:223.

50. The phrase is Disraeli's: Sutherland, "Henry Colburn," 64, 59, 72.

51. Janet Courtney, *The Adventurous Thirties: A Chapter in the Women's Movement* ([1933] Freeport, NY: Books for Libraries, 1969), 6–14.

52. Jones, "The *New Monthly Magazine*," 30; Sutherland, "Henry Colburn," 72.

53. Beattie's three-volume *Life and Letters of Thomas Campbell* provides the fullest catalog of his activities, while Redding offers revealing detail (*Fifty Years*; "Life and Reminiscences") and Miller a scholarly condensation ("Thomas Campbell and General Pepé").

54. Beattie, *Life and Letters*, 1:253.

55. Ibid., 1:262. Campbell's rare twentieth-century critics also emphasize his political and war poetry: Edmund Blunden, "Campbell's Political Poetry," *English Review* 46 (June 1928), 703–6; Peter S. Macaulay, "Thomas Campbell: A Revaluation," *English Studies* 50 (1969), 39–46; Mary Ruth Miller, *Thomas Campbell* (Boston, MA: Twayne, 1978), 81–94.

56. Thomas Campbell poems: "To a Rainbow," *NMM* 1 (Jan. 1821), 16–17; "The Last Man," *NMM* 8 (Sept. 1823), 272; "Stanzas to the Memory of the Spanish Patriots," *NMM* 8 (Dec. 1823), 480. The rainbow iconography of Whig "hope" threads throughout Byron's *Childe Harold* (Jerome J. McGann, ed., *Byron* [Oxford: Oxford University Press, 1986], 145–206).

57. Beattie, *Life and Letters*, 2:201, 352, 425. Redding repeats that Campbell was "fastidious," as in *Fifty Years*, 2:162.

58. [Thomas Campbell], "A Letter to the Rev. W.L. Bowles," *NMM* 6 (March 1822), 122–4.

59. Redding, *Fifty Years*, 2:42–62, 98–100.

60. Ibid., 2:132.

61. As Redding comments frequently and ruefully, some of his phrases were "too liberal for some of the friends of the publisher." *Fifty Years*, 2:223.

62. Ibid., 2:176–7. For a consideration of Redding as such a Cockney himself, although dissatisfied, see Parker, *Literary Magazines*, 149–50.

63. [Cyrus Redding], "Spes Rediviva, or Lines on the Death of Alexander," *NMM* 16 (Feb. 1826), 143–4; claimed by Redding, *Fifty Years*, 2:355n.

64. George Canning, "Epitaph, George Charles Canning," *NMM* 1 (March 1821), 230; 278 quoted below. See Redding, "Literary Reminiscences," *NMM* 6 (1846), 431: "Campbell's forgetfulness … put an end" to Redding's expectation that "more might have been contributed by Canning." Redding indicates that the letter went "verbatim" into the magazine's first political register, but it does not appear in the (somewhat foul) opening pages of the annualized edition (*NMM* 1821, Vol.3).

65. Redding, *Fifty Years*, 171, 223.

66. Redding, *NMM* 20 (Sept. 1827), 276.

67. Halévy, *Liberal Awakening*, 18

Abstracts

Mary Robinson, the *Monthly Magazine*, and the Free Press *by Adriana Craciun*

Mary Robinson's essay on the "Present State of the Manners and Society of the Metropolis," published in the *Monthly Magazine* in 1800, is read as a significant statement on the status of print culture and the free press at the turn of the nineteenth century. Suggesting that Robinson's "Metropolis" essay may have been an catalyst for (or at the very least an counterargument to) Wordsworth's Preface to the *Lyrical Ballads*, this essay traces one possible genealogy of "Metropolis" and its influence through different periodicals, genres, and even authors (in its pirated versions). "Metropolis" is characteristic of Robinson's later prose works in its engagement with radical print culture and its championing of the free press, particularly in reformist periodicals like the *Monthly Magazine* and newspapers like the *Morning Post*.

Correcting Mrs Opie's Powers: The *Edinburgh* Review of Amelia Opie's *Poems* (1802) *by Andrea Bradley*

The critique of Amelia Opie's *Poems* (1802) in the inaugural issue of the *Edinburgh Review* (Oct. 1802) offers a model of the periodical's practices of reading women's poetry and enacts its strategies of creating not only the *Edinburgh* reader and reviewer, but also the *Edinburgh* author. The periodical's critique of genre in the Opie article genders not only the writer under review – demarcating the bounds of appropriate form, style, and sentiment – but also genders by implicit comparison both the reader of the periodical and the *Edinburgh* reviewer: masculine, Whig, and committed to the maintenance of corporate identity.

Novel Marriages, Romantic Labor, and the Quarterly Press *by Mark Schoenfield*

The major Romantic periodicals, the *Edinburgh* and *Quarterly* Reviews, hailed the novel of manners, a genre they identified with the major female novelists of their time, as a new realism of the ordinary. These novels, often richly heteroglossic like the periodicals that sought to tame them, also offered a critique of the ordinary and an insistence on the political and historical ramifications of the lives of women, particularly the (de)valuing of women's labor. The quarterly press, however, repressed such critiques by positioning both the narrative and characterization to naturalize the genre, its mode of "observation," and its telos of marriage. As is evident in reviews of Burney's *The Wanderer* and Edgeworth's *Patronage*, an attempt to professionalize patriarchy in the midst of a reconfiguration of the marriage economy is intrinsic to the aesthetic judgments of both corporate identities such as the Edinburgh reviewer and individualized career periodical writers like William Hazlitt.

Reading the Rhetoric of Resistance in William Cobbett's *Two-Penny Trash by Bonnie J. Gunzenhauser*

At a time when the periodical was increasingly focused on superintending literary matters and instantiating class distinctions, William Cobbett's *Political Register* remained unflinchingly focused on political initiatives and injustices: Cobbett repeatedly figures the *Register* as a battlefield and his readers as soldiers fighting the good fight for political justice. This essay shows how Cobbett uses the inexpensive version of his *Political Register*, the *Two-Penny Trash*, to reanimate ancient republican ideas of both literacy and citizenship during a moment when such ideas were in danger of disappearing. Using the contemporary literary discourse of sympathy, Cobbett makes classical ideals of reading and writing accessible to a broad readership, positioning his readers as activist citizens rather than consuming subjects. Through the *Two-Penny Trash*, Cobbett enlists his readers in a campaign of discursive resistance that ultimately challenges both the periodical and the political culture of early nineteenth-century England.

"May the married be single, and the single happy:" *Blackwood's*, the *Maga* for the Single Man *by Lisa Niles*

Structuring the male homosociality of *Blackwood's Edinburgh Magazine*, the "bachelor," one of *Maga*'s most familiar "types," shapes *Blackwood's*' complex configurations of and responses to women. The series of essays analyzed here (1817–19), beginning with "Letters of an Old Bachelor," uses "feminine" issues – fashion, the marriage market, domestic topics – as tropes to mediate the larger, masculinized concerns of the periodical project. As women are both producers and consumers in periodical culture, *Blackwood's* embraces its dually-gendered audience by invoking multiple femininities through competing views of women in its pages, while carefully maintaining the primacy of its masculinity under the governing principle of a bachelor typology.

Blackwood's Edinburgh Magazine and the Construction of Wordsworth's Genius *by David Higgins*

This essay examines how and why *Blackwood's Edinburgh Magazine* represented Wordsworth as a great poet in the period from 1818 to 1822, in the context of the complex relationship between the Romantic "myth" of genius and the operations of the literary marketplace in the early nineteenth century. A number of strong commercial and ideological reasons contributed to the magazine's support of the poet: for example, its opposition to the *Edinburgh Review*, and its desire to put forward an account of poetic genius as, ideally, a locus of timeless, orthodox values, rather than a dangerous, transgressive force which threatened the sociopolitical status quo. The second part of the article focuses on the third of John Wilson's "Letters from the Lakes" (1819), a panegyrical account of Wordsworth as both private gentleman and solitary genius. But it is argued that Wilson had ambivalent feelings about his fellow "Lake Poet." He sought both to improve Wordsworth's cultural status, and to offend him by publicizing his private life, thus imbricating him in the contemporary culture of "personality" which the poet so deplored.

Detaching Lamb's Thoughts *by Peter J. Manning*

This essay speculates on the ways in which Lamb's essays seek to detach themselves from, or at any rate to resist absorption by, the particular circumstances of the *London Magazine* to which they nonetheless remain tied. Lamb draws out of periodical publishing an identity that disguises the commercial nature of that enterprise, and then seeks to elude the concretion, the historical embedding, of that identity. The name of this double process is Elia, and it is the workings of this persona that mark the unsettled situation of the text.

The *New Monthly Magazine* and the Liberalism of the 1820s *by Nanora Sweet*

In the 1820s, the *New Monthly Magazine* under Henry Colburn, Thomas Campbell, and Cyrus Redding participated in a new domain of public opinion, exploited by Tory apostate George Canning for its leverage against partisan gridlock. Current criticism takes the *New Monthly*'s refusal of partisanship as a refusal of politics, calling it an authorless institution. Yet partisanship caused the death of the *London Magazine*'s editor, and the *New Monthly* went on to dominate the London market by embracing constitutionalism abroad and middle-class reformism at home. Through its contributors, republican émigrés, offshore commentators, and women writers sharing a republican idiom, the *New Monthly* promoted institutional as well as political reform: a better term than authorless for the magazine's identity, then, is *coverture*.

Notes on Contributors

Stephen C. Behrendt is George Holmes Distinguished University Professor of English at the University of Nebraska. He has published widely on Blake, the Shelleys, the radical press, women writers of the Romantic period, and relations among the arts. His poetry is widely published as well, and includes two book-length collections.

Andrea Bradley is currently a doctoral student at Vanderbilt University. She has presented papers on subjects including Frances Burney, Caroline Bowles, and Anna Laetitia Barbauld. Her dissertation project concerns the discourse of advertising in eighteenth- and early nineteenth-century literature.

Adriana Craciun's *Fatal Women of Romanticism*, which discusses other aspects of Mary Robinson's work than those covered in this essay, was published in 2002. She is also the editor of *A Routledge Literary Sourcebook on Mary Wollstonecraft's Vindication of the Rights of Woman* (2002) and Charlotte Dacre's *Zofloya, or The Moor* (1997), and the co-editor (with Kari Lokke) of *Rebellious Hearts: British Women Writers and the French Revolution* (2001). She is currently writing a new book, *Citizens of the World: British Women Writers and the French Revolution*, and is Lecturer at University of Nottingham.

Bonnie J. Gunzenhauser is Assistant Professor of English at Roosevelt University. This essay stems from her current book project, titled *The Transformation of Virtue: Genre, Reading, and Political Identity in Late Eighteenth- and Early Nineteenth-Century Britain*. Her research focuses especially on prose fiction, periodical literature, and didactic writings of the Romantic period.

David Higgins has recently completed a Ph.D. at the University of York, England, entitled "The Cult of Genius: Magazines, Readers, and the Creative Artist, 1802–37." He is working on a book based on his thesis.

Peter J. Manning is Professor and Chair of the English Department at SUNY Stony Brook. He is the author of *Byron and His Fictions* (1978) and *Reading Romantics* (1990), and the co-editor, with Susan J. Wolfson, of the Romantics portion of the *Longman Anthology of British Literature* (1999; 2003), the Penguin *Selected Poems of Lord Byron* (1996), and the Penguin *Selected Poems of Beddoes, Praed, and Hood* (2000).

Lisa Niles is a doctoral candidate in English at Vanderbilt University specializing in nineteenth-century studies. In addition to her work on early nineteenth-century periodicals, her current research interests include the engagement between representations of aging in various print media and medical, behavioral, and legal discourses surrounding the elderly.

Mark Schoenfield, an Associate Professor of English at Vanderbilt University, is the author of *The Professional Wordsworth: Law, Labor, and the Poet's Contract* (1996), as well as a variety of essays on the periodical press and on Romanticism and the law. His "Abraham Goldsmid: Money Magician in the Popular Press" has recently appeared in *British Romanticism and the Jews*, edited by Sheila Spector. He is currently working on a book tentatively titled *British Periodicals and Romantic Identity*.

Nanora Sweet has written on Felicia Hemans and her context in *European Romantic Review*, *Romantic Praxis*, *European Journal of English Studies*, *Journal of Modern Language Studies*, *At the Limits of Romanticism*, *Approaches to Teaching Women Poets of the British Romantic Period*, *The Lessons of Romanticism*, Staël's Corinne in *Critical Inquiry*, and *Felicia Hemans: Reimagining Poetry in the Nineteenth Century*, which she co-edited with Julie Melnyk (2001). With Barbara Taylor she has edited Hemans' *The Sceptic* for the Centre for Byron Studies and *Romantic Circles* (forthcoming). She wrote on Hemans for the *Cambridge Bibliography of English Literature* (2000) and *New Dictionary of National Biography* (forthcoming).

Kim Wheatley, an Associate Professor of English at the College of William and Mary, has published essays on *Blackwood's* and the *Quarterly Review*, and is the author of *Shelley and His Readers: Beyond Paranoid Politics* (1999).

Index

Other Titles in the Series

News, Newspapers and Society in Early-Modern Britain

Joad Raymond, *University of Aberdeen* (Ed)

This collection of essays explores the impact of printed periodicals on British culture and society between 1590 and 1800.

    The relationship between newsbooks and the theatre; the use of newspapers by political radicals during the civil wars of the mid-seventeenth century; the role of women in the early periodical press; the emergence of a public sphere of popular political opinion; the use of advertising as a form of communication; the distribution and readership of newspapers in the provinces; ideas of nationhood in the Scottish periodical press; and the role of medical and philosophical journals in promoting medical reform.

240 pages 1999
0 7146 4944 9 cloth
0 7146 8003 6 paper
A special issue of the journal Prose Studies

FRANK CASS PUBLISHERS
Crown House, 47 Chase Side, Southgate, London N14 5BP
Tel: +44 (0)20 8920 2100 Fax: +44 (0)20 8447 8548 E-mail: info@frankcass.com
NORTH AMERICA
920 NE 58th Avenue Suite 300, Portland, OR 97213-3786 USA
Tel: 800 944 6190 Fax: 503 280 8832 E-mail: cass@isbs.com
Website: www.frankcass.com